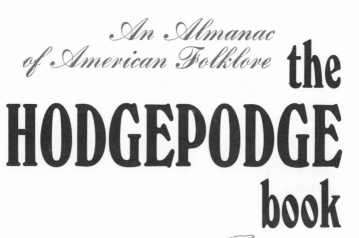

An Almanac of American Folklore

the HODGEPODGE book

FOUR WINDS PRESS • NEW YORK

Containing All Manner
of Curious, Interesting, and
Out-of-the-Way Information
Drawn from American Folklore,
and Not To Be Found
Anywhere Else
in the World;

As Well as Jokes,
Conundrums,
Riddles, Puzzles,
and Other Matter
Designed To Amuse
and Entertain;

All of It Most Instructive and Delightful.

collected by **DUNCAN EMRICH** ♥ illustrated by **IB OHLSSON**

BY THE SAME AUTHOR

The Nonsense Book
The Book of Wishes and Wishmaking
Folklore on the American Land
The Folklore of Love and Courtship
The Folklore of Weddings and Marriage

3 4 5 6 78 77 76 75 74
PUBLISHED BY FOUR WINDS PRESS
A DIVISION OF SCHOLASTIC MAGAZINES, INC., NEW YORK, N. Y.
TEXT COPYRIGHT © 1972 BY DUNCAN EMRICH
ILLUSTRATIONS COPYRIGHT © 1972 BY IB OHLSSON
ALL RIGHTS RESERVED
PRINTED IN THE UNITED STATES OF AMERICA
LIBRARY OF CONGRESS CATALOGUE CARD NUMBER: 72-77811

If this book
Should stray away,
Tie it up
And feed it hay.

If this book
Is found in Rome,
Box its ears
And send it home.

I pity the baker,
I pity the cook,
I pity the one
Who takes this book.

Hic liber est meus,
And to this I will stick,
Si aliquis rapit,
I'll give him a kick.

(That is Latin, which all students had to
study not too long ago. *Hic liber est meus:*
this book is mine. *Si aliquis rapit:* if
anyone steals it.)

CONTENTS

This book is an orderly hodgepodge, which is to say that it is a grab bag of almost anything and everything, but so arranged that you can find the particular thing you're looking for—especially when you've read through the Hodgepodge once. Then you can go back to "bees" or "doodlebugs" or "elephants" or "scratches," and there you are.

There are things in this Hodgepodge which are very, very true, or almost always true. For example: "A bee never gets wet," or "Rain before seven, stop before eleven," or "A penny saved is a penny earned."

Then there are other things here which are true, but in a quite different sort of way. Examples: "A ghost is never seen without mittens," (Have you ever seen one without mittens?), or "If you can keep your tongue out of the hole where a tooth has been pulled, a gold tooth will grow in its place."

And then there are other things which are halfway between. You can believe them or not. "If you want to get rid of your freckles, wash your face with buttermilk," or "A three-colored cat brings luck and prevents fires," or "If you have tangles in your hair, rats have slept in it." If you believe these, then they are beliefs. If you do not believe them, then they are superstitions. In either case, they are delightful funsense. Your great-great-great-grandmother—and great-great-great-grandfather as well—knew most of these and enjoyed them. Some of them they did not know (elephant jokes, for example, because they had not been invented then), but you have them all here in one great big hodge-podge grab bag. Have fun!

The Seasons of the Year

THE SEASONS OF THE YEAR

The four seasons of the year anywhere in the world begin officially on the twenty-first day of the month of March for spring, of June for summer, of September for fall or autumn, and of December for winter. But the seasons vary greatly from place to place. Spring and the robin come later in Maine, for example, than they do in Alabama, and winter and the bitter winds are much earlier in Montana than in Texas. Yet by and large everyone everywhere thinks of March as the beginning of spring and of December as the beginning of winter. So, to make remembering easy, call:

Spring: March, April, and May
Summer: June, July, and August
Autumn: September, October, and November, and
Winter: December, January, and February.

By the official seasonal calendar, these can be
read:

Spring: March   21
           April
           May
Summer: June   21
           July
           August
Autumn: September 21
           October
           November
Winter: December   21
           January
           February
Spring: March

and so on again into another year

The regular calendar year, of course, begins
with January 1, and goes on through February, March, April, May, June, July, August,
September, October, November, and ends with
December 31. But our lives—and the lives of
all animals, birds, and insects, and the lives
of trees, plants, and flowers—are much more
influenced and regulated by the seasonal calendar than by the regular calendar.

Birds, for example, don't know March from
April, but they know when spring is here. And
squirrels know when winter is coming. And
you know that when the pond is frozen, it's
time for ice skates.

The seasonal calendar is nature's calendar.
The calendar of the months and days is man's
calendar.

SPRING (March 21–June 20)

Spring: daffodils and robins and worms, and crocus and running brooks and buds on the trees, and tulips and dandelions and lilacs and violets, and just sniffing the air.

These things begin in spring: skip-rope, marbles, leapfrog, tag, baseball, tops.

Spring is sprung!

They say that if March comes in like a lion, it will go out like a lamb. And that if it comes in like a lamb, it will go out like a lion. The weather in March is very changeable. Watch the first few days and the last few days of the month to see whether this lamb-and-lion saying is true.

April showers bring May flowers.

A windy March and a rainy April make a beautiful May.

Spring has come when whippoorwills sing: "Chips fell off the white-oak tree."

BAREFOOTED (Time to go)

With the sound of the first whippoorwill in the spring, it is time to go barefoot.

Do not go barefoot until you have seen three swallows.

SUMMER (June 21–September 20)

Lie on your back in the meadow and watch the small white clouds move across the hot blue sky. Just lie there—and make wishes.

Lie on a feather bed during a thunderstorm. Chickens have never been struck by lightning.

Take a heavy blade of grass, hold it lengthwise between your thumbs, and blow hard on it. It makes a piercing, screaming sound that will give an unsuspecting aunt conniption fits. She will remember you. (It is not always good to be remembered.)

Roller-skating, swimming, cops-and-robbers, hide-and-seek, baseball (how's your team doing?), climbing apple trees.

Blueberries, popcorn, lobsters, ice cream, corn-on-the-cob (with butter running off your chin), Concord grapes, and hard, crisp, juicy apples. Wish that summer will never end.

Run your toes through summer grass or dig them into the sand on beaches.

Wish that summer will never end.

FALL, or AUTUMN
(September 21–December 20)

When you see yellow butterflies flying south, fall is coming.

Fall is the time when the leaves change from green to crimson, gold, and yellow and purple. All the woods are on fire with color. Everything is aflame, and particularly the maple trees in New England.

It is good to go walking in the woods with your dog.

Fall is the smell of burning leaves raked off the lawn and piled in the gutter, the smoke curling up slowly.

Watch the squirrels. If the squirrels are running around like crazy gathering nuts, the winter will be long and cold and hard. If the squirrels seem to be taking it easy and lollygagging about, winter will be mild and soft and open.

If you live in the city, it is good to smell the hot roasted chestnuts sold by the chestnut man, and to burn your fingers peeling off the hot shells.

Fall is football, the rival of baseball in spring.
  Rah! Rah!   Rah!
  Siss! Boom! Bah!

Did you know that the Rah! Rah! Rah! cry was invented at Harvard in 1864 and finally adopted by all the Eastern colleges in 1886? Before that the yell had been the much longer Hurrah! Hurrah! Hurrah!

WINTER (December 21–March 20)

When you hear a grouse drumming its wings on a log or a fox barking, a storm is on the way.

The snow will be as deep in winter as the weeds were high in summer.

Christmas decorations should not be left up after January 6th (Twelfth-night). Some say New Year's Day.

If you are indoors during a blizzard, it's fun to dress warmly (boots, mittens, stocking-cap) and to go out into the blizzard for several minutes. The howling wind, the bitter cold, the stinging of the snow and sleet, the cold air in your lungs! But don't go wandering off out of sight of the lighted windows of your house. Enjoy the blizzard, but don't let it get you!

When a dove sings, winter is over.

The Months
of the Year

THE MONTHS OF THE YEAR

Thirty days hath September,
April, June and November.
All the rest have thirty-one
Save February
Which alone has twenty-eight,
Excepting Leap Year—that's the time
When February's days are twenty-nine.

The Knuckle Calendar is
a very simple way of
telling which months are
the long months
(thirty-one days) and
which months are the
short months (thirty days
or February's twenty-
eight). Double your left
hand into a fist and then,
with a finger of your
right hand, touch the
knuckles and the small
depressions, at the same
time naming the months.
All the long months will be on the knuckles, and
all the short months on the depressions or
small valleys.

January,   March,   May,   July,
       February,   April,   June,
(now back to the first knuckle),
August,   October,   December.
       September,   November,

Very tricky. When you are old and gray-haired,
remember to teach that to your grandchildren.

JANUARY

Brrr-r-r-r!
To find out what the
weather will be for the
twelve months of the year,
check the weather for
each of the twelve days
after Christmas, that is,
from December 26
through January 6. The
weather on each of these
days should tell you
what the weather is likely
to be for each of the
following months.
December 26 for January,
December 27 for
February, December 28
for March, and so on
through the year. Wet,
dry, rainy, stormy,
sunny, good, bad,
terrible, hot, cold,
sleeting, showery, misty,
mixed-up, changeable.
Keep a record.

FEBRUARY

What month has twenty-eight days? All of them.

When it thunders in February, winter has broken.

MARCH

"Sap's flowin'!"

The sap begins to run in the maple trees in New England. The sap is thin and watery-colored when it is tapped from the trees. When it is boiled down over a stove, it becomes dark and syrupy, and perfect for griddlecakes and pancakes. And corn fritters. It takes fifteen gallons of sap to make one gallon of syrup.

Pussy willows! If you put long branches of pussy willows in a large vase or jug on the floor in a corner of your room, they will not die but will grow and grow—or stay the same as when you got them. For three years at least.

APRIL

April Fool jokes can be played in the morning, and only up until noontime. After that, you are the fool for trying to fool someone.

Baby lambs!
Easter eggs!
Chocolate (or real live) rabbits!
A new hat, dress, and pair of white gloves!

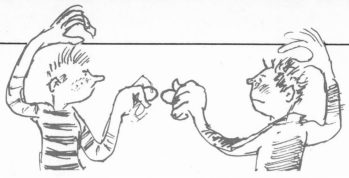

Hard-boiled egg fights: hold a hard-boiled egg in your hand and hit the point of the egg against the point of an egg held by a friend. If his egg cracks or breaks, you win his egg; if your egg breaks, he wins your egg. (This is a very, very old game played on Easter. When it is played in Greece, the eggs are dyed red.)

MAY

On May Day, pick flowers, put them in little paper baskets, and hang them on the doorknobs of neighbors' or friends' houses. Ring the bell, run and hide, and watch how surprised and pleased they are when they open the door and find them.

Move your bees on the first of May.

A cold spell in May is called blackberry winter, and it makes for a good blackberry crop.

Never eat oysters in any month that does not have the letter R in it.

JUNE

Midsummer's Day is June 24. If it rains on June 24, there will be no hickory nuts that year.

A dry June, much corn;
A wet June, no corn at all.

June, more than any other month, is the month of marriages. If you know a bride who is going to be married, tell her to enter the church with her right foot first for good luck.

JULY

Corn should be knee high
By the Fourth of July.

(Otherwise the crop will not be very good.)

Firecrackers!
Skyrockets!
Pinwheels!
Sparklers!
Roman candles!
Red devils!
Snakes!

AUGUST

Hot, hot!
Hot, hotter, hottest!

A superb month for picnics.

Menu: fried chicken (with salt and pepper shakers), potato salad (nice and vinegary), watermelon (big slices). Potato chips, hard-boiled eggs, pickles, cookies, bottles of soda pop in ice buckets. Leave some crumbs for the ants, but clean everything else up. Bad luck to leave a sloppy table.

All thunderstorms after August 24th (St. Bartholomew's Day) are more or less violent.

Freckles are sun kisses.

SEPTEMBER

Back to school. And school can be great. Consider this: every single day in school you learn something new. Every day, every day! And everything that you learn becomes part of you and your total knowledge. Every day. School is terrific! (You're lucky to be in school.)

Chrysanthemums! Your mother would like one.

OCTOBER

When you are husking corn at a "husking bee" and find a red ear of corn, you have the right to kiss the person next to you or to toss the ear to anyone in the room whom you want to kiss. He (or she) must kiss you—perhaps after a chase around the room.

It is bad luck to keep a pumpkin in your bedroom overnight.

Pumpkins! Witches! Goblins! Ghosts!
Trick or Treat!

NOVEMBER

Look forward to one thing in November: Thanksgiving. And be very, very thankful for all the blessings you may have!

You know the dinner by heart, but in case you have momentarily lost your mind, here is a reminder (mind-remind).

Beginning nibbling: Salted nuts. Celery sticks. Olives.
Roast turkey: big, fat, juicy; crisp, brown skin; drumsticks.
Stuffing: chestnut at one end, oyster at the other.
Cranberry sauce.
Sweet potatoes. Mashed potatoes.
Giblet gravy.
Squash (buttered). Peas (a bowl full).
Apple pie. Pumpkin pie. Mince pie.

You certainly don't want ice cream after all that, do you?

You do? Okay—chocolate, vanilla, pistachio, coffee, strawberry, chocolate, vanilla, coffee . . .

DECEMBER

This month should bring snow.
And snow and cold weather
should bring:

> Snowballs
> Snowforts
> Snowmen
> Snowshoes
> Sledding
> Skiing
> Skating
> (Seven S's!)

If you want your Christmas log to burn slowly, soak it first in a stream of water. It will be damp and last longer.

No two snowflakes are alike. Compare any two and you will find this to be true.

December is a good month. But what about April? If you had to choose two, which two months would you choose? (There is a Spanish proverb which says: Give me April and May, and you can have the rest of the world.) Choose your two months, and see if they agree with those your friends may choose. Good fun: have a small party and ask everyone to choose their two months, and then ask them to give their reasons for choosing the months. Do you think that any two will be alike? Not on your tintype!

Hot cider. Spiced.

Very Special Days of the Year

The Eve

On New Year's Eve place a loaf of bread, a silver dollar, and some salt on the table, and you will have bread, money, and good luck throughout the coming year.

Just before midnight on New Year's Eve, set a tub of water out in the yard and into it drop a penny. You will be lucky in money matters for the next year.

Watch closely at midnight on New Year's Eve and you can see an old man leave your house and a young child enter.

If you are up at midnight on New Year's Eve, try to be the first to say "Happy New Year!" "Happy New Year!" "Happy New Year!" "Same to you!" "I said it first!" "Happy New Year!"

On New Year's Eve, sleep with a horseshoe under your pillow and at midnight, when the bells are ringing, make a wish.

Ring out the old,
Ring in the new,
Ring out the false,
Ring in the true!

The Day

Wish *every* person you meet on New Year's Day a "Happy New Year!" and you will have good luck all year. It is a friendly thing to do.

On New Year's Day, always cook and eat some kind of food that swells, and your pocketbook will be swollen all year. Black-eyed peas and hog jowl say some, cabbage say others.

Eat green beans and dried peas
On New Year's Day,
You'll have greenbacks and silver
All your way.

On New Year's Day,
always do a little bit of
something that you hope
to continue doing during
the year. If you plan
to write a book during
the year, write a few
sentences. If you want to
knit a lot, do a few
stitches. If you want to
travel, study a map or
walk around the block. If
you plan to learn how
to cook, read a cookbook
or boil an egg. It is always
good to think ahead
and to make a start at
doing something on New
Year's Day.

VALENTINE'S DAY

Rain or shine,
This girl's mine!

To your valentine (the girl you love best) it is nice to send on Valentine's Day a very beautiful red and white valentine of bows and paper frills. She will keep it forever. You don't necessarily have to put your name on it. You can if you want to, but she will know from whom it comes in any case.

It is also nice to send a valentine to your mother. Your mother will know who sent it.

Nice gifts to give on Valentine's Day?

Flowers that you have picked yourself and tied in a bunch with a ribbon bow.

Candy that you have made yourself.

Valentine cards that you have made in secret.

Kittens and puppies. (They love love and want love, and Valentine's Day is love.)

Girls can give valentines, too. (And generally girls make better candy than boys.)

WASHINGTON'S BIRTHDAY
(February 22, 1732-1799)

George Washington died in 1799, and not long after his death schoolchildren in many parts of our country were singing this song about him in school.

———————◆▶◀◆———————

I suppose you've heard of Washington, of
    Washington the Great,
Who fought the French and Indians upon the
    northern lakes,
And when King George of Eng-e-land op-
    pressed our lovely land,
Our country fought for freedom under Wash-
    ington's command.

He captured British battleships, and tore
    their ensign down,
And raised our banner in its place, our banner
    of renown.
He drove the British from our shores, he
    whipped them good and strong,
And sent them back to Eng-e-land, the place
    where they belonged.

He was the first great President, the first to
    rule this land,
And all the people honored him down to a
    single man.
He taught the people to be good, and love
    their country, too,
And everybody sings his praise, as loudly as
    we do.

He loved the little children, too, and took
   them out to ride,
And he threw a silver dollar o'er bold Rappa-
   hannock's tide.
And when he died, they buried him beside
   Potomac's waves,
And raised a marble monument to mark a
   hero's grave.

If all the boys throughout the land his deeds
   would emulate,
They'd grow to be like Washington, like
   Washington the Great.

Whenever you have the opportunity, visit
Washington's home at Mount Vernon on the
Potomac, where he is buried. The house and
gardens are beautiful. And guess what the
weathervane is which Washington ordered
especially made for the house? A dove with
an olive branch in its beak.

PEACE

THE DERBY RAM

George Washington is supposed never to have told a lie. (That's legend and very difficult to believe.) But he did enjoy singing this song of wild exaggeration, and tradition has it that he sang it to the children of the Chief Justice of the United States. It makes him very human, doesn't it? (This is an old English song, and the pronunciation of "Derby," by the way, is "Darby.")

> Oh, as I went down to Derby Town
> All on a summer's day,
> It's there I saw the finest ram
> That was ever fed on hay.
>
> > And if you don't believe me
> > And think I tell a lie,
> > Just you go down to Derby,
> > And you'll see the same as I!
>
> Oh, the wool upon this ram's back
> It drug to the ground,
> And I hauled it to the market,
> And it weighed ten thousand pounds.

Oh, the horns upon this ram's head
They reached to the moon,
For the butcher went up in February
And never got back till June.

Oh, the ears upon this ram's head
They reached to the sky,
And the eagle built his nest there
For I heard the young ones cry.

Oh, every tooth this ram had
Would hold a bushel of corn,
And every foot he stood on
Would cover an acre of ground.

And if you don't believe me
And think I tell a lie,
Just you go down to Derby,
And you'll see the same as I!

ST. PATRICK'S DAY (March 17)

Plant sweet peas on March 17th.

My mother and father were Irish,
My mother and father were Irish,
My mother and father were Irish,
And I am Irish too!
And I am Irish too!
And I am Irish too!
My mother and father were Irish,
My mother and father were Irish,
My mother and father were Irish,
And I am Irish too!

St. Patrick chased all the snakes out of Ireland. There is not a snake in Ireland!

APRIL FOOL'S DAY

April Fool's a-coming,
And you're the biggest fool a-running.

Up the ladder and down the tree,
You're a bigger fool than me.

On April Fool
Go to school,
Tell your teacher
You're a fool.

April Fool has come and past,
And you're the biggest fool at last.

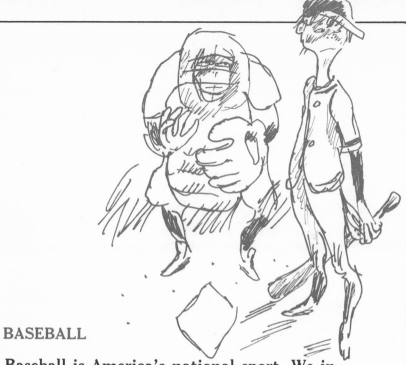

BASEBALL

Baseball is America's national sport. We invented it, and it has been picked up by Mexico and Japan. Everyone who sees it enjoys it, and hollers and yells and buys hotdogs. Have one! (Or a hot *taco*!)

The opening day of the baseball season is the first Monday in April at the ball park in Washington, D.C. All the other ball parks and teams around the country have to wait until the Washington Senators* have played their first game. The President of the United States throws out the first ball, the crowds cheer, and spring is very *officially* here in America. (The Cherry Blossom Festival in Washington usually takes place at about the same time.)

*The owner of the Senators took the team to Texas in 1971, and changed its name to the Texas Rangers. Washington fans were very upset, because it left their city without a baseball team. But that is being corrected, and Washington will again have a baseball team—in 1973, or at the very latest in 1974. It will probably be called the (new) Washington Senators, and the President will throw out the first ball.

Ever stop to think about all the words which come from baseball and which we use daily?

He'll never get to first base!
Don't die on third!
He's got two strikes on him already!
Butterfingers!
He doesn't even know the score!
A foul ball, if I ever saw one!
He's muffed it!
He's way out in left field—without sunglasses!
Kill the umpire! (Poor umpire! He's only trying to be fair in all his judgments.)

There are special days when the clubs give away bats, caps, baseballs, and other souvenirs. Be sure to know about these days. And be sure to be at the ball park on "bat day." So that you can beat your bats on the stadium floor and drive the radio and TV men crazy.

What's your favorite team? Choose one now and follow it through the season—this year or next year. These are the teams in the two leagues:

AMERICAN LEAGUE

East   Baltimore Orioles
Boston Red Sox
Detroit Tigers
Texas Rangers
New York Yankees
Cleveland Indians

West   Chicago White Sox
California Angels
Kansas City Royals
Milwaukee Brewers
Minnesota Twins
Oakland Athletics

NATIONAL LEAGUE

East   New York Mets
Pittsburgh Pirates
Chicago Cubs
St. Louis Cardinals
Montreal Expos
Philadelphia Phillies

West   Atlanta Braves
San Francisco Giants
Houston Astros
Los Angeles Dodgers
San Diego Padres
Cincinnati Reds

BIRTHDAYS

Monday's child is fair of face,
Tuesday's child is full of grace,
Wednesday's child is sour and sad,
Thursday's child is merry and glad,
Friday's child is loving and giving,
Saturday's child must work for a living,
But the child that is born on the Sabbath day
Is blithe and bonny, good and gay.

He who is born on
New Year's morn
Will have his own way as
sure as you're born.

He who is born on an
Easter morn
Shall never know want,
or care, or harm.

If you blow out all the
candles on your birthday
cake with the first try,
whatever you have wished
will come true.

Born under the light of
the moon, you will
grow tall.

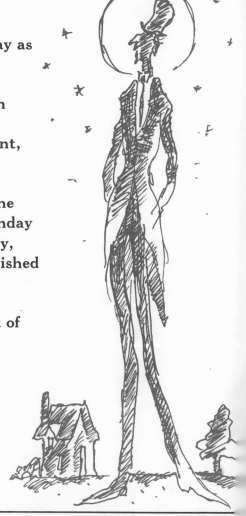

THE FOURTH OF JULY: INDEPENDENCE DAY

I've got a rocket
In my pocket,
I cannot stop to play.
Away she goes!
I've burnt my toes!
'Tis Independence Day!

The United States of America will be two hundred years old on July 4, 1976, which is just around the corner. You will be here to celebrate it, and there will be rockets and firecrackers and bells ringing and cannon booming and parades and bands and flags

from one end of the country to the other.
(There probably will be a few speeches, too.)
Anyhow, one song that you must know in
honor of the days of 1776 is "Yankee Doodle."
At least a few stanzas of it. It's great good fun!
And it *is* your country's birthday!

Father and I went down to camp
Along with Captain Goodwin,
And there we saw the men and boys
As thick as hasty pudding.

    Yankee Doodle, keep it up,
    Yankee Doodle dandy!
    Mind the music and the step,
    And with the girls be handy!

There was Captain Washington
Upon a slapping stallion,
Giving orders to his men,
I guess there was a million.

And there they had a swamping gun
As big as a log of maple,
On a deuced little cart,
A load for father's cattle.

And every time they fired it off,
It took a horn of powder;
It made a noise like father's gun,
Only a nation louder.

And there I saw a little keg,
Its heads were made of leather—
They knocked upon it with little sticks
To call the folks together.

The troopers, too, would gallop up
And fire right in our faces,
It scared me almost half to death
To see them run such races.

But I can't tell you half I saw,
They kept up such a smother,
So I took off my hat, made a bow,
And scampered home to mother.

Yankee Doodle, keep it up,
Yankee Doodle dandy!
Mind the music and the steps,
And with the girls be handy!

And then there are other stanzas which you
already probably know:

Yankee Doodle went to town
A-riding on a pony,
He stuck a feather in his hat
And called it macaroni!

Yankee Doodle went to town,
He bought a bag of peaches,
He rode so fast a-coming back,
He smashed them all to pieces!

Yankee Doodle, find a girl,
Yankee Doodle dandy,
Take her to the fair today
And buy a box of candy!

Some people say that it always rains on the
Fourth of July, and they believe that the rain
is caused by all the firecrackers popping across
the country and disturbing the clouds.

HALLOWEEN WITCHES

I'm going to town to smoke my pipe,
I won't be back until Saturday night—
Be sure and don't let the witch in!

Witches can only come out at midnight and they must be gone by the time the first morning star appears.

Witches are very curious, and they stop to count everything. You can protect yourself from witches by placing a broom or a bowl of salt outside your door. The witch will stop to count the straws in the broom and the grains of salt in the bowl. Before she can finish counting them, the morning star will appear, and then she will have to leave. You can also sleep with a sieve over your face. The witch will try to count all the holes in the sieve, but she will be unable to. (Just try it yourself sometime!)

Another very good way to keep witches at a distance is to hang a horseshoe over the door of your house or room. Witches cannot enter a house where there is a horseshoe, because before doing so they must travel every bit of the road that the horseshoe has traveled. This takes time, and the morning star will be palely shining just before dawn, and the witch will have to go.

Witches do not like the color blue because it is the color of the heavens. If you wear a blue bracelet or a blue bead, a witch cannot get you. If you paint your windowsill blue, a witch cannot come into your room.

If you carry a penny in your pocket or wear a new dime in each shoe, witches can't harm you.

Witches have fun on Halloween.

Always crush eggshells. The only way a witch can cross water is in an eggshell. When you have finished eating a soft-boiled egg out of the shell, push your spoon through the bottom of the shell and say, "Save a shipwreck!" If you do not do this, a witch may ride in the shell and cause a shipwreck.

A CHARM AGAINST EVIL SPIRITS

Hippitty pippitty trae me trow,
I went to the river to wash my toe,
But when I got there my chicken was dead:
Hey, biddy, jing shang, snake root, poke
root, lil, oppy, dill, dock, penny royal tea!

(The last words are the names of herbs,
plants, and roots which evil spirits cannot
abide. Some of the words are misspelled:
jing shang probably stands for *ginseng* and
oppy may be *poppy*. But that is the way
rhymes are passed on from one person to
another—by the sound and meaning, not
necessarily by the spelling. The evil spirits
understand the meaning! And they move!)

GHOSTS

A ghost is never seen without mittens. (Ask anyone if they have ever seen a ghost without mittens.)

Ghosts travel in a mantle of warm air. You sometimes feel a sudden warmth in the temperature while walking or riding in the country on a cool summer evening. This whiff of warm air that passes over you is the ghost traveling in its protective mantle.

If you count nine stars and nine bricks, and then look into a dark room, you will see a ghost.

A horse can see ghosts,
and dogs with seven toes
can see them.

People born at night never
see ghosts.

If you count seven stars,
and then count seven
alleys, in the seventh
alley you will see a ghost.

Ghosts vanish at cock crow.

CHRISTMAS (December 25)

Christmas is coming,
The geese are getting fat,
Please to put a nickle
In an old man's hat.
If you haven't got a nickle,
A penny will do,
And if you haven't got a penny,
God bless you!

Any girl standing under
mistletoe may be kissed.

What do you think of when you think of Christmas? Make a list: holly, ivy, mistletoe, Christmas wreaths, trees, carols, red, green and gold, snow, candy canes, popcorn balls, Santa Claus, stockings, fireplaces, plum pudding, hardsauce, colored lights, candles, ribbons, bright wrapping paper, packages, toys, a star, a manger, the Three Wise Men, gifts, sleds, skates, sleigh bells, reindeer, red berries, Jack Frost, ribbon candy . . . . See how many things you and two or three friends can list in half an hour's time. And Greetings: Merry Christmas! Merry Christmas to you!

The cows kneel down at midnight on Christmas Eve, and many people believe that they talk at that time. If you go out to the barn, you may hear them. All the roosters are supposed to crow at midnight also.

"UPON A CHRISTMAS MORNING"

This is a very gentle and lovely song. Your mother or teacher will know the tune. It is the same tune as "Mulberry Bush" and "London Hill," both of which are in this book. So, you have three songs to the same tune.

Two little ships were sailing by,
Were sailing by, were sailing by,
Two little ships were sailing by
Upon a Christmas morning.

Guess who was in one of them,
One of them, one of them,
Guess who was in one of them
Upon a Christmas morning.

The blessed Virgin and her Son,
And her Son, and her Son,
The blessed Virgin and her Son
Upon a Christmas morning.

Guess who was in the other of them,
Other of them, other of them,
Guess who was in the other of them
Upon a Christmas morning.

George Washington and his son,
And his son, and his son,
George Washington and his son
Upon a Christmas morning.

I wash my face in a golden vase,
A golden vase, a golden vase,
I wash my face in a golden vase
Upon a Christmas morning.

I wipe my face on a lily-white towel,
A lily-white towel, a lily-white towel,
I wipe my face on a lily-white towel,
Upon a Christmas morning.

I comb my hair with an ivory comb,
An ivory comb, an ivory comb,
I comb my hair with an ivory comb
Upon a Christmas morning.

This very nice Christmas Star story about a
girl named Susie comes from North Carolina,
and you will probably want to tell it to friends
on Christmas Day. You need paper and
pencil:

Susie lived in the big house on the hill
overlooking the village. See, there it is.
(Make a dot to represent the house.) It
was the day before Christmas, and Susie
was very busy wrapping presents for her

young friends. "Are there no children in the village that may be forgotten on Christmas?" her mother asked. Susie thought of this question for several minutes. She then picked four presents which she put on her sled and left the house. As she went, the sled left two lines behind in the snow.

First, she took a book to lame Timmy, who lived at the foot of the hill. (Make a dot to represent Timmy's home, and two lines to represent those left by the sled.)

Next, she went across the village to give a doll to Meg, whose father had recently died. (Make a dot to represent Meg's home, and lines to represent the sled's tracks.)

From there, she went to the home of Julie, the daughter of the laundress, who got only very practical presents. To Julie, she gave the tiny china tea set she had intended for Helen, her friend who had everything.

Last, she took a large bag of fruit and nuts to Mrs. Jones, who was old and alone.

Susie was tired, but happy, as she made her way home. Just as she reached her door, she looked up at the evening sky. And there was the Star of Bethlehem.

Hiccups, Warts, and
Health and Beauty

BACKACHE

If your back aches in the springtime, lie on the ground and roll over three times toward the sound of the first dove that you hear. You probably will not have backaches yourself, but you can tell this to older people who will be grateful to you for the information.

BEE STINGS

For a bee sting, chew the leaves of three non-poisonous plants and put the pulp on the sting. It will soothe the sting very quickly. Chew the leaves of roses, clover, licorice root, nasturtiums, or any other plants that happen to be handy.

Another way to cure a bee sting is to put some mud on the sting right away.

Don't let the same bee sting you twice!

BEAUTY HINTS

A maid who on the first of May
Goes to the fields at break of day
And washes in the dew from the
    hawthorn tree
Will ever after handsome be.

To make yourself attractive, eat a chicken
gizzard while standing on your head in a
corner of the room.

To bleach your skin, wash your face with
cucumber juice, or with buttermilk mixed
with horseradish roots or tansy leaves, or
with cow's milk.

Eat cooked chicken feet
behind a door and throw
or poke the bones
through the crack of the
door. This will make
you pretty.

DIMPLES

Dimple in the cheek,
Mild, gentle, and meek.

Dimple on the chin,
Devil within.

or

A dimple on the chin,
Many lovers you will win.

A dimple is the mark left by an angel's finger
when it turned up the baby's face to kiss it
while it was asleep.

CRAMPS

When you get a cramp or a stitch in your side
from running hard, stop for a minute, lift up
a rock or stone lying on the ground, spit
under it, and put the rock back just as you
found it. When you do this, do not lift the
stone completely off the ground, but let an
edge always rest on the ground.

If you occasionally have cramps at night, you
can help stop them by turning your shoes
upside down under the bed before you go to
sleep. This precaution helps to relax you, and
if you are relaxed, you won't have cramps.

EARS

When your ear burns, it may mean that someone is either saying good or bad things about
you. If you think that a person is talking
badly about you, put some salt in the fire, and
it will give him a headache.

When your ear burns, you can also wet your
finger, make a cross on your ear, and say:

> If it's good,
> May the Lord bless you;
> If it's bad,
> May the Devil take you.

or

> If good,
> Good betide you;
> If bad,
> May the Devil ride you.

When your ear burns, name three persons
whom you think are talking about you. The
name on which your ear stops burning is the
name of the person doing the talking.

Large ears show that you have a generous
nature. Very small ears mean that you are
stingy.

EYES

If your right eye itches, twitches, or jumps, it is a sign that you will cry soon. If it is your left eye, you will laugh.

Blue-eyed persons are faithful, black-eyed persons are not always to be trusted, and gray-eyed persons are greedy:

> Blue-eye beauty,
> Do your mammy's duty!
> Black-eye, pick a pie,
> Run around and tell a lie!
> Gray-eye greedy gut,
> Eat the whole world up!

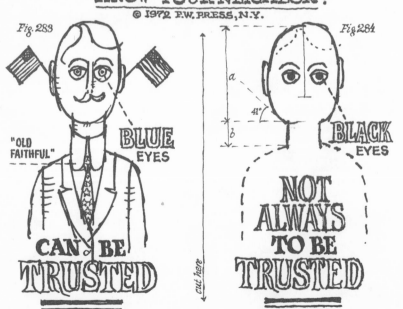

A Guide For The Perplexed

REPRINTED, WITH PERMISSION, FROM PROFESSOR WILHELM Von OSTERHASE:

KNOW YOUR NEIGHBOR!

© 1972 F.W. PRESS, N.Y.

Fig. 283

Fig 284

"OLD FAITHFUL"

BLUE EYES

CAN BE TRUSTED

BLACK EYES

NOT ALWAYS TO BE TRUSTED

Remember: GRAY-EYED PERSONS ARE GREEDY !!! (*All Rights Reserved*)

Right eye, cry eye,
Left eye, laugh eye.

If you wash your eyes with the blood of a bat,
you will be able to see on the darkest nights.

Heavy eyebrows are a sign of a long life.

A person with long eyelashes will always have
good luck.

FINGERNAILS

Cut them on Monday, cut them for wealth,
Cut them on Tuesday, cut them for health,
Cut them on Wednesday, cut them for news,
Cut them on Thursday, a new pair of shoes,
Cut them on Friday, cut them for woe,
Cut them on Saturday, a journey to go,
Cut them on Sunday, cut them for evil,
And be all the week as cross as the Devil.

For Friday and Saturday, some say:

Cut them on Friday, cut them for sorrow,
Cut them on Saturday, see your
    sweetheart tomorrow.

Cut your nails on Monday morning, without
thinking of a red fox's tail, and you will get
a present before the week is out.

If you cut your fingernails on Sunday, you
will have a pain in the neck for seven days.
You will also blush before the day is out.

It is very bad luck to bite your fingernails. Some people believe that if fingernails are eaten, they will stick in your heart and kill you.

Some say that each white spot on the finger-nails stands for a lie that has been told. Others say that each spot represents a letter which you will receive. As the white spot grows out toward the end of the nail, the letter comes closer and closer, and you will receive it when the spot reaches the tip of the nail.

A white spot on the nail means a present. You will get the present when the spot reaches the end and is cut.

If you count the white spots on your finger-nails between December 20th and December 25th, they will show the number of presents you will receive on Christmas Day.

Count the spots on your fingernails, saying:

> Friends, Foes,
> Money, Beaux,
> Friends, Foes . . .

The last one counted
tells your fortune.

Another way of counting:

> A friend, A foe, A gift,
> A beau, A journey to go.

FRECKLES

Freckles come from looking into tiger lilies or smelling them.

A person with freckles has good health.

Even though they are a sign of good health, some people want to get rid of their freckles, and there are many "cures" for doing this. Here are ten:

1. Bottle the last snow of winter and use it as a lotion for washing away freckles.

2. Put lemon-rind juice and ten raisins in a bottle filled with water that has run or dripped from the eaves of a house. Shake the bottle daily for nine days. After the ninth day, use the liquid as a lotion to wash away your freckles.

3. Go to a brook, catch a frog, and rub him alive on your face. Then let him go. He will take your freckles.

4. If you get up before sunrise on the first three mornings of May and wash your freckles in the dew from red clover, your freckles will soon vanish.

5. Wash your face with rainwater that is standing in a hollow stump.

6. Wash the freckles with buttermilk.

7. Go to a crossroads, kneel down, and wash your face three times in the dust that lies exactly in the middle of the roads. Then go to a creek and wash your face.

8. Take the dew from growing wheat and mix it with rose water and oil of lilies. This lotion will drive away freckles.

9. Rub your freckles with a penny and then throw it away. Whoever picks up the penny will get your freckles.

10. The dew of wild roses gathered on Midsummer's Night will cause freckles to disappear if used as a lotion.

I'm not a Northern beauty,
I'm not a Southern rose,
I'm just a little girl
With freckles on her nose.

HAIR

If you cut your hair in the dark of the moon, it will grow out slowly. This saves on haircuts.

If you are a girl, cut a half inch from the end of your hair at the time of the full moon, and it will grow so long that you can sit on it.

I wish I had a nickel,
I wish I had a dime,
I'd send you to get a haircut
Just like mine.

To make your hair curly, eat carrots or crusts of toasted bread.

Rain falling on your bare head will make hair grow. Grapevine sap is also very good for strengthening the hair and making it grow in a rich and healthy way.

If you have tangles in your hair, rats have slept in it.

A person with a cowlick will be lucky.

It is unlucky to comb your hair after dark. Some people say that if you do so it will make you crazy. There is also a saying:

> To comb your hair after dark
> Brings grief and sorrow to the heart.

When you drop a comb, step on it, then pick it up and kiss it to avoid bad luck.

There is a warning rhyme:

> Trust no man though he be your brother,
> Whose hair is one color, and his beard another.

Pull a hair from someone's head, and draw it sharply between two fingernails. If it curls, the one from whose head it was taken has a bad temper. If it remains straight, the person is sweet-tempered.

HEADACHES

If a bird picks up the combings of your hair and makes a nest of them you will have a headache. Do not throw the combings of your hair out of doors where a bird can get them. It may also make you forgetful, and give you a "wandering mind."

To sit in the house with your hat on will cause a headache.

To prevent headaches or to make them go away, carry a buckeye in your pocket, or carry a small potato until it dries up and withers, or wear rattlesnake rattles in your hatband. You can also put cabbage leaves on your forehead, or wear a match in your hair.

HEALTH MEASURES

Don't go swimming in the spring until the cottonwood leaves are as big as squirrels' ears.

> Cocks crow in the morning
> To tell us to rise,
> And he who lies late
> Will never be wise;
> For early to bed
> And early to rise
> Is the way to be healthy,
> Wealthy and wise!

To avoid catching cold, it is best not to take your long underwear off until the Fourth of July. (This is for children in the very northern states and does not apply in Florida, Louisiana, or Georgia.)

An apple a day
Keeps the doctor away;
An onion a day
Keeps everybody away!

An apple a day is 365 a year.

If you are rained on and get wet during a May rain, you will not be sick the following summer.

> After breakfast, work awhile;
> After dinner, sit awhile;
> After supper, walk a mile.

HICCUPS

> Hiccups, hiccups, go away,
> Come again another day;
> Hiccups, hiccups, when I bake,
> I'll give you a butter cake.

If you have the hiccups, it means that you have told a lie. (Some people say that, but you know best.)

To stop the hiccups, say these words quickly nine times:

> Hiccups, sticcups,
> Stand right straight up!

When a friend of yours has the hiccups, you can stop them by scaring him. You can suddenly hit him on the back and scream "FIRE!" Or tell him that his dog is dead. Or that there is an earthquake around the corner. Or that the roof is falling in. Anything that will scare him is good to stop his hiccups.

To stop the hiccups drink three swallows of water while holding your breath, and at the same time say under your breath:

Three sups up
Will cure the hiccups up.

Concentrate very hard on holding the tips of your forefingers together as closely as possible without letting them touch, and your hiccups will go away. So close that there's not a hair's breadth between them!

Put a small cube of ice on the lobe of your right ear.

Put your thumbs in your ears and press your little fingers against your nostrils. Then sip water out of a cup that someone holds for you.

Say this three times to cure hiccups:

Hee-cup, teacup,
Jump up, Jacob!

For hiccups, make the person angry by picking on him or aggravating him.

Eat plum preserves.

Pull a hair out of your ear.
Put a penny between your toes.
Think of seven bald-headed men.

ILLNESS or SICKNESS

For every illness under the sun
There is a cure or there is none.
If there is a cure, go and find it.
If there is none, never mind it.

POP! WENT THE MEASLES!

I went up to Mary's house,
Mary had the measles.
This is the way the measles go:
Pop! went the measles!

ONIONS-BUNIONS

Roses smell
And so do onions,
Corns are sore
And so are bunions.

If you eat onions for breakfast,
you will marry a bald-headed man.

ITCHES

Peaches, peaches,
My nose eetches,
Somebody's coming
With a hole in their breeches!

If your nose itches, you will kiss a fool.

When the left side of your nose itches, you
will have good news.

When the right side itches, you'll quarrel
with someone.

When the palm of either hand itches, put it
in your pocket before you touch anything,
and your pocket will soon be full of money.

If the right hand itches just below the index
finger, you will get a job of work to do.

If the soles of your feet itch, you are going
to travel.

SCRATCHES

A scratch up and down is a lover found,
A scratch across is a lover lost.

A scratch on the arm or leg is a sign of a trip
or a journey. If it is a short scratch, it will be
a short trip. If it is a long one, the trip will
be long.

When you are scratching someone's back, use this rhyme:

> Going on a treasure hunt,
> X marks the spot,
> Three big circles
> And one big spot.
> Go up, go down,
> Follow the dotted line,
> Take three steps
> And squeeeeeeze!

MOLES

> Mole on the arm,
> You're a gentleman's charm.
>
> Mole on the neck,
> Money by the peck.
>
> Mole on the arm,
> You'll live on a farm.
>
> or
>
> Mole on the back,
> Money by the sack.
>
> Mole on the lip,
> You're a little too flip.

A mole on the right cheek is a mark of beauty.

A mole on either cheek is a sign of wealth.

A chin mole means a long life.

A mole on the nose stands for success.

SNEEZING

Sneeze on Monday, sneeze for danger,
Sneeze on Tuesday, kiss a stranger,
Sneeze on Wednesday, sneeze for a letter,
Sneeze on Thursday, something better,
Sneeze on Friday, sneeze for sorrow,
Sneeze on Saturday, joy tomorrow.
Sneeze on Sunday, your safety seek,
Or the Devil will have you the rest of the week.

When anyone sneezes, always say "God bless you." This will keep the Devil from flying down the person's throat. You can also say, "God bless you and may the Devil miss you."

If you feel like sneezing and cannot, either look at a bright light or walk into another room. You will sneeze.

To stop a sneeze, press a finger hard against your upper lip under your nose.

Very often you will hear people say *"Gesundheit"* after a person has sneezed. This is a German word meaning *health*. The person who has sneezed should answer at once, *"Gesundheit ist besser wie krankheit"* (health is better than sickness). It is, of course.

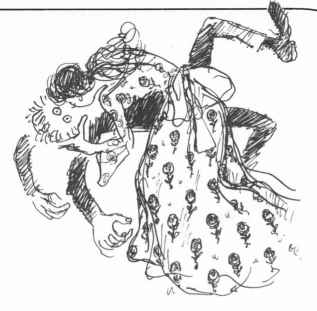

Two sneezes before breakfast generally means that you will have a new sweetheart that week. Or that you will soon be kissed.

What paper is most like a sneeze?
    Tissue.

What nut is most like a sneeze?
    Cashew.

If you sneeze while you are thinking, what you are thinking will come true.

Sneeze before seven,
Company before eleven.

Sneeze before you eat,
See your sweetheart before you sleep.

Anyone sneezing will soon be kissed.

STIES

To cure a sty, stand at a crossroad and say:

Sty, sty, leave my eye,
Go to the next one passing by.

The next person coming by will get it, and your sty will disappear.

You can cure a sty by rubbing it three times with the tip of a black cat's tail.

Another way to cure a sty: Have an older person hold a warm, gold ring as close to the sty as possible without actually touching it. The warmth of the ring will soothe the sty and cure it. The ring can be heated either by rubbing it very hard on a piece of heavy cloth or by holding it with a glove near a lighted match.

TEETH

It's best not to throw a tooth away outdoors. If a rabbit runs over it, your next tooth will be a rabbit's tooth. If a dog or a rat finds it and takes it away, you will get a dog or a rat tooth.

When a tooth has been pulled or when you have lost it in any other way, put it under your pillow or in a glass of water by your bed. In the morning the tooth will be gone, and in its place there will be a dime or a quarter.

If you can keep your tongue out of the hole where a tooth has been pulled, a gold tooth will grow in its place. (This is almost impossible to do.)

A toothpick made from the splinter of a tree struck by lightning is better than any regular toothpick. It is supposed to be of help against toothaches.

WARTS

Warts come from handling toads or from lying on your back and pointing at stars while you are counting them. When you are counting stars, it's best not to point at them.

There are a million cures for warts. Doctors often do not know why these cures work, but it is probably because those who use the cures really believe in them. If you try one of these cures and believe that it will work, your warts may go away. If they don't, you can try another cure. Here are ten:

1. Wear a straw hat for two days, and then burn it.

2. Steal a dirty dishrag, rub your warts with it, and then bury it secretly. When the dishrag rots, your warts will go away.

3. Sell your warts to a sailor for a penny. When he gives you the penny, put it down your dress or inside your shirt, and then run around the outside of the house until you lose the penny.

4. "You can get rid of a wart by making a rhyme while your head is stuck in a rain barrel." Any rhyme will do, and it is best when the rain barrel is about half full.

5. When you see the new moon, rub your hands over your warts while looking at the moon, and say:
   > What I see, increase,
   > What I feel, decrease.

6. When you are walking in the fields, pick a stem of milkweed, break the stem, and rub your warts with the milk. Do this every morning for seven days, and your warts will disappear.

7. Tie a knot in a string for each wart that you have. If you have seven warts, tie seven knots; if you have six, tie six. Then rub the warts with the string, and put the string on the ground under the eaves of the house where the rainwater can fall on it. When the string rots, your warts will be gone.

8. Rub your warts with a kernel of corn, and then feed the kernel to a black chicken.

9. Take nine beans, rub each one over your warts, and then throw the beans in a well.

10. If you happen to have your warts in the month of May, rub your warts and say:
    Beautiful flowers in May,
    Beautiful flowers in May,
    Beautiful flowers in May.
    After the May flowers have stopped blooming, your warts will have gone.

Love and Kisses

A I LOVE YOU BETTER THAN A PIG LOVES SLOP

LOVE

I love you vip,
I love you vop,
I love you better
Than a pig loves slop.

That is perhaps not quite as delicately stated as it might be, but no one can deny that love is there.

Houston is a knockout,
Galveston is a pain,
The way I love you, honey,
Would make a bulldog break his chain.

(If you happen to live in Galveston, put Galveston in the first line and Houston in the second.)

I used to be a little girl
Playing in the sand,
Now I am a great big girl,
All I need's a man.

Red and yellow,
Catch a fellow,
Black and white,
Hold him tight.

A rooster crowed in Boston,
He was heard in Spain,
The way I love you, darling,
Is a dirty shame.

I love you, I love you,
I love you so well,
If I had a peanut,
I'd give you the shell! (Tsk! Tsk!)

What care I for gold or silver,
What care I for house or land,
What care I for ships on the ocean,
All I want's a nice young man.

The roads are long and muddy,
The sea is wide and deep,
I think of you, my darling,
Ten thousand times a week.

Snow or blow,
I'm bound to go
With my beau.

Sugar is sweet,
Butter is greasy,
I love you,
So don't be uneasy.

For to meet him, for to meet him,
For to meet him I will go,
For to meet my love William,
The young man that I love.

Get up on the first day of May and count the
live things you see, and it will be that many
years till you marry.

Put your stockings under your pillow on Friday night, and say this little rhyme, and you
will dream of your husband-to-be:

> Now I lay me down to sleep
> With my stockings under my head,
> And I hope that I will dream
> Of the one that I am to wed.

Wear a piece of goldenrod, and you will see
your love before tomorrow.

"The moon shines bright,
May I carry you home tonight?"
"The stars are shining, too,
I don't care if you do."

Peaches in the summertime,
Apples in the fall,
I've been loving this pretty girl
Ever since I learned to crawl.

Isn't love wonderful? In the springtime? Or at any time?

Let a girl fold up the last letter from her sweetheart and wear it next to her heart for three days and nights. If on the third night she dreams of beautiful trees, he is true; if of water, false.

The girl who can eat eight green gooseberries without making a face can make any boy she wants fall in love with her.

LONDON HILL

When I was going up London Hill,
London Hill, London Hill,
When I was going up London Hill
On a cold and frosty morning.

I met my true love coming down,
Coming down, coming down,
I met my true love coming down
On a cold and frosty morning.

What do you think she gave to me,
Gave to me, gave to me,
What do you think she gave to me
On a cold and frosty morning?

A snow white cake and a Guinea gold ring,
Guinea gold ring, Guinea gold ring,
A snow white cake and Guinea gold ring,
On a cold and frosty morning.

MRS. VICKERS' DAUGHTER

Johnny Thomson, so they say,
Goes a-courting every day,
Sword and pistol by his side,
Lizzie Vickers for his bride.

Oh, dear doctor, can you tell
What will make poor Lizzie well?
She is sick and she may die,
That would make poor Johnny cry.

Johnny here and Johnny there,
Johnny o'er the water,
Johnny's got the sweetest girl,
Mrs. Vickers' daughter.

KISSES

Crackers is crackers,
Cheese is cheese,
What is a kiss
Without a squeeze.

Here I stand
On two little chips,
Come and kiss
My sweet little lips.

Wish I had a nickel,
Wish I had a dime,
Wish I had a pretty girl
To kiss me all the time!

I SAW A SHIP A-SAILING

I saw a ship a-sailing,
A-sailing on the sea,
And oh! but it was laden
With pretty things for thee.

There were comfits in the cabin,
And kisses in the hold;
The sails were made of silk,
And the masts were all of gold.

The four-and-twenty sailors
That stood between the decks
Were four-and-twenty white mice
With chains about their necks.

The captain was a duck
With a packet on his back,
And when the ship began to move,
The captain said, "Quack! Quack!"

A boy with eyes of brown
Will kiss you once and turn you down;
A boy with eyes of black
Will kiss you once and not come back;
A boy with eyes of blue
Will kiss you once and ask for two.

Here I stand
All ragged and dirty,
Kiss me quick
And I'll run like a turkey!

(*A skip-rope rhyme:*)

Dolly, Dolly, where are you?
—Up the Hudson Bay.
What are you doing there, dear?
—Kissing a sailor.

When a young girl dreams of sour pickles, it is a sign she is going to be kissed.

If a boy kisses his girl on the nose, he may expect trouble.

POSTAGE STAMPS ON LETTERS

There are messages you can send to your sweetheart through the way you place a postage stamp on a letter:

An upside-down stamp means: *I love you*, or *I want a kiss*.

Two stamps side-by-side on an envelope means: *My love for you has doubled.*

One stamp above the other: *I will see you Saturday afternoon.*

When you use two stamps where only one is needed: *My love for you will stop at nothing.*

If you cut a stamp in half and paste the two halves at the upper right-hand corner of the envelope so that they are separated by a small space, it means: *Our friendship is at an end.* If you place the two halves in the left-hand corner: *You have broken my heart.*

If you place the stamp on the lower right-hand corner of the envelope, you are warning your sweetheart that: *Father has caught on.*

A circle at the end of a letter is a hug.

A cross or an X at the end of a letter is a kiss.

It is nice to mix them up: OXOXXXOOO-XOOXOO, and then put the stamp upside down on the envelope.

STUBBING YOUR TOE

If you stump your toe,
And kiss your thumb,
You'll see your sweetheart
Before the sun goes down.

Stub your toe,
Kiss your finger, and touch blue,
You'll see your fellow
Before the day is through.

NOBODY LOVES ME

Nobody loves me,
Everybody hates me.
I'm down in the garden eating worms:
Big, fat juicy ones,
Long, slick, slimy ones,
And some woolly ones, too.

Riddles, Jokes, Knock-Knocks, Elephants, and Problems- Problems-Problems

RIDDLES

I went to the garden and got it,
Came to the house and cried with it.
> *An onion.*

Only the size of a nut, yet without feet it
climbs the mountain.
> *A snail.*

Big as a cucumber and with a blond beard.
> *An ear of corn.*

An old lady with a single tooth calls all her
people.
> *A bell with its clapper.*

My father had so much money he couldn't
count it.
My mother had such a large sheet she
couldn't fold it.
I had a ball and couldn't bounce it.
> *The stars, sky, and moon.*

The greater it is, the less it can be seen.
> *Darkness.*

As an act of charity, whom should we always
kill?
> *Hunger.*

If a cow fell in the river, how would you take
her out?
> *Wet.*

It increases and decreases,
And no one sees it.
It is not a fire,
And yet it can be quenched.
>*Thirst.*

Don't meddle, don't touch,
Little girl, little boy,
Or the world will lose
Some of its joy.
>*A bird's nest.*

What loves a dog
And rides on his back,
Travels for miles
And leaves not a track?
>*A flea.*

I have a little house,
And a mouse couldn't fit in it,
And all the men in our town
Couldn't count the windows in it.
>*A thimble.*

How many wells does it take to make a sea?
>*One, if it's big enough.*

What runs without stopping and never needs
winding up?
>*A creek or brook.*

A body met a body
In a bag of beans,
Said a body to a body,
"Can a body tell a body
What a body means?"

> Two bugs in a bag of beans. (That doesn't make much sense, does it? But do you want sense every single minute of the day? Of course not!)

WHAT DID ONE SAY TO THE OTHER?

What did one eye say to the other eye?
> What's that that smells between us?

What did one ear say to the other ear?
> Do you live on this block, too?

What did one tonsil say to the other?
> Get dressed. The doctor's taking us out tonight.

What did one flea say to the other when they came out of the theater?
> *Shall we walk or take a dog?*

What did one carrot say to the other carrots?
> *Silly, carrots don't talk!*

What did the big rose say to the little rose?
> *Hiya, bud.*

What did the big frying pan say to the little frying pan?
> *Hiya, small fry.*

What did one hen say to the other hen?
> *"I think I'm going to have a baby."*

What does a two-hundred-pound mouse say?
> *"Here, kitty, kitty, kitty."*

WHEN IS IT NOT?

When is a door not a door?
When it's ajar.

When is a sailor not a sailor?
When he's afloat.

When is a cat not a cat?
When it's a kitten.

When is a Ford not a Ford?
When it's turning into a driveway.

When is a hat not a hat?
When it becomes a pretty lady.

When is a boat like a pile of snow?
When it's adrift.

CRISS-CROSS JOKES

What do you get when you cross a duck and a cow?
Quackers and milk.

What do you get when you cross a cat and a lemon?
A sourpuss.

What do you get when you cross an octopus and a bale of hay?
Eight straw brooms.

What do you get when you cross a parrot and an elephant?

> *An animal that not only remembers, but can tell what it remembers.*

What do you get when you cross a canary and a tiger?

> *I don't know, but when it sings, you'd better listen.*

BANANAS ETC.

What's long and yellow and wears diapers?

> *A baby banana.*

What's yellow and writes?

> *A ballpoint banana.*

What's yellow and flies through the air?

> *Superbanana.*

What's orange, goes click–click, and is good for the eyes?

> *A ballpoint carrot.*

What's Smoky the Bear's middle name?

> *The.*

WHY?

Why did the crow sit on the telephone line?
He wanted to make a long distance caw.

Why did the bear climb up the telephone pole?
He wanted to call his mother.

Why are Boy Scouts so chubby?
'Cause scouting rounds a guy out.

Why are Boy Scouts so chubby?
From eating so many Brownies.

Why is Mr. Timothy More, since he lost his hair, like an American city?
Because he is bald Tim More.

Why is Samuel Smith like an underdone cake?
Because he is not Brown.

Why do white sheep eat more than black ones?
Because there are more of them.

Why is 1860 like 1862?
Because the one is 1860 and the other is 1862.

Why are the tallest people the laziest?
They are always longer in bed than others.

Why is a person bathing in the river in Paris like a madman?
> *Because he's insane.*

Why did the lady sue the department store?
> *Because she bought a living bra and it bit her.*

Why does the ocean roar?
> *You'd roar, too, if you had crabs on your bottom.*

COLORS

What's white and black with a cherry on top?
> *A police car.*

What's white and flies up?
> *A retarded snowflake.*

What's green and has a big mouth?
> *A Girl Scout that talks a lot.*

What's gray and comes in a can?
> *Campbell's Elephant Soup.*

What's brown and wears a mask?
A raccoon.

What's green on the inside and white on the outside?
A frog sandwich.

What's black and blue and goes ding-dong?
A black and blue ding-dong.

What's black and white and read all over?
A newspaper.

What's black and white and red all over?
A blushing zebra.

What's black and white and black and white and black and white?
A nun rolling down hill.

What's purple and green with yellow and black stripes and also has a hundred legs?
I don't know.
I don't know either, but it's crawling up your neck.

DIFFERENCES

What's the difference between a blind man and a sailor in prison?
One can't see to go, and the other can't go to sea.

What's the difference between a summer dress in winter and an extracted tooth?
One is too thin, the other is tooth out.

partly after Degas.

What's the difference between a ballerina and a duck?

> *One goes quick on her beautiful legs, and the other goes quack on her beautiful eggs.*

What's the difference between a legal document and a cat?

> *One has pauses at the end of its clauses, and the other has claws-es at the end of its paws-es.*

What's the difference between a gardener and a billiard player?

> *One minds his peas and the other his cues.*

What's the difference between a storm cloud and a spanked child?

> *One pours with rain, the other roars with pain.*

What's the difference between a glass of water and a glass of Coke?

> *Fifteen cents.*

What's the difference between a match and a cat?

A match always lights on its head, and a cat always lights on its feet.

What's the difference between a new penny and an old dime?

Nine cents.

What's the difference between a hen and a man?

A man can lay an egg on a red hot stove without burning himself, and a hen can't.

What's the difference between illegal and un-lawful?

One is a sick bird, and the other is against the law.

What's the difference between an elephant and a grape?

A grape is purple.

What's the difference between a deer fleeing from its pursuers and a midget witch?

One is a hunted stag, and the other a stunted hag.

TIME

What time is it?

Half past kissing time and time to start again.

What time is it?

Time all dogs were dead. Don't you feel sick?

What time is it?

Same time it was this time yesterday.

What time is it?
> *Ten to.*

Ten to what?
> *Ten' to your own business.*

What time is it?
> *Ten hairs past a freckle,*
> *Ten hairs past a freckle . . .*

What time is it?
> *Daytime, going on nighttime.*

What time is it?
> *Half past biscuit, going on cornbread.*

What time is it?
> *Half past twelve, ticking like crazy to get to one.*

DINGLE-DANGLES

What's red and dingle-dangles
from the ceiling?
> *A red dingle-dangle.*

What's green and dingle-dangles
from the ceiling?
> *A green dingle-dangle.*

No! They don't come in green.

INFIR TARIS

> Infir taris,
> Inoak noneis,
> Inmud eelsare,
> Inclay noneare.
> Goatsea tivy,
> Maresea toats.

More reasonably spelled, that becomes:

> In fir, tar is,
> In oak, none is,
> In mud, eels are,
> In clay, none are.
> Goats eat ivy,
> Mares eat oats.

But say it rapidly, and you will fool most listeners. They will think it is Latin or Portuguese or Old French. Or that you are off your rocker.

FIRE ENGINES

Why are fire engines painted red?

> *Books are read. Magazines are read, too. Two and two are four. Three times four is twelve. There are twelve inches in a ruler. Queen Elizabeth is a ruler. Queen Elizabeth is also a ship that sails the sea. Little fishes swim in the sea. Fishes have fins. Finns fought Russians. Russians are called Reds. Fire engines are always rushin'. That's why they are painted red.*

EATERS

What's purple and eats people?

> *A purple people eater.*

What is a Vatican usher called?

> *A papal people seater.*

What's big and red and eats rocks?

> *A red rock eater.*

What's purple and eats worms?

> *A purple worm eater.*

ELEPHANTS

How can you tell when there's an elephant in the back seat of your car?

> *You can smell the peanuts on his breath.*

Why do ducks have flat feet?

> *From stamping out forest fires.*

Why do elephants have flat feet?

> *From stamping out burning ducks.*

How can you lift an elephant?
> *Put an acorn under him and wait twenty years.*

What has a trunk and is gray?
> *A mouse on vacation. (You thought I was going to say an elephant, didn't you?)*

Why did the mouse bite the elephant's ear?
> *He thought it was a gray potato chip.*

If an elephant were to sit on a fence, what time would it be?
> *Time to get a new fence.*

Why do elephants squirt water through their noses?
> *It's cheaper than beer.*

What is gray and blue?
> *An elephant holding his breath.*

How do you talk to an elephant?
> *Use big words.*

How do you capture elephants?
> *Put up a sign reading "Water for ELFANTS." The elephants will gather around and laugh at it. Look at them through a telescope held backwards. Pick them up with tweezers and drop them in a bottle.*

How do you make an elephant float?
> *Two scoops of ice cream, an elephant, and some root beer.*

How do you get six elephants in a Volkswagen?
Three in front and three in back.

How do you get six giraffes in a Volkswagen?
Well, first you have to get the elephants out, and then you trade the hardtop model for a convertible, because the giraffes' necks are longer than elephants and if you had six giraffes' necks inside a hardtop it would be more crowded than a pitcherful of eels, and all of them would be looking in different directions because of the poor accommodations. And after you have the convertible, then three giraffes sit in the front seat and three in the back. And if the giraffes don't like it, even with the top down, then you send them home and invite the elephants back in. They were there in the first place.

Why are elephants poor dancers?
They have two left feet.

Why don't elephants like martinis?
Did you ever try to get an olive out of your nose?

How can you tell if there's an elephant in the refrigerator?
By the letter E on his sweater.

What's the difference between an elephant and peanut butter?
An elephant doesn't stick to the roof of your mouth.

What did the little stream say when the elephant sat down in it?
Well, I'm dammed!

How can you tell an elephant from a grape?
Jump up and down on it for a while. If you don't get any wine, it's an elephant.

Why was the man on the bus throwing paper out the window?
To keep the elephants away.

But there are no elephants within miles!
That proves how effective it is.

Have you heard the last elephant joke?
I hope so.

What did the Lone Ranger say when he saw his horse coming?
Here comes my horse.

What did Tarzan say when he saw a herd of elephants coming?
Here come the elephants.

What did Jane say when she saw the herd of elephants coming?
Here come the grapes. (She was color blind.)

GRAPES

What's purple and surrounded by water?
Grape Britain.

What's purple and conquered the world?
Alexander the Grape.

What's purple and swims?
Moby Grape.

What color is a grape's belch?
Burple.

What's purple and rides on a white horse?
General Grape.

ICE

Spell hard water in three letters.
> *I-C-E.*

Why doesn't the Devil skate?
> *Where in hell would he find ice?*
> *(That isn't swearing. You are talking about a specific place: hell.)*

RIDDLE-JOKES

What did the man step on when it was raining cats and dogs?
> *A poodle.*

What should you do when you feel run down?
> *Get the license number.*

What is an old lady in the middle of a river like?
> *Like to be drowned.*

What is a very good definition of nonsense?
> *Bolting a door with a boiled carrot.*

To what two cities of Massachusetts should little boys go with their boats?
> *To Fall River and Salem.*

What kind of animals can jump over houses?
All kinds of animals. Houses can't jump.

If a little girl is enjoying herself and doing no harm, what letter in the alphabet would you name?
Letter B.

What is that from which if you take all its letters it remains the same?
A postman.

When is a man ahead of himself or in advance of his age?
When he's knocked into the middle of next week.

What has two heads, four ears, six feet, and one tail?
You, when you ride a donkey.

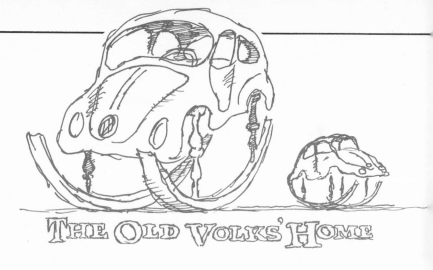

THE OLD VOLKS' HOME

Where do old Volkswagens go?
> *To the old Volks' home.*

If a tree were to break several windows, what would the windows say?
> *Tremendous.*

If I were in the sun and you were out of it, what would the sun become?
> *Sin.*

What did Jack Frost say when he kissed the violet?
> *Wilt thou, and it wilted.*

What is the wickedest city of America?
> *Sin-sin-naughty.*

If Mississ-ippi should lend Miss-ouri her New Jersey, what would Dela-ware?
> *Alaska.*

What two things can you never eat for break-fast?
> *Lunch and supper.*

What's the biggest pencil in the whole world?
Pennsylvania.

What's the greatest feat of strength ever performed?
Wheeling, West Virginia.

What's the happiest State in the Union?
Merry-land.

What does Washington, D. C. stand for?
Washington, Daddy of his Country.

A question to which you can never answer "yes."
"Are you sleeping?"

Three enormously fat ladies were under a tiny umbrella. It started thundering and lightning. Why didn't they get wet?
It wasn't raining.

What gives milk and has one horn?
A milk truck.

What do you call a monkey that eats potato chips?

A chipmonk.

When did the fly fly?

When the spider spied her.

If you wished a Doctor of Divinity to play on your violin, what would you say?

Fiddle, D. D.

What is the best thing that you can put in a pumpkin pie?

Your teeth.

When is the soup likely to run out of the saucepan?

When there's a leek in it. (Eek!)

What is the most difficult river on which to get a boat?

Arno, because they're Arno boats there. (Eek! Eeek!)
(The Arno is a river which flows through the very great and wonderful city of Florence in Italy. Forget the joke if you can, but try to visit Florence some time.)

KNOCK, KNOCK

Knock, knock.
Who's there?
Banana.
Banana who?

Knock, knock.
Who's there?
Banana.
Banana who?

Knock, knock.
Who's there?
Banana.
Banana who?

Knock, knock.
Who's there?
Orange.
Orange who?
Orange you glad I didn't say banana?

Knock, knock.
Who's there?
Bob.
Bob who?
Bob, Bob, black sheep, have you any wool?

Knock, knock.
Who's there?
Caesar.
Caesar who?
Caesar jolly good fellow, Caesar jolly good
fellow.

Knock, knock.
Who's there?
Oswald.
Oswald who?
Oswald my gum.

Knock, knock.
Who's there?
Ether.
Ether who?
Ether bunny.

Knock, knock.
Who's there?
Duane.
Duane who?
Duane the bathtub, mama, I'm dwowning.

Knock, knock.
Who's there?
Yah.
Yah who?
That's right. Ride 'em cowboy!

Knock, knock.
Who's there?
Emerson.
Emerson who?
Emerson nice shoes you've got on.

Knock, knock.
Who's there?
Chesterfield.
Chesterfield who?
Chesterfield my leg, so I slapped him.

Knock, knock.
Who's there?
Amsterdam.
Amsterdam who?
Amsterdam tired of
these knock-knocks,
I could scream.

PROBLEMS, PROBLEMS, PROBLEMS

How long is a piece of string?
*Twice the distance from the middle to
the end.*

How long is the stinger of a bee?
*About one thirty-second (1/32) of an inch. The
other foot and a half is imagination.*

**A farmer had seventeen sheep. All but nine
died. How may did he have left?**
Nine.

**How can ten horses be put into nine stalls
with only one horse in each stall?**

Take the numbers from 1 to 7, and mix them up and add them in any way, but use each number only once, and come up with a total of 100.

1 + 2 + 34 + 56 + 7 = 100

A man lives in a one-story building. He is out in his yard one day, and sees a bear roller-skating. He runs inside his house to get his own roller skates. He finds the roller skates, but has to go upstairs to get the key. What is wrong with this story?

He couldn't go upstairs because he lived in a one-story building.

What's one and one?   Two.
What's four minus two?   Two.
What's the name of the author of *Tom Sawyer*?   Twain.
Now say all the answers together.

Two, two, Twain.

How can you subtract 45 from 45 and still leave 45?

$$\frac{\begin{aligned}987654321 &= 45\\ 123456789 &= 45\end{aligned}}{864197532 = 45}$$

How many feet are there on a lamb if you call a tail a foot?

> *Four. Calling a tail a foot doesn't make it one.*

There were seven copycats sitting on a fence. One jumped off. How many were left?

> *None.*

How far can a person go into the woods?

> *Half-way. After that he would be coming out.*

A man cashed a $63.00 check at a bank and received in change eight bills. No one of them was a dollar bill. What were the bills?

$$\frac{\begin{aligned}2-\$20&-40\\ 1-\$10&-10\\ 1-\ \$5&-\ 5\\ 4-\ \$2&-\ 8\end{aligned}}{8 \qquad 63}$$

Within a time limit of twelve seconds name twelve animals from Africa.

> *Nine lions and three elephants.*

How can anyone live eighty years and have only twenty birthdays?

> *Be born on February 29th.*

Add five lines to six and have nine.

If a woman has ten apples and eight children, how can she fairly divide the apples and give each child the same amount?
Make applesauce.

John gave Mike thirty cents in two coins, one of which was not a quarter. How did he do it?
One is a nickel, the other is a quarter.

If Mr. Cheever had fifty-seven fish, what would a boat-load come to in Newburyport?
A wharf.

Which is bigger, Mr. Bigger, or Mr. Bigger's baby?

The baby is a little Bigger.

How can you arrange the numbers from 1 to 9 in a magic square so that the sum of any row—horizontal, diagonal, or vertical—will always total 15?

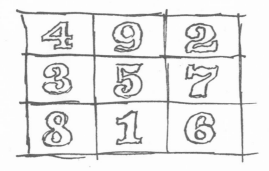

If it takes a woodpecker with a rubber bill two days to peck a hole through the branch of a birch tree, how long will it take a grass-hopper with a cork leg to kick all the seeds out of a dill pickle?

Three and a half days. (Don't you believe it!)

What has two feet and no legs?

Twenty-four inches.

Mr. Gray is a butcher. He is six feet tall, wears a size ten shoe, and his waist measurement is forty-four. What does he weigh?

Meat.

Cats, Dogs, Mice, Lions, Rats

CATS

Spell "mouse trap" in three letters.

C-A-T.

What do people in Tennessee call little gray cats?

Kittens.

If you put a kitten under the covers of your bed and leave it there until it crawls out by itself, it will not leave you.

Butter the front paws of a cat. When the cat has licked the butter off, it will never leave home. You can also stick the cat's front paws into cream. When the cat has licked the cream off its paws and then lapped up the rest of the cream in the saucer, it will not desert you.

You can break a cat from the habit of catching birds by burning a match and rubbing the charred wood three times over the cat's nose.

If a cat walks to the front door and then comes back into the room and lies down in the center of the room with all four feet in the air, you will have company from out of town that same day.

What is there that never was and never will be?

A mouse's nest in a cat's ear.

When a cat jumps up on the table and laps cream, visitors are coming to stay for a time.

Along the East Coast they say that when it is ebb tide, the slits in a cat's eyes are horizontal; when it is flood tide, they are vertical. (Take a cat with you when the tide is changing, and have a look into its eyes!)

Happy as a cat on Friday! (You know what that means? FISH!)

FISHES

Fishy, fishy,
Come bite my hook,
I'll go Captain,
And you'll go cook!

(Which is a sneaky way of telling the fish that he will go *cook*-ed in the pan.)

Some people believe that when a bald person dies, he becomes a fish, and he remains a fish until he collects enough hair to make a wig. He can collect only one hair a month. So he remains a fish for a considerable length of time. (If you catch a hairy fish, it may actually be a bald-headed uncle or schoolteacher.)

Fish bite best when the mockingbird sings.

Spit on your bait for good luck.

What's long and green and hangs on the wall?
> *I don't know.*
A fish.
> *But a fish isn't long.*
It is if you stretch it.
> *But a fish isn't green.*
It is if you let it sit long enough.
> *But a fish doesn't hang on the wall.*
That's right. It doesn't.

DOGS

"A dog is a man's best friend." Be a friend to him, and he will always be faithful to you.

When a dog moans or whines in his sleep, or when he barks small barks in his sleep, he is dreaming. To learn his dream, pull a whisker from the dog's lip and put it under your pillow. That night you will dream what the dog dreamed. You can also put your hat over the head of a dreaming dog, and that night you will have his dreams.

Jumping over a dog will bring you bad luck.

When a dog chases a cat up a weeping willow tree, it means that your sorrows have been chased away.

If a dog is given to you, scrape his paws on the back of the chimney, and he will never run away. You can also cut a few hairs from his tail and bury them under the front porch. This has the same effect.

Scratch a dog where he is unable to scratch himself, and he will not run away from home.

You can make a dog savage by feeding him gunpowder.

Dogs growl because they have never learned to swear.

When a dog's ears are turned inside out, it means that a visitor is coming or that you will get a telephone call from a friend.

After a dog has rolled on the floor, gotten up and shaken himself, visitors will come from the direction he faces.

A barking dog never bites, but you can't tell when he will quit barking.

The dog's nose is cold because he helped Noah drive all the other animals aboard the ark. The dog went on board last, and because there was very little room, he had to stand squeezed in with the others, but with his nose out in the cold rain for forty days. (Your nose would be cold, too. Forty days!)

Whenever you see a lost dog, particularly in the city or in town, try to help him.

THE LION AND THE MOUSE

One fine day a lion was strutting through the forest when he suddenly came upon a small pool. Noticing his reflection in the unrippled surface, he stopped to admire himself. Being a vain animal, he decided to find out why the other animals were not as beautiful as he.

First he saw a giraffe and asked him why he was not as big, strong, and beautiful as he. The giraffe couldn't answer, but merely

shrugged his shoulders and walked on.

Next the lion saw a bear and inquired, "Why aren't you as big and brave and beautiful as I am?" The bear answered, "I don't know," and went on.

Then the lion met a hippopotamus and asked him the same question. The hippopotamus also replied, "I don't know."

Next the lion met a mouse and asked him, "Why aren't you big and brave and beautiful like me?"

The mouse looked up at the lion and said, "I've been sick."

GUINEA PIGS

Pick up a guinea pig by the tail and its eyes will drop out. (This is absolutely true. Why? Because guinea pigs don't have any tails. So, if you could pick one up by the tail . . .)

CLAMS

You've heard the expression "happy as a clam." That's not the full expression. The full expression is "happy as a clam at high tide." Why? Because when it's high tide, a clam is very, very happy. No enemies can get at him; he's as safe as a clam can be. You could get at him at low tide, but not at high!

THREE FRIENDLY LITTLE FISH

Here are three very friendly little fish. Start with the letter Y:

Now make half
their bodies:

Now make their
heads:

and eyes:

and tails:

and scales:

Three friendly little fish!

MICE

All the cats consulted.
  What was it about?
How to catch a little mouse
  Running in and out.

RATS

To rid a house of rats, catch and paint one red and turn it loose. The rest will be horrified at the sight of a red rat and will leave.

Another way to make rats leave is to write a serious letter to them in which you ask them to go to a house down the street or in the next block. (Be sure to give the exact address.) Push this letter inside the rat hole. The rats will read it and do as you ask.

Rats desert sinking ships.

In the western gold and silver mines (Nevada, Montana, Utah, Arizona, California), whenever the rats begin running out of the tunnels, the miners also leave, because the rats are warning of a cave-in.

Somewhat after Monsieur Géricault

WHITE HORSES

When you meet a white horse, make a wish, and say:

> White, white, white horse,
> Ding, ding, ding,
> Where I go,
> I'll find something.

Count three white horses and one red-haired woman, and whatever wish you have made will come true.

If you meet two white horses in the same block, you may make a wish on them.

Birds,
Birds,
Birds

BIRDS

White head, yellow toes,
Tell me this riddle
Or I'll ring your nose.
    A duck.

When you see a buzzard in the sky, say:

Poor old lonesome turkey buzzard,
Fly to the east, fly to the west,
Fly to the one I love the best.

If the buzzard flaps his wings, you will see
your sweetheart before Saturday night.

When you see a redbird, throw it a kiss and
make a wish. The wish will come true.

If my peacock lays an egg in your yard, who
owns the egg?
    Peahens lay eggs.

A hoot owl crying at
night is bad luck. To
offset the bad luck, throw
salt in the fire, turn
your pockets inside out,
or place a broom across
the doorway. To stop his
hooting, grasp the wrist
of one hand with the
fingers of the other. This
chokes the hoot owl and
makes him silent.

If you want to hoodoo a person with hoot owls, go to his house when he is away and turn his shoes upside down under the bed. Hoot owls will come and torment him with their hooting, and they will not stop until he finds the shoes and turns them right side up again.

How long can a goose stand on one leg?
Try it and see.

If a white pigeon flies to your window and sits upon the sill, it is a sign of good luck. It is particularly lucky if the pigeon's name is Gertrude.

Jay bird, jay bird
Settin' on a fence,
Tryin' to make a dollar
Out of fifteen cents.

Some people believe that the jay bird is a devil bird, and that every Friday he gathers sticks and carries them to hell to keep the fires going.

People also believe that the robin's breast is red because he carries water in his beak to hell to put the fires out, and that the fires burn his breast a red color.

It is very, very good luck to find an eagle feather.

If an owl speaks or hollers "Who?" at you, always answer with your full name.

CHICKENS AND HENS AND ROOSTERS

Children and chickens
Must always be pickin'.

My Grandfather Ben
Has a Shanghai hen,
And you can bet she's a hummer.
She laid ninety-nine eggs
On the Fourth of July,
And now she's laid up for the summer!

Never worry about why a black hen lays a white egg. Get the egg!

A frizzly chicken or hen is one that has its feathers ruffled or frizzled in the wrong direction. Evil spirits and witches do not like frizzly hens, and it is good luck to keep one around the yard.

The rooster always crows at midnight two weeks before Christmas.

CROWS

When you see crows:
One's unlucky,
Two's lucky,
Three is health,
Four is wealth,
Five is sickness,
And six is death.

or

See one crow, sorrow,
Two crows, joy,
Three crows, a letter,
Four crows, a boy.

or

One crow, sorrow,
Two crows, mirth,
Three crows, a wedding,
Four crows, a birth.

As straight as the crow flies. Which is a more direct and faster way of getting there than going all around Robin Hood's barn.

(Do you know why they say "all around Robin Hood's barn"? Because Robin Hood didn't have any barn. His barn was Sherwood Forest. If you tried to go around his barn, you would be going around and around Sherwood Forest and probably be getting lost as well. You'd never get there. But as straight as a crow flies is a different matter. Watch a crow fly. You're there in a direct line, in no time at all.)

RED BIRDS

If you see a redbird on a holiday, you will marry a sailor.

Little Bugs and Crawlin

hings

ANTS

There are a hundred workers in the road, but they raise no dust.

     Ants.

An ant can carry as much as seven times its own weight. (A horse can't, a human can't.) Take time to watch ants at work in the summer. Their energy and concentration on their work is astonishing.

BEES

Bees never get wet. By the time it rains they are all snug in their hives counting their honey.

What's a boobee?

A little bug that runs up the leg of a bee and yells: "Boo! Bee!"

BUTTERFLIES

Wish on the first butterfly you see in the spring, and you will get your wish.

The color of the first butterfly you see will be the color of your next dress.

Butterflies are very lovely and beautiful.

CATERPILLARS

If you sit in the sun and look at a yellow caterpillar, you will have a chill.

CRICKETS

It is always lucky to have a cricket chirping about the house. When they chirp, they are telling you about your future success. It is especially lucky when you hear them chirping after you have gone to bed.

Never kill a cricket. It will bring very bad luck.

Also, if you kill a cricket, all the other cricket friends of the dead cricket will come and eat holes in your clothes and socks and stockings. A lady says: "I always sweep the crickets out, and never kill them, for the others will come and eat up your woollen clothes."

Another woman said: "I am seventy-five years old and this is an old saying of my grand-mother: if you kill a cricket, your teeth will all rot and drop out." (The moral is very clear: *Never kill a cricket!*)

When you actually see a cricket coming into the house, it is a sign of very good luck.

When you hear a cricket chirping in the summer, count the number of chirps it chirps during a fifteen second period of time. Then add 37 to that figure, and you will have the temperature of the day. So, with a watch and a cricket, you can be your own weather reporter. This sounds wild and incredible, but it has been proven again and again. (And who first figured such things out? Eh?)

DADDY-LONGLEGS

You will lose a friend if you kill a daddy-longlegs.

Daddy-longlegs can tell where lost cows are. When you are on a farm and the cows are lost, simply catch a daddy-longlegs and hold him by his hind legs. Then say, "Tell me where my cows are." The daddy-longlegs will point with his front legs in the direction where the cows can be found.

Or you may ask a very different question:

> Daddy-, daddy-longlegs,
> Tell me where my true love is,
> And then I'll let you go.

He will point toward your true love. Daddy-longlegs are very good at this sort of thing.

DOODLEBUGS

The doodlebug is a small round gray bug about the size of a pea. He lives in the ground, usually in soft sandy soil around very old houses. The boring of the hole in the earth causes a small cone-shaped pile of sand to form, which makes the roof of the doodlebug house, and away down below lives the bug. If you kneel by the hole and call the doodlebug, the loose earth will begin to stir and the bug will scamper backwards out of the hole. The odd expression on his brow is caused not by fear, but by disgust at having been fooled by you.

You can make a doodlebug come out of his hole by repeating over and over:

Doodle up, doodle up, doodle up.

And you can make him go down again by saying:

Doodle down, doodle down, doodle down.

Or you may say:

Doodle up, Johnnie Brown, doodle up, Johnnie Brown, doodle up, Johnnie Brown.

And after the bug has appeared and you want it to return into its hole, say:

Doodlebug, doodlebug, go down;
Go down, Johnnie Brown, go down.

Another way to make him come out of his hole is to alarm him by repeating:

Doodle, doodle, doodle,
Your mother and granddaddy are dead.

Or threaten him:

Doodlebug, doodlebug, come out of your hole;
If you don't, I'll beat you as black as a mole.

Still another way to make the doodlebug come out is to take a hollow straw, poke it down the doodlebug hole, and blow through it gently. The doodlebug will grab hold of the end of the straw, and you can pull him up out of his hole.

A man in Illinois wrote: "When I was a boy, I would get down on the ground and whistle and whistle down one of these doodlebug's holes in the ground, and they would crawl out to see what I wanted."

FLEAS

Two fleas got married. They were determined to work hard and save their money. Unlike most other fleas, they didn't squander their time and savings on frivolous pleasures. Instead, they worked, economized, and planned their future. Finally came the day when they had accumulated ten dollars. Overjoyed, they went out and bought their own dog.

Why was the mother flea so upset?
   All her little children were going to the dogs.

What is the difference between Texas fleas and other fleas?
   Texas fleas have their own dogs.

Bye-bye Fly

FLIES

If you kill a fly, ten flies will come to its funeral.

GRASSHOPPERS

When you catch a grasshopper, hold him gently by the hind legs and say:

> Grasshopper, grasshopper,
> Grasshopper gray,
> Have you any molasses
> To give me today?

He will give you some molasses, and then you can let him go.

You can also say to the grasshopper:

> Spit, spit tobacco juice,
> Spit, spit tobacco juice,
> Spit tobacco juice,
> And I'll turn you loose.

If you could jump in one jump as far as a grasshopper can hop in one hop, you could jump the length of your block or street.

When you're describing a much smaller brother or youngster, one often says, "He's about knee-high to a grasshopper."

LADYBUGS

Bad luck will come to the person who kills a
ladybug.

When a ladybug lights on you, say one of these
rhymes to her, and she will depart:

Ladybug, ladybug,
Fly away home,
Your house is on fire,
Your children are burning,
All except little Anne,
And she crawled under
the marble stone.

Ladybug, ladybug,
Your house is burning,
And your children are crying.

Ladybug, ladybug,
Go home quick,
Your house is on fire,
And your children are sick.

Ladybug, ladybug,
Your house is on fire,
Your children will burn
In half an hour.

If a ladybug lights on your hand, it means
you will have new gloves. If on your head, a
new hat. If on your dress, a new dress. On
your coat, a new coat. On your shoes, new
shoes. On trousers, new trousers. On stockings, new stockings.

LIGHTNING BUGS

I wonder, I wonder
Why lightning bugs don't thunder.

On hot summer nights you can make a lantern by catching lightning bugs and putting them in a glass jar. Be gentle with them and do not hurt them. Otherwise they will not light up for you.

When a firefly enters the house, it is a sign that a visitor is coming.

It wasn't the moon,
It wasn't the stars,
But it lighted the fields.
Fireflies.

LIZARDS

If you kill a lizard, its mate will come and count your teeth and you will surely die. When you see a lizard, it is always a wise thing to keep your mouth closed.

(Lizards are really very nice. They can climb walls and run across ceilings upside down, which is more than you can do.)

SNAKES

When a black snake rises up two feet on its tail, looks in the doorway of a house, and whistles, it means that something terrible will happen to the house.

When you sleep outdoors on the ground, always put a hair rope around your bed to keep the rattlesnakes away. The prickly hairs of the rope tickle the rattlesnake's stomach. He does not like to be tickled, so he will not cross the rope.

Some people say that snakes swallow their young. When the baby snakes are in danger, the mother opens her mouth wide, and all the baby snakes run into her mouth to hide. The mother then crawls away into the grass, and when the danger has passed, the baby snakes come out again.

Snake, snake, run in the grass,
And I'll not hurt you as you pass.

A hoop snake can take its tail in its mouth
and roll down hill like a hoop. This is much
faster than crawling, slithering, or skittering
downhill.

If you pull a hair from a horse's tail and put it
in a puddle of rain water just after it has
rained, it will turn into a snake in nine days.

Snakes sleep in the winter, and the first thunder in spring—usually in March—wakes
them.

If you kill a snake and hang it on a rail fence,
it will rain within three days. Also, if you kill
a snake, its tail will wiggle until sundown.

SNAILS

Speak these words, and a snail will stick out
its head:

> Snail, snail, poke out your horn,
> And I will give you a barrel of corn.

Say these words, and the snail will draw in
its head:

> Snail, snail, pull in your head,
> Or else I'll beat you till you're dead.

To find the initials of your true love, place
one or two snails on a large piece of heavy
brown wrapping paper. As the snails move,
they will leave shiny marks on the paper
which will make fairly crude initials. You will
discover the initials of your loved one in these
marks. (Give the snails plenty of time to do
this. Even overnight.)

MOSQUITOES

Mosquitoes were the very
first to practice and profit
from blood transfusion.

SPIDERS

If you wish to run and thrive,
Let the spider run alive.

It is bad luck to kill a
spider, and it will also
bring rain. To kill a baby
spider will bring the
worst luck of all.

If you see a spider at night,
It will bring you joy and delight.

If you see a spider in the morning,
It is a warning.

Small spiders, especially
the little red ones and
black ones, are called
money spiders and bring
good fortune if they are
not disturbed or injured.

A spider crawling over a garment means a
new garment of the same kind. When you see
a spider spinning its web, it is also a sign that
a new dress is being woven for you.

It is always good luck to see a spider, and also
to have a few spiders around the house.

Some say that if you see a black spider, you will have bad news; brown, good news; white, good luck; or:

> Black, sad,
> Brown, glad,
> White, good luck attend you.

THE WORMS CRAWL IN

Did you ever think
As the hearse rolls by
That some day in it
You will lie?
They'll bury you deep
In the cold, cold ground,
Where it's inky black
And there's never a sound.
And the worms crawl in
And the worms crawl out,
And they crawl all over
Your chin and mouth.
And they call their friends,
And their friends' friends, too,
And you look like hell
When they're through with you!

Spooky, eh? Hoo, boy! Well, try to be good until next Monday.

Weather
and the Sun and Moon

WEATHER

Everybody talks about the weather, but nobody does anything about it. (Mark Twain said that, or Will Rogers, or both of them.)

Everybody talks about the weather. In some way or another, you (and everyone else) probably mention the weather every single day of the year. "What's it like out?" "Boy, it's hot!" "I wish it would stop raining." "I hope tomorrow's a good day." "It smells like snow." "I bet it's over 100 degrees." "Looks as though it might storm." "Beautiful day, isn't it?" "If the weather's good, we can have a picnic." "It's probably below freezing right now." "It's so nice, I think I'll go for a walk." Just for the fun of it, keep track within your own family and see if one day goes by in the week without mention of the weather. As soon as it is mentioned on one day, chalk that day off and wait for the next. And the next. And the next. Want to bet?

When the weather is wet,
You must not fret;
When the weather is dry,
You must not cry;
When the weather is cold,
You must not scold;
Whatever the weather,
Be happy together!

Evening red and morning gray
Sets the traveler on his way,
But evening gray and morning red
Brings down rain upon his head.

RAIN

When the dew is on the grass,
Rain will never come to pass.

When a cat sneezes, there will be a misty rain.

Rain before seven,
Stop before eleven.

When your hair curls, it is a sign of rain.

If chickens roll in the sand,
Rain is at hand.

Accidentally stepping on a dog's tail will cause rain.

If chickens sit on a fence after dark and flap their wings, rain will fall before morning.

If a hen goes singing to bed,
It will get up with a wet head.

When cows or horses huddle in a pasture, expect rain.

If you can hear a train whistle or any other distant sound more clearly than usual, rain is at hand. (This is because the sound is bent back towards the earth by the damp air and clouds, instead of going up and away into the clear air and being dispersed.)

It's raining pitchforks and barn shovels.

It's raining cats and dogs.

It's raining stove lids and hammer handles.

It's raining fish and little froggies.

Rainy, rainy, rattlestone,
Don't you rain on me,
Rain on Johnny Groat's house
Far across the sea!

It's raining,
It's pouring,
The old man
Is snoring!

Ring around the moon,
Rain soon;
Ring around the sun,
Rain none.

If the sun goes pale to bed,
It will rain tomorrow—
It is said.

"I can always tell when it's going to rain. I
always feel lazy the day before."

When a cow tries to scratch her ear,
It's a sign that rain is very near.

If you hear a hoot owl during the day, it will
rain within three days.

SUNSHINE SHOWERS

A sunshine shower
Never lasts an hour.

If it is sunshining at the same time that it is
raining, it will rain again at the same time
tomorrow.

Some people say that when it rains and sun-
shines at the same time, the devil is beating
his wife with a codfish. If you put your ear to
the ground, you can hear them fighting.

Rain and sunshine in one day
Brings more rain the following day.

When the sun shines while it is raining, a
sailor is going to heaven.

WIND

When the wind is in the east,
It's good for neither man nor beast;
When the wind is in the north,
Old folks should not venture forth;
When the wind is in the south,
It blows the bait in the fishes' mouth;
When the wind is in the west,
Of all the winds it's the best.

In the days of the old sailing ships, sailors believed that you could buy the wind. When there was no wind and the ship was becalmed, the captain would throw a dime or a quarter or half dollar overboard, depending upon how much wind he wanted. Another way to get wind was to stick a knife in the mast, sticking the point in the direction from which you wanted the wind to come.

Some people believe that pigs can see the wind, and that the color of the wind is red. Pigs do not like the color red, and they run around and squeal and are restless before a wind storm.

When cats run up and down and are frisky, wind is on the way.

The howling blizzards that sweep the Great Plains from Montana and the Dakotas to Texas come from the north in winter.

When stars tremble and seem brighter than usual, it is a sign the wind will blow.

THUNDER AND LIGHTNING

When you see a flash of lightning begin counting as fast as possible. Keep on counting until you hear the thunder. The number that you have counted tells the number of miles between you and the place that the lightning struck.

Thunder in the morning,
All the day storming.

If it thunders in winter, colder weather is coming.

They say that "Lightning never strikes twice in the same place."

It is not wise to stand in an open field or under a tree—especially a lone tree—during a thunderstorm.

If it thunders both in February and March, crops will be abundant—especially fruit crops. Early thunderstorms bring wonderful crops:

> Winter's thunder,
> Summer's wonder.

Thunder on the left is a sign of good luck.
Thunder on the right is a sign of bad luck.

———

Dora R. Elam, a schoolteacher of a third grade class at Fairview School, Boulder, Colorado (and it really thunders over the Rockies!) collected these beliefs from her students in 1959. She asked the students for their explanation of what caused thunder. And here are their wonderful answers:

1. I think thunder is a cartwheel with a lot of sticks in it dropping out. I have also heard that it is a potato bag with potatoes dropping out.

2. I have heard that thunder is a dog barking and a lion roaring.

3. I think thunder is a big man with a gun shooting.

4. Some of them say that thunder is God washing his clothes.

5. Daddy says it is old man Joe moving his furniture.

6. I think thunder is the angels getting mad.

7. I've been told that it is angels bowling and that it is dogs mumbling to themselves, but I really think it is people fighting.

8. It is the thunder man pounding rocks in the sky.

9. I was told that thunder is two clouds running together.

10. Thunder is a volcano in the sky erupting. Or it might be a giant walking across the Milky Way.

I like the "mumbling dogs" and "old man Joe" and the "giant walking" and the "potatoes dropping out" and the "lion roaring" and "God washing his clothes." I like them all.

FROST AND FOG

When you hear the first katydid, it will frost in sixty days.

It will frost as many times in May as it thunders in February.

The number of fogs in August determines the number of snows in winter. If fogs in August are light, a light winter; if they are heavy, a heavy winter.

A foggy morning will fade away,
A foggy afternoon will stay.

Much autumn fog,
Much winter snow.

The day on which a fog occurs in January will be the date of a frost in May.

There will be neither freeze nor frost after doves have cooed in the spring.

Jack Frost. Have you seen him? On the windowpane?

SNOW

If snow sticks to trees, it won't stay. If it does not stick to trees, it will stay.

Stick, no stick;
No stick, stick.

Big, wet snowflakes are a sign of a short storm. The very small, powdery, "dry" flakes are a sign of a long storm.

The day of the month on which the first snow falls tells you the number of storms for that winter. If it first snows, for example, on December 12, you will have twelve snowstorms.

When it begins to snow, they say that an old woman up in the sky is shaking her feather bed. Some also say that the old woman up there is picking geese. Others believe that angels are having a pillow fight.

I wish I was a snowflake
And an apple was another,
Oh, what a pretty pair we'd make
Upon a tree together!

Real spring will not come until it snows on the daffodils in bloom. This is known as a daffy snow.

MAINE WEATHER

Weather in the State of Maine is rather special, and people have special things to say about it:

> In Maine there are three months of cold weather and nine months of winter.

or:

> Maine has thirteen months of winter, and the rest of the year is summer.

or:

> There are two seasons in Maine—winter and the Fourth of July.

or:

> Dirty days hath September,
> April, June, and November.
> From January up to May,
> The rain it raineth every day.
> All the rest have thirty-one
> Without a blessed gleam of sun,
> And if any of them had two-and-thirty,
> They'd be just as wet and twice as dirty.

Not true! When you visit Maine in the summer, you will discover beautiful country: sea and sand and woods. The names are wonderful: Ogunquit, Pemaquid Point, Kennebunkport, Bar Harbor, Frenchman Bay, Ironbound Island, Penobscot, Biddeford, Passamaquoddy, Portland . . .

THE SUN

No matter how bad or rainy or stormy the weather, the sun will shine at the end of three days. The sun will shine always on every fourth day. The sun never hides more than three days.

The sun always shines on some part of Saturday every Saturday in the year—except one.

Sunshine on Monday,
Sunshine all week.

In Baltimore they say that if you get up early on Easter morning and look to the east, you will see the sun "dancing" as it rises.

THE MOON

I see the moon
And the moon sees me,
And the moon sees somebody
I want to see.

When you see the new moon for the first time, bow to it three times and make a wish.

When the crescent moon is lying on its back so that the horns point up, the month will be a dry one because the water can not run out of it. When the crescent is tilted or when the points turn down, the month will be a wet one, because then the water can run out. There is an old saying: "When an Indian can hang his powder horn on the moon, the month will be dry. When he cannot, it will be wet."

New moon, new moon,
Truly and trusty,
Tell me who
My true love must be.

New moon, true moon,
True and bright,
If I have a lover,
Let me dream of him tonight.

When you see a halo or ring around the moon, count the stars inside the ring. The number of stars stand for the number of days before the weather changes or for the number of days of bad weather you can expect. One or the other, or maybe both.

What goes up and down, but never goes to town?

The moon.

If you sleep with the full moon shining on your face, you will either go stark raving mad or just plain crazy. Other people say that if you sleep in the moonlight, it will make you beautiful.

I see the moon
And the moon sees me,
God bless the moon,
And God bless me.

I see the moon
And the moon sees me,
God bless the parson
That baptized me.

The moon is positively not made of green cheese. Ask any astronaut.

Plants and Flowers

PLANTING VEGETABLES

Some farmers believe that plants which grow aboveground (like peas, beans, cucumbers, or melons) should always be planted in the morning, so that they will grow upwards with the rising sun; and that plants which grow underground (like potatoes, onions, and radishes) should be planted in the afternoon, so that they will grow downwards with the sinking sun.

Some farmers also believe that plants which grow underground should be planted in the dark of the moon, and that plants which grow aboveground should be planted in the light of the moon.

Place cornbread crumbs about your cucumber plants. They will attract the ants, and these will destroy the cucumber bugs.

Stretch a yarn string over beans and other young plants in the early spring, and they will not be injured. The frost will collect on the yarn, and the plants will not be touched.

(If you have four square feet of earth, you can always have a small garden. Your own. And do your planting according to what a good farmer-neighbor tells you, because planting times and weather vary from one part of the country to another. It is very satisfying to watch things grow that you have planted yourself.)

Good planting days? Some say:

> Bed sweet potatoes on the 8th of April.
> Watermelon should be planted on the 10th of May.
> March 22—28 are good days for planting Irish potatoes.
> Plant corn when dogwood is in full bloom. Or on the 15th of May.
> Always plant beans in the morning.
> Plant flowers on the 14th, 15th, and 16th of May.

PLUM SEEDS (OR STONES)

If a small child swallows a plum seed, a plum tree will grow out of the top of his head. (This, of course, bears watching. When you see it happening, report it to your mother or to some other responsible person. They will take care of it for you.)

DANDELIONS

When you see the first yellow blossom of a dandelion in the spring, say to it, "Hello, sunny!" and a new sweetheart will soon appear.

If you blow all the seeds off a dandelion seed-ball with one breath, your sweetheart loves you. A thistle seed-ball will give you the same information.

If you blow all the seeds from a dandelion with one breath your mother wants you to come home. If some seeds are left, you can stay out and play longer.

DAISIES

Pluck the petals from a daisy while telling your fortune:

> One I love, two I love,
> Three I love I say,
> Four I love with all my heart,
> Five I cast away.
> Six he loves, seven she loves,
> Eight they want to wed,
> Nine they tarry, ten they marry
> Is what the daisy said.

Or you can be much briefer:

> He loves me, he loves me not,
> He loves me, he loves me not,
> He loves me . . .

The last petal tells your fortune.

Proverbs, Wise Sayings, and "Happy as a Lark"

PROVERBS

A proverb is a wise saying that contains a great deal of truth in a very few words. You will hear people using them from time to time, and you will also run across them in books. Often there is a great deal more to them than meets the eye at first reading. For example, "The early bird catches the worm" is quite true. He does. The worms are up in the damp early morning, and they will not be during the hot part of the day. Therefore, the early birds will get them, and the birds that come later will not. But you can apply that proverb in many ways. It can mean: The student who gets up early and studies his lesson will learn it and be tops in his class. It can mean: The first person in line at the store which is having a sale will be the one who gets the best bargain. It can mean: The first person who applies for a job has the best chance of getting the job. It can mean many things. Most proverbs can and because they can, they add richness to our language. Here are several:

The early bird catches the worm.

One swallow doesn't make a summer. (One could say also: One robin doesn't make a spring. But it never has been said and consequently it isn't a proverb. Proverbs must be widely known.)

You can lead a horse to water, but you can't make him drink.

Don't wait for your ship to come in. Row out and get it!

A stitch in time saves nine.

A new broom sweeps clean.
    (But an old broom gets in the corners.)

A tree is known by the fruit it bears.
    (And bears are known by the fur they wear.)

Never trouble trouble till
trouble troubles you.

Two heads are better
than one.

Better late than never,
But better never late.

You can't have your cake
and eat it, too.

You can catch more flies
with molasses than
you can with vinegar.

If you don't do any more than what you are
paid for,
You won't get paid for any more than you do.

If you believe all you hear,
You can eat all you see.

A bird in the hand is worth two in the bush.

It's an ill wind that blows no good. (At the
edge of a hurricane, the wind is gentle and
blows sailing ships on their way. Every wind
blows some good, and it would be a very ill
wind that blew no good.)

You can't teach an old dog new tricks.

A rolling stone gathers no moss.

Make hay while the sun shines.

'Tis as it is and it can't be any 'tiser.

And a batch of others:

It's a daft dog that bites itself.
(*Daft* is Scotch for *Crazy*.)

He who talks constantly does his thinking aloud. (Everything he thinks is said in his words, and there's no other thought behind them.)

She was just as good as nobody. (She was no help whatsoever.)

She's awful nice to your face. (But she might say some nasty things behind your back!)

You can't tell a book by its cover.

The troubles that we worry about are the ones that never happen. (Those that happen, we do something about right away, and we don't worry about them because we're doing something about them.)

A small leak will sink a big ship.

The smallest thing in the world is the little end of nothing whittled down to a point.

Keep your chin up.

The world is your cow, but you have to do the milking.

Reach for the high apples first; you can get the low ones anytime.

PROCRASTINATION

That's the most high powered word in this book. There is a proverb: Procrastination is the thief of time. Which means that if you keep putting things off, they'll never get done. Procrastination robs time of things that might be done. It is much more easily said in other words, and these you certainly know:

Never put off till tomorrow what you can do today.

PROVIDENCE

Trust in Providence and you'd fetch up in Rhode Island. (Somebody from Maine can tell you precisely what that means.)

PENNIES

A penny saved is a penny earned.

Take care of the pennies and the dollars will take care of themselves.

To have good luck, carry a penny that was minted in the year of your birth.

To receive pennies in change on Monday means you will have money all week.

When you find a penny,
do not spend it, but wear
it in your shoe for luck.

Save your pennies for a rainy day.

A bad penny always returns.

A penny for your thoughts.

WORK

(Everyone must: you don't often get something for nothing.)

If it's worth doing, it's worth doing well.

"We don't want cats here that can't catch mice." (No lazy persons wanted on this job.)

It's better to make two
trips than to kill yourself
trying to do it in one.
(Better to make two trips
carrying three logs for the
fireplace each time than to carry
six in one and break your neck falling
over the steps or up the cellar stairs.
Common sense, common sense . . .)

When the sun is in the west, lazy folks work
the best.

(Just before quitting time, at a quarter to
five, someone who has been loafing all day
will suddenly pretend to be very busy, in
order to give the impression that he is winding
up a hard day's work. This phrase came from
the haying fields where the lazy workers, who
had been loafing under shade trees and avoid-
ing the hard work in the sun during the day,
came out in the cool of the afternoon to do
just a little work before quitting time. The
real workers knew who they were; the "lazy
folks" weren't fooling anybody but themselves.)

Today is short.
Yesterday has gone.
Tomorrow may never come.
If you have anything to do,
   Get Busy!

The half of doing a job is getting at it.

Stand up and grow tall!

Good, better, best!
Never let it rest
Until your good is better
And your better, best.

LIFE

Sich is life and it grows sicher and sicher every day.

While we live,
We live in clover,
When we die,
We die all over.

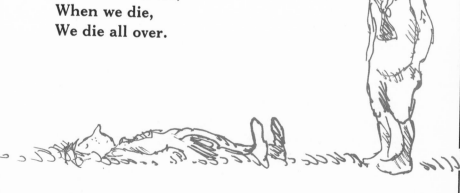

COMPARISONS

Hot as a little red stove

Smooth as silk

Good as gold

Strong as an ox

Busy as a bee

Comparisons are a way of making language lively and colorful.

It's easy enough to say "I'm warm." But better to be "as warm as toast." It's nice to be "snug" in bed. But better to be "as snug as a bug." And even better to be "as snug as a bug in a rug."

These expressions and comparisons come to us simply from hearing them. We don't learn them by studying them; they are not taught to us; we don't try to memorize them.

They are handed down to us from generation to generation—from grandfather to father to son; from grandmother to mother to daughter—without our even being aware of it.

You have heard all of these, and so have your father and mother. But you can't tell (and neither can anyone else) when you first heard any one of them. Can you? Or your father? Or mother?

Blind as a bat

Slick as an eel

Hungry as a bear

Crazy as a loon

Flatter than a flounder

Slick as a weasel

Sly as a fox

Stubborn as a mule

Slick as a whistle

Thin as a rail

Warm as toast

Dead as a doornail

Fit as a fiddle

Sweet as honey

Sweet as a rose

Pretty as a picture

Pretty as a little red wagon with blue wheels

Slow as molasses in January

Quick as a wink

Green as grass

Clean as a hound's tooth

Poor as a church mouse

Mad as a wet hen

Easy as falling off a log

Crooked as a dog's hind leg

Cool as a cucumber

White as a sheet

Black as pitch

Crooked as a rail fence

Darker than a stack of black cats

Plain as the nose on your face

Clear as crystal

Clear as mud (meaning that
it's not clear at all)

Brown as a berry

Red as a beet

Weak as a kitten

Happy as a lark

Tall as a Georgia pine

Crazy as a bedbug

Sound as a dollar

Proud as a peacock

Light as a feather

So weak that when he tried to raise the window shade he got all wound up in it

So gentle he'd go out of his way nine miles to keep from stepping on an ant hill

So tall he could wade the Mississippi and never get his ankles wet

DUMB AS THEY COME

He can count to twenty if he takes his shoes off. (Ten fingers, ten toes makes twenty.)

He hasn't the brains God gave geese.

He hasn't the sense of a skunk-chasing dog.

He doesn't know how many beans make five.

He doesn't know beans from bird eggs.

He doesn't know twice around a broomstick.

He doesn't know enough to pull his head in when he shuts the window.

If his brains were in a bird's head, the bird would fly backwards.

He doesn't know if he's going, coming, or standing still.

But watch out whom you're calling dumb or foolish, and remember: If all fools wore white caps, we should all look like geese!

Cumulative Storie

CUMULATIVE OR SNOWBALL STORIES

Cumulative stories are like snowballs that you roll along the ground. They grow and grow and grow. The first two stories here, "The Old Hen" and "The Old Woman and Her Pig," come from England and are probably more than two hundred years old. "The Old Hen" was found in the United States in Searsport, Maine, and "The Old Woman and Her Pig" in Durham, California. They are meant to be read aloud. Everyone in any family loves them—from grandmother to small sister. Try them and see. "The Little Old Lady Who Swallowed a Fly" comes from Denver, Colorado, but is also found elsewhere in this country. You may have heard it, or some version of it. It's pretty crazy! And "The Tree in the Wood", which is a song, does grow and grow right up to the "mosqueetee" of the last stanza. (It's on a Library of Congress record—and Doney Hammontree, who sings it, is completely out of breath when he finishes the very last "growing all around." You will be, too.)

THE OLD HEN

Once upon a time there was an old cock and an old hen, and they lived happily together underneath a hazelnut bush.

One day the old hen choked upon a hazelnut burr, and was like to die. So the cock ran to the stream, and he said:

"Stream, stream, gi' me water,
That I may give the water to my old hen
That lies half-dead 'neath the hazelnut
bush!"

But the stream wouldn't give him any water till he fetched it some leaves. So he went to the linden tree and said:

"Linden tree, linden tree, gi' me leaves,
That I may give the leaves to the stream,
Stream may give me water,
I may give the water to my old hen
That lies half-dead 'neath the hazelnut
bush!"

But the linden tree wouldn't give him any leaves till he fetched it some red-and-gold ribbons. So he went to St. Mary and said:

"St. Mary, St. Mary, gi' me red-and-gold
ribbons,
That I may give the red-and-gold ribbons
to the linden tree,
Linden tree may give me leaves,
That I may give the leaves to the stream,
Stream may give me water,
I may give the water to my old hen
That lies half-dead 'neath the hazelnut
bush!"

But St. Mary wouldn't give him any red-and-gold ribbons till he fetched her some French shoes. So he went to the shoemaker and said:

"Shoemaker, shoemaker, gi' me shoes,
That I may give the shoes to St. Mary,
St. Mary may give me red-and-gold ribbons,
That I may give the red-and-gold ribbons to the linden tree,
Linden tree may give me leaves,
That I may give the leaves to the stream,
Stream may give me water,
I may give the water to my old hen
That lies half-dead 'neath the hazelnut bush!"

But the shoemaker wouldn't give him any shoes till he fetched him some bristles. So he went to the boar and said:

"Boar, boar, gi' me some bristles,
That I may give the bristles to the shoe-
    maker,
Shoemaker may give me shoes,
That I may give the shoes to St. Mary,
St. Mary may give me red-and-gold rib-
    bons,
That I may give the red-and-gold ribbons
    to the linden tree,
Linden tree may give me leaves,
That I may give leaves to the stream,
Stream may give me water,
I may give the water to my old hen
That lies half-dead 'neath the hazelnut
    bush!"

But the boar wouldn't give him any bristles
till he fetched it some corn. So he went to the
miller and said:

"Miller, miller, gi' me some corn,
That I may give the corn to the boar,
Boar may give me bristles,
That I may give the bristles to the shoe-
  maker,
Shoemaker may give me shoes,
That I may give the shoes to St. Mary,
St. Mary may give me red-and-gold rib-
  bons,
That I may give the red-and-gold ribbons
  to the linden tree,
Linden tree may give me leaves,
That I may give the leaves to the stream,
Stream may give me water,
I may give the water to my old hen
That lies half-dead 'neath the hazelnut
  bush!"

But the miller wouldn't give him any corn
till he fetched him some bread. So he went to
the baker and said:

"Baker, baker, gi' me some bread,
That I may give the bread to the miller,
Miller may give me corn,
That I may give the corn to the boar,
Boar may give me bristles,
That I may give the bristles to the shoe-
  maker,
Shoemaker may give me shoes,
That I may give the shoes to St. Mary,
St. Mary may give me red-and-gold rib-
  bons,
That I may give the red-and-gold ribbons
  to the linden tree,

Linden tree may give me leaves,
That I may give leaves to the stream,
Stream may give me water,
I may give the water to my old hen
That lies half-dead 'neath the hazelnut
    bush!''

But the baker wouldn't give him any bread
till he fetched him some wood. So he went to
the woodcutter and said:

"Woodcutter, woodcutter, gi' me some
    wood,
That I may give the wood to the baker,
Baker may give me bread,

That I may give the bread to the miller,
Miller may give me corn,
That I may give the corn to the boar,
Boar may give me bristles,
That I may give the bristles to the shoe-
  maker,
Shoemaker may give me shoes,
That I may give the shoes to St. Mary,
St. Mary may give me red-and-gold rib-
  bons,
That I may give the red-and-gold ribbons
  to the linden tree,
Linden tree may give me leaves,
That I may give the leaves to the stream,
Stream may give me water,
I may give the water to my old hen
That lies half-dead 'neath the hazelnut
  bush!"

But the woodcutter wouldn't give him any wood till he fetched him an axe. So he went to the smith and said:

"Smith, smith, gi' me an axe,
That I may give the axe to the wood-
    cutter,
Woodcutter may give me wood,
That I may give the wood to the baker,
Baker may give me bread,
That I may give the bread to the miller,
Miller may give me corn,
That I may give the corn to the boar,
Boar may give me bristles,
That I may give the bristles to the shoe-
    maker,
Shoemaker may give me shoes,
That I may give the shoes to St. Mary,
St. Mary may give me red-and-gold rib-
    bons,
That I may give the red-and-gold ribbons
    to the linden tree,
Linden tree may give me leaves,
That I may give the leaves to the stream,
Stream may give me water,
I may give the water to my old hen
That lies half-dead 'neath the hazelnut
    bush!"

(Now, chant with increasing rapidity.)

So the smith gave him an axe, and he gave the axe to the woodcutter, and the woodcutter gave him wood, and he gave the wood to the baker, and the baker gave him bread, and he gave the bread to the miller, and the miller gave him corn, and he gave the corn to the boar, and the boar gave him bristles, and he gave the bristles to the shoemaker, and the shoemaker gave him shoes, and he gave the shoes to St. Mary, and St. Mary gave him the red-and-gold ribbons, and he gave the red-and-gold ribbons to the linden tree, and the linden tree gave him leaves, and he gave the leaves to the stream, stream gave him water, and he gave the water to his

(Very slowly, with emphasis)

OLD HEN,

(Now rapidly)

And she got well and went home again!

THE OLD WOMAN AND HER PIG

An old woman was sweeping her house, and she found a little crooked sixpence. "What," said she, "shall I do with this little sixpence? I will go to market and buy a little pig." So she went to market and bought a little pig. As she was coming home, she came to a stile. The pig would not go over the stile.

She went a little farther, and she met a dog. So she said to the dog:

"Dog, dog, bite pig,
Piggy won't go over the stile,
And I shan't get home tonight."

But the dog would not. She went a little farther, and she met a stick. So she said:

"Stick, stick, beat dog,
Dog won't bite pig,
Piggy won't go over the stile,
And I shan't get home tonight."

But the stick would not. She went a little farther, and she met a fire. So she said:

"Fire, fire, burn stick,
Stick won't beat dog,
Dog won't bite pig,
Piggy won't go over the stile,
And I shan't get home tonight."

But the fire would not. She went on a little farther, and she met some water. So she said:

"Water, water, quench fire,
Fire won't burn stick,
Stick won't beat dog,
Dog won't bite pig,
Piggy won't go over the stile,
And I shan't get home tonight."

But the water would not. She went a little farther and she met an ox. So she said:

"Ox, ox, drink water,
Water won't quench fire,
Fire won't burn stick,
Stick won't beat dog,
Dog won't bite pig,
Piggy won't go over the stile,
And I shan't get home tonight."

But the ox would not. She went a little farther, and she met a butcher. So she said:

"Butcher, butcher, kill ox,
Ox won't drink water,
Water won't quench fire,
Fire won't burn stick,
Stick won't beat dog,
Dog won't bite pig,
Piggy won't go over the stile,
And I shan't get home tonight."

But the butcher would not. She went a little farther, and she met a rope. So she said:

"Rope, rope, hang butcher,
Butcher won't kill ox,
Ox won't drink water,
Water won't quench fire,
Fire won't burn stick,
Stick won't beat dog,
Dog won't bite pig,
Piggy won't go over the stile,
And I shan't get home tonight."

But the rope would not. She went a little farther, and she met a rat. So she said:

"Rat, rat, gnaw rope,
Rope won't hang butcher,
Butcher won't kill ox,
Ox won't drink water,
Water won't quench fire,
Fire won't burn stick,
Stick won't beat dog,
Dog won't bite pig,
Piggy won't go over the stile,
And I shan't get home tonight."

But the rat would not. She went a little farther, and she met a cat. So she said:

"Cat, cat, kill rat,
Rat won't gnaw rope,
Rope won't hang butcher,
Butcher won't kill ox,
Ox won't drink water,
Water won't quench fire,

Fire won't burn stick,
Stick won't beat dog,
Dog won't bite pig,
Piggy won't go over the stile,
And I shan't get home tonight."

But the cat said to her, "If you will go to yonder cow and fetch me a saucer of milk, I will kill the rat." So away went the old woman to the cow, and said:

"Cow, cow, give me a saucer of milk,
Cat won't kill rat,
Rat won't gnaw rope,
Rope won't hang butcher,
Butcher won't kill ox,
Ox won't drink water,
Water won't quench fire,
Fire won't burn stick,
Stick won't beat dog,
Dog won't bite pig,
Piggy won't go over the stile,
And I shan't get home tonight."

But the cow said to her, "If you will go to
yonder haymakers and fetch me a wisp of hay,
I'll give you the milk." So away the old woman
went to the haymakers, and said:

"Haymakers, haymakers, give me a wisp
   of hay,
Cow won't give milk,
Cat won't kill rat,
Rat won't gnaw rope,
Rope won't hang butcher,
Butcher won't kill ox,
Ox won't drink water,
Water won't quench fire,
Fire won't burn stick,
Stick won't beat dog,
Dog won't bite pig,
Piggy won't go over the stile,
And I shan't get home tonight."

But the haymakers said to her, "If you will
go to yonder stream and fetch us a bucket of
water, we will give you the hay." So away the
old woman went, but when she got to the
stream, she found the bucket was full of
holes. So she covered the bottom with pebbles,
and then filled the bucket with water, and
away she went back with it to the haymakers
and they gave her a wisp of hay.
As soon as the cow had eaten the hay, she
gave the old woman the milk, and away she
went with it in a saucer to the cat. As soon as
the cat had lapped up the milk—

The cat began to kill the rat,
The rat began to gnaw the rope,
The rope began to hang the butcher,
The butcher began to kill the ox,
The ox began to drink the water,
The water began to quench the fire,
The fire began to burn the stick,
The stick began to beat the dog,
The dog began to bite the pig,

The piggy in fright jumped over the stile,
And so the old woman got home that
   night.

THE LITTLE OLD LADY
WHO SWALLOWED A FLY

There was an old lady—she swallowed a fly.
I don't know why she swallowed a fly.
Poor old lady, I thought she would die.

She swallowed a spider.
It wriggled and wriggled and wriggled inside
her.
She swallowed the spider to eat up the fly.
But I don't know why she swallowed the fly.
Poor old lady, I thought she would die.

She swallowed a bird. How absurd! She swallowed a bird.
She swallowed the bird to eat up the spider
That wriggled and wriggled and wriggled inside her.
She swallowed the spider to eat up the fly.
But I don't know why she swallowed the fly.
Poor old lady, I thought she would die.

She swallowed a dog. What a hog! She swallowed a dog.
She swallowed the dog to eat up the bird.
How absurd! She swallowed the bird.
To eat up the spider
That wriggled and wriggled and wriggled inside her.
She swallowed the spider to eat up the fly.
But I don't know why she swallowed the fly.
Poor old lady, I thought she would die.

She swallowed a cow. I don't know how
She swallowed a cow. She swallowed the cow
To eat up the dog. What a hog!
She swallowed the dog to eat up the bird.
How absurd! She swallowed the bird
To eat up the spider
That wriggled and wriggled and wriggled inside her.
She swallowed the spider to eat up the fly.
But I don't know why she swallowed the fly.
Poor old lady, I thought she would die.

She swallowed a horse.
She died,
Of course.

THE TREE IN THE WOOD

On the ground there was a tree,
The prettiest little tree you ever did see.
The tree's on the ground
And the green grass growing all around-
round-round,
And the green grass growing all around.

On the tree there was a limb,
The prettiest little limb you ever did see.
The limb's on the tree
And the tree's on the ground
And the green grass growing all around-
round-round,
And the green grass growing all around.

On that limb there was a nest,
The prettiest little nest you ever did see.
The nest's on the limb
And the limb's on the tree
And the tree's on the ground
And the green grass growing all around-
round-round,
And the green grass growing all around.

On that nest there was a bird,
The prettiest little bird you ever did see.
The bird's on the nest
And the nest's on the limb
And the limb's on the tree
And the tree's on the ground
And the green grass growing all around-
round-round,
And the green grass growing all around.

On that bird there was a wing,
The prettiest little wing you ever did see.
The wing's on the bird
And the bird's on the nest
And the nest's on the limb
And the limb's on the tree
And the tree's on the ground
And the green grass growing all around-round-round,
And the green grass growing all around.

On that wing there was a flea,
The prettiest little flea you ever did see.
The flea's on the wing
And the wing's on the bird
And the bird's on the nest
And the nest's on the limb
And the limb's on the tree
And the tree's on the ground
And the green grass growing all around-round-round,
And the green grass growing all around.

On that flea there was a mosqueetee,
The prettiest little mosqueetee you ever did see.
The mosqueetee's on the flea
And the flea's on the wing
And the wing's on the bird
And the bird's on the nest
And the nest's on the limb
And the limb's on the tree
And the tree's on the ground
And the green grass growing all around-round-round,
And the green grass growing all around.

The President

THE PRESIDENT

Every four years there is a great deal of screeching up and down the country. We are electing a President. And you can add your voice to the hullaballoo with either one of these two rhymes, depending upon which party you are for:

Coffee and gingerbread hot from the pans
We'll serve to good Republicans!
Fried rats and pickled cats
Are good enough for Democrats!

1 2 3 4 5 6 7,
All good Democrats go to Heaven!
When they get there they will yell,
All bad Republicans go to Hell!

After everything is said and done, never forget
that the President (Republican or Democrat)
is your President and the President of these
United States of America.

If I were the President
Of these United States,
I'd eat molasses candy
And swing upon the gates!

Wishes, Dreams, and Good and Bad Luck

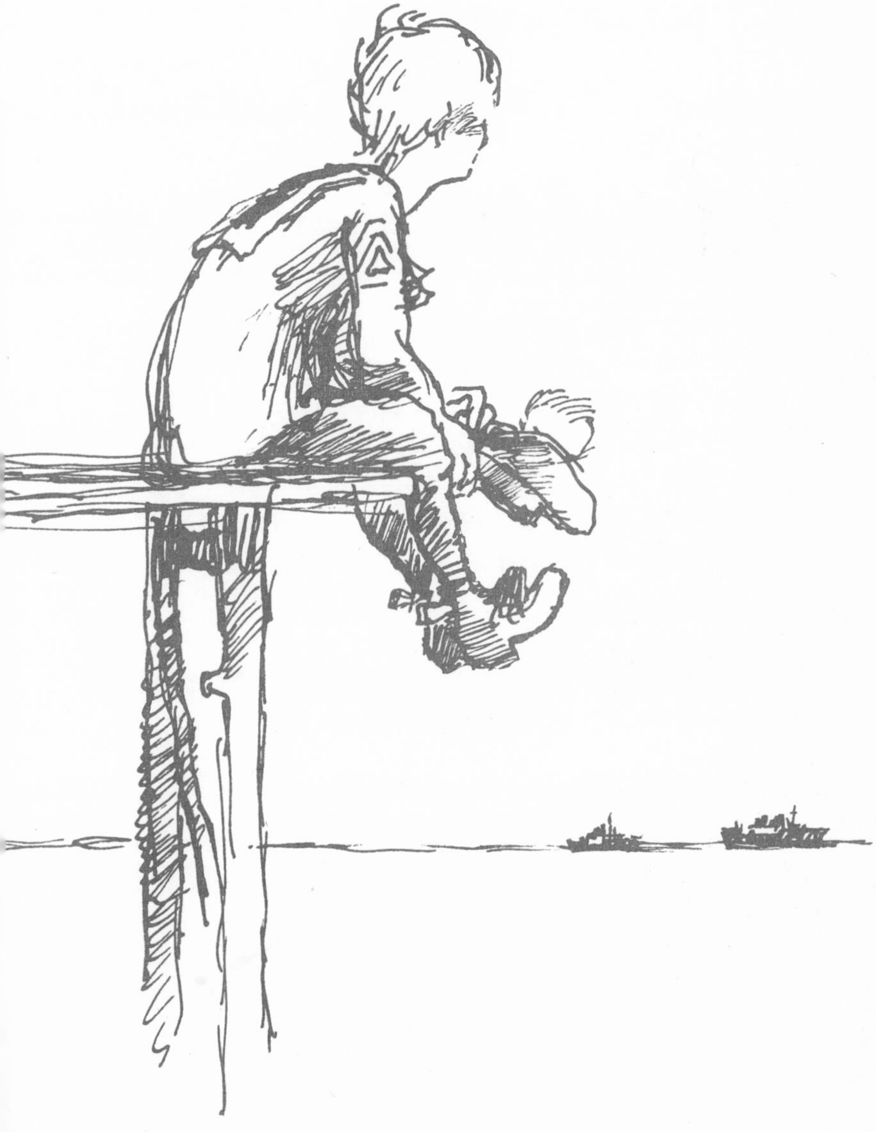

WISHES

To know whether a wish that you have made will come true or not, take a deck of cards and turn the cards over one by one. If a red ace comes up before a black ace, your wish will come true. If a black ace comes up first, your wish will not come true.

Another way to learn the outcome of your wish is to write the wish on a piece of paper and put it under your pillow. If you dream about your wish that night, it will come true.

At sunset time:

> A sky of red mixed with blue,
> Make a wish with closed eyes,
> And it's sure to come true.

When you cross a bridge, make a wish and throw a raw potato in the water. Your wish will come true.

This will keep you busy: Stamp one hundred robins before summer comes and then make a wish.

I see stars
And stars see me,
I wish I may,
I wish I might
Get this wish
I wish tonight.

When you see the first star in the evening, walk towards it and say:

> Star light, star bright,
> The first star I see tonight,
> I wish I may, I wish I might
> Have the wish I wish tonight.

Then stop, make your wish, and continue walking and stopping until you have recited the rhyme three times.

> Load of hay, load of hay,
> Make a wish and look away.

If you have a blister on your heel, spit on a piece of cotton while making a wish, and then tie the cotton on the blister. After the blister heals, your wish will be granted.

When you see the first of any kind of flower in the spring, you may make a wish. Daffodils, violets, jonquils, anemones, pussy willows . . .

If you find a bruise or a lump and don't know how you got it, you may make a wish.

Tie your two big toes together and make a wish while walking backwards to bed. (Is that possible? How can you walk?)

If two girls tie their big toes together, make separate wishes, and go to bed without laughing or speaking, the one having the longest piece of string attached to her big toe the next morning will get what she wished.

"A lady friend of mine found a rusty nail one day, picked it up, and made a wish. She only went half a block and found $8.00."

After you have swept your room, take the dirt outside and throw it up in the air while making three wishes. (Three wishes!)

You can make a wish while turning a ring around eighteen times on someone's finger.

If, when you start to go through a tunnel or cross a bridge, you make a wish and keep your eyes closed and hold your breath until the other end is reached, your wish will come true.

If you make a wish while you are making a fruitcake and stirring it, the wish will come true before another fruitcake is made.

"I remember once I had a beau and I put my petticoat on wrong side out, and I made a wish. I wished he would kiss me that night and he did."

You may make a wish if a woodpecker pecks on your house before daybreak.

Always wish on a white horse Or a red-haired woman.

You may make a wish while burying a stolen dishrag.

DREAMS

New moon, true moon,
Star in the stream,
Pray tell my fortune
In my dream.

Some people believe that dreams go by contraries or opposites. If you dream of finding money, you will lose money; if you dream of losing money, you will find money. If you dream of rain, the weather will be dry. If you dream of a dog, it means a cat. If you weep tears in a dream, it means happiness.

Saturday night dreams
Sunday morning told
Will come true
Before the week's old.

If you do not wish a dream to come true, do not tell anyone about it.

To dream of roses shows that you have many friends.

If you dream of a half-starved duck, someone who pretends to be a friend is actually your enemy.

The girl who dreams of a kitten purring at her feet will soon get a letter from a young man.

If you dream of a lion, you need not fear anyone.

If you go fishing in your dream and fall in the water, it is a sign that someone wants to see you.

Whoever dreams of gathering ripe apples off a tree and eating them will soon be lucky.

Whoever dreams of playing a guitar and singing will be lucky in love.

Dream of a buzzard flying across the moon
Is a sure sign of sadness coming soon.

To dream of fruit out of season
Means trouble without reason.

The girl who dreams of a redbird will see her sweetheart on Saturday.

If a bad dream wakes you, sit up in bed, raise your right hand several times straight above your head, and you will return to a peaceful sleep.

If you dream of fresh or sweet milk, you will soon fall in love. If you dream of sour milk or buttermilk, you will fall out of love.

SIGNS AND OMENS OF GOOD AND BAD LUCK.

A corn cob worn behind the ear is good luck.

It is bad luck to pass through the house with a bucket of water on your head.

To own a white rabbit is good luck.

Never buy a broom in August. You will have bad luck if you do.

It is good luck to find a button. As many holes as there are in the button, you will have that many months of good luck.

If you see a woolly worm and don't spit, you will have bad luck.

When you are riding in an automobile and pass under a bridge, hit the roof of the car with your right fist and at the same time blow the horn of the car for good luck.

Always raise your feet when riding over a county line if you want good luck. Or when you are crossing railroad tracks.

If you carry a cat through town, it is bad luck.

When you see a red car, pinch your companion. If you do not, you will have bad luck. Say:

> Red car, pinch,
> No pinch back.

It is unlucky

to fall down

the cellar steps.

If it hasn't rained for two weeks and water in some pond five miles away is a blackish color, something bad will happen to you in the next week or two. (Beware! Beware! And check that pond!)

It is bad luck to have two clocks in the same room.

If you fall upstairs, it is a sign your credit is getting better. (Maybe you can borrow a dime from an older sister or a quarter from an uncle.)

Never start anywhere on the left foot. Very bad luck. If you notice that you have started on the left foot, go back, sit down, and start over.

It is good luck to find money, and very good luck to find a penny in a silver horseshoe.

It is bad luck for a skunk to get under the house.

It is good luck to carry a rabbit under your arm.

Always take off the left shoe first; you'll have bad luck if you take off the right one first.

It is bad luck to watch anyone until he is out of sight.

It is bad luck to harm hummingbirds. And if you throw rocks at swallows, the cows will give bloody milk. (Swallows eat harmful insects and should always be protected.)

PINS

If you find a hairpin and
hang it on a nail, you will
receive a letter.

It is a sin to steal a pin,
It is a greater to steal a 'tater.

See a pin and let it lie,
Before the night you will cry.

See a pin and let it lay,
Bad luck follows through the day.

If you pick up a pin as you walk along,
You'll have good luck all day long.

See a pin and pick it up,
All that day you'll have good luck.

Find a pin and let it lie,
You shall want before you die.

Never pick a pin up when it is pointing toward
you. Always walk around it to pick it up by
its head. Otherwise you will have bad luck.

If you find a pin pointing toward you, pick it
up with your right hand, stick the pin into
the left shoulder of whatever clothing you
are wearing, and make a wish while doing it.
Let the pin stay there for a while, and then
take it out and give it to someone.

SHADOWS

Step on your shadow. It will bring you good luck.

As big as a house, yet lighter than a feather?
The shadow of the house.

DIMES

It is good luck to show a new dime to the full moon.

Wear a dime in each shoe on New Year's Day, and you will have money all year.

If an older sister or cousin or aunt is getting married, be sure that she wears a new dime in the heel of her left shoe at the wedding. This will bring her luck and happiness.

Some Game Rhymes and Teases

TAUNTS AND TEASES AND GENERAL IMPERTINENCE

Every time it rains,
I think of you:
  Drip, drip, drip!

Your ears are like flowers.
  Cauliflowers!

Your hair is like a movie star's.
  Rin-Tin-Tin!

 Tommy loves Mary!
 Tommy loves Mary!
 Tommy loves Mary!

Teacher's pet, teacher's pet!
Never missed a lesson yet!

 You're a wit,
 A half-wit!
 You're a wit,
 A half-wit!

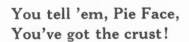

You tell 'em, Pie Face,
You've got the crust!

You tell 'em, Coffee
You've got the grounds!

Roses are red,
Violets are blue,
Garlic stinks
And so do you.

Roses are red
Violets are blue,
Skunks have instincts
And so do you.

Marguerite,
Go wash your feet!
The Board of Health's
Across the street!

Three, six, nine,
A bottle of wine,
I can lick you
Any old time!

Wipe your nose.
Your brains are leaking!

I know a fellow by the name of Bill,
Lives on top of a garbage hill,
Never took a bath and never will.
Ach, pooh! Dirty Bill!

When a friend happens to have a short haircut:

The sun shines red
On Frankie's baldy head!

What's eating you?
Termites. Want a bite?

REPLIES TO TAUNTS AND
BAD NAME CALLING

When anyone calls you a bad name, tell him:

It takes one to know one!

or yell at him:
Don't call me by your family name!

or simply say:
Same to you, and many of them!

If you have the time, you can really tell him
off:

You insignificant piece of humanity,
How dare you insult a lady of my dignity!
You're worse than the very ground I tread
upon!
Born in a flood of ignorance!
If my words are too copious
For your comprehension,
Consult the dictionary,
You sawed-off, hammered-on, knock-
kneed, pigeon-toed monkey!

TEASING GAMES

Name your friend's forehead "rooster," his nose "pullet," and his chin "hen." Then ask him what his forehead is called. He will say, "rooster." Then ask him what his nose is called. When he says "pullet," give his nose a pull.

When you meet a friend, hold out your fingers, then fold them into the palm of your hand and show your thumb, then fold your thumb over your fingers to make a fist. As you do this, say:

> See my fingers,
> See my thumb,
> See my fist,
> You hummy, hum, hum?

If your friend knows the game, he will duck or jump away. If he does not, you can sock him one with your fist. If you do all this very quickly, you can probably catch him even before he has a chance to jump out of reach.

When you see a friend whom you haven't seen for a little while, say, "I'm glad to see you back, I haven't seen you for a year, and I hardly knows you." When you say "back," slap him a good one on the back; when you say "year," tweak his ear; and when you say "knows," pull his nose. You must do all this very quickly, or he will be all over you, pounding and yelling.

When you are outdoors with a group of friends and have eaten an apple down to the core, turn to one of your friends and say:

> Apple core,
> Baltimore,
> Who's your friend?

Throw the apple core at the person he names. All your friends will be listening for the name, and the person named will, of course, try to duck or run so that he won't be hit.

Put your hands over your face and leave just your nose sticking out, then holler, "Bus driver, bus driver, open the door!" or "Elevator boy! Elevator boy!"

Tell a person to stand up and to put his hands out in front of him as though he were holding some handlebars. Then tell him to stamp his right foot twice. Then ask him, "What's the matter? Can't you get your motorcycle started?"

COUNTING-OUT RHYMES

These are some of the oldest counting-out rhymes in America. They all come from Maryland.

One's all, two's all, zigger's all, zan,
Bobtail nanny goat, tickery tall tan.
Harum scarum, virgum, marum,
Zinctum, zanctum, Washington, Buck!

One's all, two's all, zig's all, tan,
Ticks in a twaddle, twenty-one,
Backs in a barram, ferro fan,
Harum scarum, nugen, narum,
Twiddle twaddle, out!

One zall, two zall, zickery zan,
Bobtail, bobtail, tickulum tan,
Harum scarum, segun sarum,
Frances!

One's all, two's all, zigzag zan,
Backram bellum tenofam,
Harum scarum, hugen karem,
Turkey buzzard!

Henry, menry, deeper, dee,
Delia, dalia, nomine,
Hotcher, potcher, number notcher,
Hi-pon-tus!

Ailie, mailie, tribily, trick,
Treely, trily, O me nick,
Uncle Bro, Tom I no,
I sunt tuz!

Brier, brier, limber lock,
Three geese in a flock,
One flew East, one flew West,
And one flew over the cuckoo's nest,
O-U-T, out with a greasy dishcloth, out!

Intery, mintery, cutery corn,
Apple seed and apple thorn,
Wire brier, limber lock,
Five geese in a glock,
Sit and sing, by a spring,
O-U-T, out, and in again!

Lucky, minchy, cuchy cow,
Apple seed and berry thorn,
Briar, briar, limber lock,
Ten mice on a clock.
The clock fell down,
The mice went round.
Tee, tee, turn me out
To get a bottle of wine!

Iggany offany, box of gold,
I had a house seven years old,
Seven and seven and seven to that,
I thought the old fellow would never get fat,
I inched him, I pinched him,
I made his back smart;
If ever I catch hold of him,
I'll tear-out-his-h-e-a-r-t!

Peter Matrimety was a good waterman,
He caught hens and put them in pens,
Some laid eggs and some laid none,
White foot, speckle foot, trip and be gone!

And a very short one:

> The sky is blue.
> How old are you?

If the player answers "eight," then count around to the eighth person. If "nine," count around to the ninth.

BALL BOUNCING RHYMES

> I am a little Dutch girl,
> Five years old.
> My mother made a petticoat
> All trimmed with gold.
> A penny in my pocket,
> A dolly in my hand,
> Ain't I cute?

She must have been very cute. This next is a candy cane:

> Bright and red,
> Spicy and sweet,
> We don't last long,
> But we're very sweet!
>
> Oho! Lily, Lily, Lily,
> You ought to be ashamed
> To marry, marry, marry
> A boy without a name!
>
> All around the butter dish,
> One, two, three,
> If you want a pretty girl,
> Just pick me!

JUMP-ROPE RHYMES

One, two, three, four,
Close the window, shut the door,
One, two, three, four,
Wash the ceiling, scrub the floor.
How many jobs shall we do today?
Why don't we count to find the ways?
One, two, three, four, five, six, seven . . .

Cinderella, dressed in yellow,
Ran upstairs to kiss her fellow.
On the way her girdle busted—
How many people were disgusted?
1, 2, 3, 4 . . .

Cinderella, dressed in yellow,
Ran upstairs to kiss her fellow.
Made a mistake and kissed a snake—
How many doctors will it take?
1, 2, 3, 4 . . .

1-2-3 Olary,
My first name is Mary!
Don't you think I look cute
In my papa's bathing suit?

Nine o'clock is striking,
Mother, may I go out?
All the boys are waiting
For to take me out.
Some will give me apples,
Some will give me pears,
Some will give me fifty cents
And kiss me on the stairs.

Hello, hello, hello, sir!
Can you come out and play, sir?
No, sir. Why, sir?
Because I've got a cold, sir.
Where'd you get the cold, sir?
At the North Pole, sir.
What were you doing there, sir?
Catching a polar bear, sir.
How many did you catch, sir?
One, sir; two, sir; three, sir . . .

Peaches, plums, pumpkin butter,
Little Johnny Green is my true lover,
Little Johnny Green, give me a kiss,
When I miss, I miss like this.

Red, white, and blue,
Tap me on the shoe;
Red, white, and green,
Tap me on the bean;
Red, white, and black,
Tap me on the back.

Red, white, and blue,
Columbus lost his shoe
In fourteen-hundred-and-ninety-two!

HOPSCOTCH

Hopscotch, let us hop,
Hopscotch, let us stop,
Let us hop, then you stop,
Let us stop, then you hop,
Hopscotch, hopscotch,
Let us hop!

LAST ONE THERE!

Last one there
Is a monkey!

Last one there
Is a rotten egg!

THE MULBERRY BUSH

When you sing this, go through the motions
of walking around, washing, ironing, mend-
ing, baking, sweeping, scrubbing, and going
to church. When you go to church, you simply
march off and away, and that's the end. This
is usually considered a song for small child-
dren, but I'm not so sure that it is. And even
if it is, you can have the pleasure of teaching
it to the younger ones.

Here we go 'round the mulberry bush,
Mulberry bush, mulberry bush,
Here we go 'round the mulberry bush
So early in the morning.

This is the way we wash our clothes,
Wash our clothes, wash our clothes,
This is the way we wash our clothes
So early Monday morning.

This is the way we iron our clothes,
Iron our clothes, iron our clothes,
This is the way we iron our clothes,
So early Tuesday morning.

This is the way we mend our clothes,
Mend our clothes, mend our clothes,
This is the way we mend our clothes
So early Wednesday morning.

This is the way we bake our bread,
Bake our bread, bake our bread,
This is the way we bake our bread
So early Thursday morning.

This is the way we sweep our room,
Sweep our room, sweep our room,
This is the way we sweep our room,
So early Friday morning.

This is the way we scrub our floor,
Scrub our floor, scrub our floor,
This is the way we scrub our floor
So early Saturday morning.

This is the way we go to church,
Go to church, go to church,
This is the way we go to church
So early Sunday morning.

MRS. MURPHY'S CHOWDER

(You and a friend begin this with whispers, but raise your voices each time you repeat, until you are screaming at the top of your lungs.)

Who put the overalls in Mrs. Murphy's chow-
der?
    I can't hear you, so speak a little louder.
Who put the overalls in Mrs. Murphy's chow-
der?
    I can't hear you, so speak a little louder!
Who put the overalls in Mrs. Murphy's chow-
der?
    I can't hear you, so speak a little louder!!
WHO put the overalls in Mrs. MURPHY's
Chowder?
    I can't HEAR you, so speak a little
    LOUDER!!!
WHO put the OVERALLS in Mrs. MURPHY's
CHOWDER?
    I CAN'T HEAR YOU, so SPEAK a little
    LOUDER!!!!
               and so on,
                  and on, and on.

TWENTY-NINE MEN
IN A BOARDING HOUSE BED.

(This is a good one to chant or sing with two
or three friends, or even more.)

Twenty-nine men in a boarding house bed,
All would roll over when any one said:
Roll over, roll over!
One of them thought it would be a good joke
Not to roll over when any one spoke,
And in the confusion he got his neck broke.
Roll over, roll over!
Twenty-eight men in a boarding house bed,
All would roll over when any one said:
Roll over, roll over!
One of them thought it would be a good joke
Not to roll over when any one spoke,
And in the confusion he got his neck broke.
Roll over, roll over!
Twenty-seven men in a boarding house bed
. . . and so on.

(When you come towards the end, change it
a bit.)

Two men in a boarding house bed,
Both would roll over when either one said:
Roll over, roll over!
One of them thought it would be a good joke
Not to roll over when the other one spoke,
And in the confusion he got his neck broke,
Roll over, roll over!

(The one man left sleeps peacefully until you
start out again with the twenty-nine, and
then he has to start rolling all over again.)

Words and Words

TONGUE-TWISTERS

What is a rainbow?
A sure sign of sunshine.

**I saw Esau kissing Kate,
And Kate saw I saw Esau,
And Esau saw that I saw Kate,
And Kate saw I saw Esau saw.**

He ran from the Indies to the Andes in his undies.

Sixty-six sick chicks.

Does this shop stock short socks?

Double bubblegum bubbles double.

Six snakes slid slowly southward.

A big blue bucket of blueberries.

CIRCULAR JINGLES AND JOKES

These run on in an endless circle, or at least keep going for a considerable length of time. Some can be said or sung by one person, but most require two people.

WHODO

You remind me of a man.
What man?
The man Whodo.
Who do?
You do.
Do what?
Remind me of a man.
What man?
The man Whodo.
Who do?
You do . . . and so on.

YIM YONSON

My name is Yim Yonson.
I come from Wisconsin.
I work in the lumberyard there.
Every girl that I meet
As I walk down the street,
I stop her and say:
My name is Yim Yonson,
I come from Wisconsin
I work in the lumberyard there,
Every girl that I meet . . . and so on,
and on,
and on.

LIFE

That's tough.
What's tough?
LIFE.
What's that?
A magazine.
Where can you get it?
At the corner drugstore.
How much?
Ten cents.
That's too much.
That's tough.
What's tough?
LIFE.
What's that? . . . and so on.

I LAUGHED SO HARD

I laughed so hard I thought I'd die.
I did die.
They buried me, and flowers grew on my
    grave.
The roots grew down and tickled me.
I laughed so hard I thought I'd die.
I did die.
They buried me, and flowers grew on my
    grave.
The roots grew down . . . and so on.

TRANSPOSITIONS

Take a two, three, or four word phrase and transpose the letters so that they become one word:

> **Grin, O ant.**
> *Ignorant.*

Easy? Then tackle a more difficult one:

> **Our big hens.**
> *Neighbours.*

"Grin, O ant" has almost the sound of "ignorant," but "our big hens" bears no relation to "neighbours." The sound, therefore, is not important; the letters are. And, of course, the way the transpositions came into being was not to begin with "grin, O ant," but to begin with "ignorant" and work backwards to find the words contained in "ignorant." Riddles are made the same way: the answer is there first (a path) and the riddle-question is made to fit the answer (what goes through the field but when it comes to a stream breaks its neck?) So with transpositions. You know the answers and you ask the questions. (You have to use pencil and paper with these.)

> **A mild bear.**
> *Admirable.*

> **Yes, lambs.**
> *Assembly.*

Cool cheat.
Chocolate.

The wig.
Weight.

To love ruin.
Revolution.

Mad retort.
Rotterdam.

A noble car.
Barcelona.

I bring a treat.
Great Britain.

With those last three, tell the person you are questioning that the answer has to be a foreign city or country.

There we sat.
Sweetheart.

Moon starers.
Astronomers.

It is a fact, son.
Satisfaction.

And a most difficult one:

Saint Lucy heals it.
Enthusiastically.

Mind Your Manners!

SPANKINGS AND WHACKINGS

Not too long ago (and perhaps in some places it is still done) teachers spanked the smaller children when they were either unruly in class or had not done their lessons. Older students were sometimes whacked across the open palm of the hand with a ruler or spanked with a ruler. Children made up these rhymes about their real teachers, but you can bet your last nickel they never recited them so that the teacher could hear them!

Mr. Sinclair is a very good man,
He goes to church on Sunday.
He prays to God to make him strong
To beat the boys on Monday!

Here I stand
Before Miss Blodgett.
She's going to hit,
And I'm going to dodge it!

UNTIDY

Your head (or room) looks like a hairy wick-ett's nest.
(If you say that to someone, they are not apt to forget it. A wickett is a bird which builds a very untidy nest.)

He looks like an accident going somewhere to happen.
(You've seen people like that. Most distress-ing.)

He looks as though he'd been beaten with a stocking full of soot with a hole in the toe.

TABLE MANNERS

Stir with a knife
Is to stir up strife.

If you stir milk with a knife or fork, the cow will go dry.

In New England they say that you "take the manners" if you take the last of any kind of food from a plate.

Eat slowly: only men in rags
And gluttons old in sin
Mistake themselves for garbage bags
And tumble victuals in.

Go to the clam, thou wriggler,
Consider her ways and be wise.

LUNCHEON DATE

'Tis meet that friends who meet to eat
Should eat their meat on meeting.

SPILT MILK

Never cry over spilt milk!

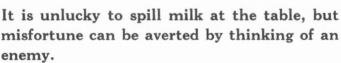

It is unlucky to spill milk at the table, but
misfortune can be averted by thinking of an
enemy.

TEMPER, TEMPER!

When angry, say the alphabet.

or:

When you are cross
And feel very naughty,
Look in the glass
And count up to forty.

BREAD AND BEER

Oh, dear!
Bread and beer!
If I were home
I wouldn't be here.

(You probably will not want to say that very
often, but you can say it when you are very,
very bored at some place where you are not
having a good time. But say it under your
breath! Don't ever let your host or hostess
hear you! Bad manners!)

YAWNING

If you do not cover your
mouth with your hand
when you yawn, the Devil
will jump down your
throat and you will have
bad luck. It is very bad
manners to yawn with an
uncovered, wide-open
mouth. It is uncouth and
boorish. ("Mother, where
is the dictionary?")

When one person yawns,
three or four others in the
room will yawn also.
Yawning is catching. It is
very odd that this is so,
but it is.

School's In,

School's Out!

GEOGRAPHY

To remember how to spell "geography," simply remember the first letter of each word in this sentence:

George Edwards' old grandmother rode a pig home yesterday.

Many years ago in the country schools of America, children learned their geography with sing-song rhymes which they chanted aloud. The whole class joined in. To remember the peninsulas in North America, for example, they chanted:

> Peninsulas we now will sing,
> Alaska leads the rhyme,
> And Nova Scotia follows next,
> All in the northern clime;
> In southern regions Florida
> And Yucatan we meet,
> Then California follows next
> To make the rhyme complete.

The rhythm made things easier to remember.
They chanted the states and their capitals in
the same way:

> State of Maine, Augusta,
> On the Kennebec River;
> State of Maine, Augusta,
> On the Kennebec River.
>
> Concord, New Hampshire,
> On the Merrimac River;
> Concord, New Hampshire,
> On the Merrimac River.
>
> Massachusetts, Boston,
> On the Charles River;
> Massachusetts, Boston,
> On the Charles River.
>
> New York, Albany,
> On the Hudson River;
> New York, Albany,
> On the Hudson River.
>
> Pennsylvania, Harrisburg,
> On the Susquehanna;
> Pennsylvania, Harrisburg,
> On the Susquehanna.
>
> Bismarck, North Dakota,
> On the Missouri River;
> Bismarck, North Dakota,
> On the Missouri River.

State of Texas, Austin,
On the Colorado River;
State of Texas, Austin,
On the Colorado River.

California, Sacramento,
On the Sacramento;
California, Sacramento,
On the Sacramento.

Almost all capital cities are located on a large river, or by a bay, lake, or other body of water, but where they are not, the children sang "inland." Wyoming, for example:

Cheyenne, Wyoming,
Is an inland city;
Cheyenne, Wyoming,
Is an inland city.

Or it could be sung also by placing it near the mountains:

Cheyenne, Wyoming,
Near the Rocky Mountains,
Cheyenne, Wyoming,
Near the Rocky Mountains.

Carson City, Nevada,
By the Sierra Nevada;
Carson City, Nevada,
By the Sierra Nevada.

Try all the states. All you need is a good map of the United States which shows the capitals, a sing-song tune (which is easy), and then make up the fifty different stanzas. That takes care of one rainy afternoon!

There is one other geography rhyme (not sung or chanted) which comes from a special part of Maine about which the people who live there seem to be very, very proud. At least they boast about it this way:

You haven't seen the world
Till you've seen the United States;
You haven't seen the United States
Till you've seen Maine;
You haven't seen Maine
Till you've seen Aroostook;
You haven't seen Aroostook
Till you've seen the sun set
On the St. John River Valley!

Now don't let those people in Aroostook County get away with that! You can do the same thing for your state and county, and river or valley or mountain or whatever your nearby countryside landmark is. And it doesn't have to be the sun setting. It can be the sun rising on the Rocky Mountains, or a rainbow over the Black Hills, or enormous thunderclouds over Kansas. Describe whatever it is that you like best, wherever you happen to live. You can even make it very personal in the last lines by saying:

Till you've seen the flaming maple tree
In my front yard!

Texas is a fairly large state, and people driving across it sometimes jokingly say:

> The sun is riz,
> The sun is set,
> And here we is
> In Texas yet!

SPELLING TRICKS

If you have a small brother or sister (or neighbor) who cannot possibly remember how to spell "arithmetic," all you have to do is to tell them to remember (as they did with "geography") the first letter of each word in the following sentence: *A rat in the house might eat the ice cream.* ARITHMETIC. Very simple. Try the same trick with other words—and you will have your teacher wondering about you.

Here are some other tricks. How do you spell stationary/stationery? With an "a" or an "e"? With an "e"! Stationery ends with "-er," like paper.

How about "believe?" Never believe a lie. There is a *lie* in be*lie*ve.

And "cemetery?" There are no "a's" buried in the cemetery. We can get there with ease ("e's"). (Pretty terrible, eh? But pun's fun.)

Now try this one, and it may be true. About words ending in "-eed" and "-ede." Remember: "To succ*eed*, ind*eed*, see that proc*eed*s exc*eed* expenses." All others end in "-ede." Prec*ede*, rec*ede*, sec*ede* . . .

DROPPING SCHOOLBOOKS

If you accidentally drop your schoolbooks on the way to school, step on them before you pick them up, or have someone else pick them up for you. Otherwise you will miss your lesson.

SCHOOL'S OUT!

School's out,
School's out!
The teacher's let
The monkeys out!

Tattoos

TATTOOS

Tattoo designs are worn chiefly by sailors, but they have been worn by other people as well. They are a form of folk art. They are pricked into the skin with an electric needle and indelible inks. Some of the designs and patterns are very beautiful, but the drawback to them is that you can't get rid of them in the event you change your mind and want the tattoo removed. It is fun, however, to make "pretend" tattoos on your hands or arms, and you can do it now with the fine-pointed felt pens that come in different colors—red, green, blue, black. Draw them on in the summer when you can scrub them off while swimming or in the shower. There are many designs, but the sailors always used:

Sailing ships

Anchors

Pierced hearts with the
initials of their True Loves

**Butterflies, snakes,
Skulls, daggers**

The names of their ships

Stars, roses

**And almost anything
else that you can
think of**

Up and Down the Street, and Hither and Yon,

and Odds and Ends

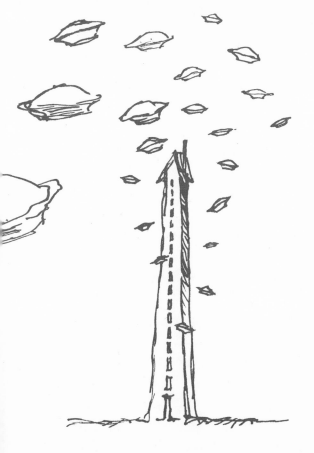

A HOUSE IN BALTIMORE

I had a house in Baltimore,
Sixteen stories high,
And every story in that house
Was filled with chicken pie!

VISITORS
(Company's Coming)

When you drop a small spoon, a little girl is coming to visit you.

If the fire sparkles, someone is coming full of chatter.

I see one buzzard,
And I don't see two;
I'm going to see someone
I didn't expect to.

If you have company on Monday, you will have company every day of that week.

If a buzzard's shadow hits you, a stranger will visit you that day.

Drop a spoon,
Company soon.

Drop a fork, a woman; drop a knife, a man. But some say that these visitors will be just the opposite. In any case, they will come from the direction in which the fork and knife point.

SHIRTS

A man without a wife,
A ship without a sail,
But the very worst of all
Is a shirt without a tail.

LETTERS

If you find a two-holed button, you will get
a letter with two pages.

When two people say the same words at the
same time, one of them will get an important
letter—provided her companion pinches her.

If a spark from the fireplace flies at you, you
will get a letter soon. The next day, maybe.

SHOES

When you are buying new shoes, always try on the right one first for luck.

Wear your shoes out at the toe,
You'll spend money as you go.

What's the news?
> *The cat has new shoes.*

New shoes greased with opossum fat last twice as long.

A HEE-HEE EGG

When your hear people laughing and don't know why they are laughing, you can say to your friend: "They must have found a hee-hee egg in a haw-haw nest." That takes care of that!

CLOTHES

It is good luck when you accidentally put on your socks (or any other piece of clothing) wrong side out. Wear them wrong side out until noon, or even all day, without changing them. Otherwise the good luck will change to bad.

If your petticoat hangs below your dress,
'Tis a sign your daddy loves you best.

It is very bad luck to put your hat on a bed or on a table.

It's raining, it's snowing,
Your petticoat is showing!

When your right shoestring comes untied, it means that someone is thinking nice things about you. If it is your left shoestring, bad things.

"Little boy, little boy,
Where did you get those britches?"
"Father cut them out
And mother sewed the stitches."

"Little boy, little boy,
What 'came of your britches?"
"Caught them on a nail
And tore out all the stitches."

BATHS AND TOWELS

Unless you take a bath on New Year's Day itself, you will be dirty all year.

Two people wiping their hands and faces on the same towel at the same time will quarrel. To avoid the quarrel, each of them must shake the towel over his/her head.

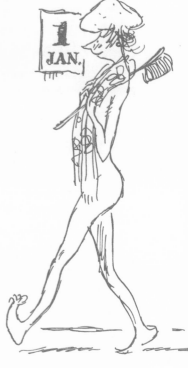

If you dry your hands together, You will be friends forever.

Do not hang a towel over a picture frame. Bad luck!

HATS

It is unlucky to be hit with a hat.

It is unlucky to hang a sunbonnet on a door-knob.

If you take a boy's hat and put it on your head, it is a sign that you want that boy to kiss you, and he must kiss you in order to get his hat back. (Suppose you were to hang on to it with both hands and pull it down over your ears!)

DRESSMAKING

A measuring worm can be
helpful. Have you seen
them? They measure an
inch, then draw themselves
up, and when they're
ready measure another
inch. They are measuring
you for a dress or other
piece of clothing.

To measure for a dress,
remember also:
> Twice around your thumb
> is the size of your wrist.
> Twice around your wrist
> is the size of your neck.
> Twice around your neck
> is the size of
> your waist.

SALT

Salt is a preservative and, because of its last-
ing quality, is a symbol of friendship. Whenever salt was spilled, the Greeks believed that
quarrels would result and friendship come to
an end. In the Middle Ages (six hundred years
ago) people believed that evil spirits spilled
the salt. So, whenever salt is spilled, immediately take a pinch of the salt and throw it
over your left shoulder in order to hit the
invisible devil in the eye and prevent him
from doing further mischief.

Because it is a symbol of friendship, salt must be the first thing placed on the table and the last thing removed. (The Romans placed no dish on the table until the salt was first in position.)

Witches detest salt.

If you wish to see your sweetheart, throw a little salt in the fire on three successive Friday nights, and each time say:

> It is not this salt I wish to burn,
> It is my lover's heart to turn,
> That he may neither rest nor happy be
> Until he comes and speaks to me.

On the third Friday, he should appear.

You can catch a rabbit or a bird by shaking fresh salt on its tail. (This is true.)

When the soup is too salty, it is a sign that the cook is in love.

TAKING A TRIP

Bless your house when you leave on a journey so that it will not burn down when you are gone.

A small sack of salt (about the size of a teabag) in your suitcase will bring good luck.

When you are away from home on a trip, place three pennies under your pillow each night—with the Lincoln head up—and your trip will be a lucky one.

Have a good trip! (And bring home some souvenirs.)

THE CROOKED LITTLE MAN

There was a crooked man
Who walked a crooked mile,
And he found a crooked sixpence
And climbed a crooked stile.
He bought a crooked cat
That caught a crooked mouse,
And they all lived together
In a crooked little house.

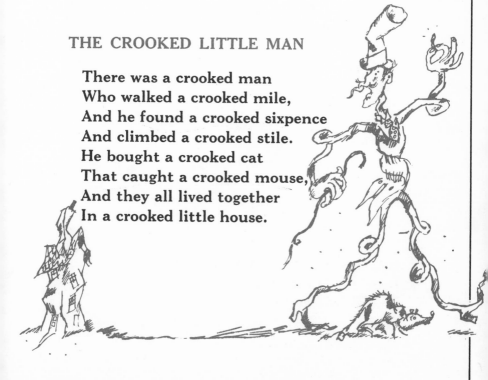

LICORICE

Licorice is made from old rubber boots.

POET

If you accidentally or by happenstance make
a rhyme when you are talking, say:

> I'm a poet
> And don't know it.

Or if your friend does, say:

> You're a poet
> And don't know it.

SOLOMON GRUNDY

Solomon Grundy,
Born on Monday,
Christened on Tuesday,
Married on Wednesday,
Took ill on Thursday,
Worse on Friday,
Died on Saturday,
Buried on Sunday,
This is the end
Of Solomon Grundy.

A SQUARE DANCE CALL

This dance call comes from the year 1880 from Midland, Texas. If you've never seen a square dance or taken part in a square dance, you will want to after listening to this one. A fiddle tune goes with it.

Salute your partner! Let her go!
Balance all and do-se-do!
Swing your gal, and all run away!
Right and left, and gents sashay!
Gents to right and swing or cheat!
On to the next gal and repeat!
Balance to the next and don't be shy!
Swing your partner and swing her high!
Bunch the gals and circle around!
Whack your feet until they sound!
Form a basket! Break away!
Swing and kiss and all git gay!
All gents to the left and balance all!
Lift your hoofs and let 'em fall!
Swing your opp'sites! Swing again!
Kiss the sage-hens if you can!
Back to your partners, do-se-do!
Gents salute your little sweets!
Hitch up and promenade to your seats!

A FOOLISH ANSWER TO A FOOLISH QUESTION

When it's perfectly
obvious that you're
knitting a scarf or making
a sandwich or whittling
a toy, and someone asks "What are you making?" come right back at them with the answer they deserve:

"A whim-wham for a goose's bridle."

WHAT HAVE YOU BEEN PLAYING?

What have you been playing?
Store.
How did you get so ragged?
I was the Swiss cheese.

WHY ARE YOU CRYING?

Why are you crying?
  Because my brother has an eight-day vaca-
  tion and I don't.
Why don't you?
  Because I'm not in school.

STREET CRIES

Call them selling cries. They are the cries
vendors use to sell whatever they have to sell—
such as hotdogs at a baseball game, watermelons at a country fair, salt water taffy, spun
sugar, souvenir flags and buttons at a football
game, apples on a stick. This cry was made up
and used by an eight year old girl (named
Rose, who lived in the Bronx in New York
City) in 1930, during the Great Depression
(ask your teacher about that). Rose made tiny
wool flowers, and she scented them with a
drop of perfume or cologne from her mother's
perfume bottle. Then she sold them for ten
cents each on the street corner in a tray which
she carried, and she had this street selling-cry
to attract customers:

> Buy my pretty flowers,
> They smell very sweet,
> And they always look well
> Worn on the street!

> Nice?

And have you ever sold lemonade on your front lawn in the hot summer? Stirring it with a silver spoon?

> Ice cold lemonade!
> Made in the shade!
> Stirred with a silver spade!
> Sweetened with the fingers
> Of a pretty little maid!

YOURS TILL

Yours till Niagara Falls (everyone knows that!).

Yours till the butterflies.

Yours till the Catskill Mountains have kittens.

Yours till Bear Mountain gets dressed.

Yours till the kitchen sinks.

Yours till the lipsticks.

Yours till the lollipops.

Yours till the milkshakes.

Yours till the cows give chocolate milk.

Yours till the mountain peaks to see the salad dressing.

Yours till the ocean waves.

Yours till the soda pops.

Yours till the moonbeams.

Notes and Bibliography

NOTES

This *Hodgepodge Book* complements the earlier (Four Winds Press, 1970) *Nonsense Book* for children in the field of American folklore. The *Nonsense Book* contained riddles, puzzles, conundrums, tongue-twisters, game rhymes (jump-rope, hide-and-seek, counting-out, ball bouncing), autograph album rhymes, and other general fun rhymes. A few added examples of some of these are included here, but the emphasis in the *Hodgepodge Book* shifts to beliefs and superstitions and to customs and traditions belonging particularly to children and which contribute to making up their very special and delightful world. The librarian, teacher, and student will recognize many of these out of his or her own childhood, while others will be quite as new and fresh as a city sidewalk-rhyme is to a country child or as a doodlebug is to a Brooklynite.

BELIEFS AND SUPERSTITIONS

A belief is a belief if you believe, and it is a superstition if you do not. The dividing line is not always an easy one: You do not necessarily believe that walking under a ladder is bad luck, but nevertheless you do not walk under it because it might be. Where is the line? You reject the superstition, but still you do not tempt the Fates—or the bucket of paint that might fall on your head.

The very great majority of the belief–superstitions in this book are gentle and lovely. They were part of our youth, and that youth was good. There is very little here of terror and fear and what there is is fun-terror and fun-fear, and we had to have that also to bring balanced excitement and shivers to our growing up: Witches come out at midnight, but they must be gone by cock crow; a black snake standing up two feet on its tail and whistling in the doorway of a house means that something terrible will happen to the house; never let a lizard count your teeth—they will all drop out.

There are four solid collections of beliefs and superstitions: Vance Randolph's *Ozark Superstitions* (Columbia University Press), New York, 1947, reissued in paperback by Dover, 1966; Harry M. Hyatt's *Folklore from Adams County, Illinois* (Memoirs of the Alma Egan Hyatt Foundation), New York, 1935, with a second and revised edition, Hannibal, Missouri, 1965 (privately printed and now out of print, but available at most university libraries); Ray B. Browne, *Popular Beliefs and Practices from Alabama* (Folklore Studies, no. 9, University of California Press), Berkeley, 1958; and two volumes (VI and VII, 1961 and 1964) of *Popular Beliefs and Superstitions from North Carolina* edited by Wayland D. Hand in the multiple volume *Frank C. Brown Collection of North Carolina Folklore* (Duke University Press), Durham, North Carolina. Randolph's work is the most readily available and highly readable; Hyatt's is the greatest single collection ever made in the United States (16,537 entries from one county!); Browne's work is representative of a single state; and Hand's editing of the Frank C. Brown material sets a high standard of comparative scholarship for beliefs and superstitions, also from a single state.

I have suggested elsewhere (*Folklore on the American Land*, Little, Brown, and Company, 1972) that there are some fifty million quite *different* beliefs and superstitions now circulating in the United States. (Consider those in the field of folk medicine alone. Each family has at least one.) To control this enormous body of material, subdivisions of it have been made, and the chief ones follow. I give with them, by way of *lagniappe*,* a few examples reflecting superstitions and beliefs by and for children rather than the more seriously believed ones of adults. (For the full range of adult superstitions and beliefs, see the books cited above as well as the works in the bibliography.)

I Birth, Infancy, and Childhood

[The field covered here ranges from prenatal influences (a birthmark due to fright, or longing for special food) through cradle-care and into prognostics about the child's future (if it crawls across the floor and picks up a coin, it will be rich; if a bottle, a drunkard; if a book, a preacher). As with all of the other subdivisions, the field is vast.] For and by children, and from Maryland: New babies are found in a cabbage head. "Many a time I have hunted among the cabbages in my mother's garden to find the little sister I longed for."—"The stork brings the baby to the roof, and the doctor finds it and brings it to mother."—A child of five said to me, "God made me, and I came down to the apple tree, and hung there eight weeks, and then the stork brought me."—"A little Baltimore girl told me that if you put a box of pure, fine, silver-sand on a closet shelf, you will soon find a baby in it." From Iowa: Babies are found in straw piles.— When a baby smiles in its sleep, it is talking with angels. Illinois: Ugly babies/ Make pretty ladies. Texas: Ugly in the cradle,/ Beautiful in the

---

lagniappe: A Creole word (combined from French and Spanish) readily used in New Orleans as an equivalent to the more common "a baker's dozen." It means "a small gift (of any kind) added to a basic purchase."

saddle. General: A baby never has any sense until it has fallen out of bed three times. (This, of course, is based on sound observation: The child must be healthy, active, and curious to fight its way out of its enclosed crib.)—To ease teething, rub the baby's gums with a silver thimble.—To insure that the baby rises in the world, it must be carried upstairs (even if it means going into the attic) before it is carried downstairs.—When you call on a baby for the first time, put a silver coin in its hand, close its fist over it, and hold the baby's fist in your own—to bring luck to the baby and to yourself as well.

II   Folk Medicine and the Human Body

Remedies for warts, hiccups, cramps, bee stings, and other minor disasters are given in the text. These separate nosebleed items are from letters sent me from around the country. San Rafael, California: "For severe nosebleed, put a bunch of cold keys down your back next to the skin. Also for nosebleed, fold a piece of brown paper and put under the lip. The brown paper was used exclusively in butcher shops to wrap meat."— Beaumont, Mississippi: "To stop nosebleed, sit in a pan of cold water." Laton, California: "Just the other day I saw a little girl wearing a punctured dime around her neck to stop nosebleed. The nosebleed seems to have stopped—but so has our hot weather."—Washington, D.C.: "Put a penny under the upper lip and press on it to stop the nosebleed."— Superstitions and beliefs about the Human Body are found in the text under fingernails, eyes, hair, dimples, ears, and moles. An added one which bears noting: If a girl kisses her elbow, she will immediately turn into a boy, and if a boy kisses his elbow, he will at once turn into a girl.

III   Domestic and Household Superstitions

Alabama: It is bad luck to hop down stairs on one foot. (Probably parentally inculcated as a belief to avert breakage to neck and limb, just as it also is sound advice "not to kill toads," since they help to keep the grounds clear of mosquitoes and harmful insects.)—The one who takes the last of anything from a plate has to kiss the cook.—It is bad luck to eat in bed unless you're sick.—If you break a mirror, you will have seven years bad luck.—It's bad luck to take or move a broom with you when you move.— It's bad luck to move a pig trough.—It's bad luck to take ashes out of the fireplace during Christmas week.—And in this *Hodgepodge* text, there are items on salt, pins, table manners, clothes, dressmaking, baths and towels, and other odds and ends. From the time one rises in the morning ("He got out of the wrong side of the bed") until one goes to sleep at night

("Go to bed laughing, wake up crying"), household folklore is with us. And remember: "You will have as many years bad luck as you twirl a chair around on one leg."

IV Travel and Communication

In the text this subdivision is represented by the Postage-Stamps on Letters and Taking a Trip entries, but there are other items also throughout. A few added ones from Alabama: If you find a two-holed button, you will get a letter with two pages.—A lightning bug in the house at night says there is a letter in the office.—When you drop a small spoon, a little girl is coming to visit you.—If the left side of your nose itches, a boy is coming to see you.—If the fire sparkles, someone is coming full of chatter. —If you get up with a feather in your hair, it is a sign you will walk a mile.—When a gray squirrel crosses the road in front of you, your journey will be safe.

V Economic and Social Relationships

In the *Hodgepodge* these are represented by itches, pennies, dimes, salt, black-eyed peas on New Year's Day, temper! temper!, and others. Some added ones, generally known: It is bad luck to give anyone a sharp instrument, since it will cut your friendship.—Don't start a job on Friday unless you can complete it that same day. Start it instead on Saturday.— Quit work when the whippoorwill calls.—Specks on the thumbs,/Fortune surely comes.—When you see a shooting star, say "money" three times. If you can complete saying it before the star falls out of sight, you will be rich before you die.

VI Love, Courtship, and Marriage

Kisses, love, Valentine's Day, daisies, and scattered items throughout the book reflect this most important segment of folklore. I have done two small books on the subject (gift books, actually) for American Heritage Press, both of them sensitively illustrated by Tomie de Paola of San Francisco: *The Folklore of Love and Courtship* and *The Folklore of Weddings and Marriages*. (I cannot, of course, do less than recommend them.) From them and with the permission of American Heritage Press: If you think of a particular man while swallowing a four-leaf clover, you will marry him.—If you can walk around the block with your mouth full of water, you may be married that year.—Run three times around the house, and on the third round a vision of your husband will rise before you.—On the first day of Spring, shout into a rain barrel. If you hear an echo, you will marry the first unmarried man who comes around the corner of the house.—If a girl wishes a young man to fall in love with her, she may offer him a glass of beer, cider, or lemonade, into which she has stirred a teaspoonful of her fingernails, which have been ground into powder.—"If you marry on a pretty day, you will live happy."—It is a sign of very good luck for the bride to find a spider crawling on her wedding dress.—It is bad to have a gray horse at a wedding.—"If your husband leaves the house in an angry mood, go to a friend's house and eat applesauce. When he comes home, everything will be forgotten."

VII   Death and Funeral Customs

Except for "The Worms Crawl in and the Worms Crawl Out" and the short rhyme under Life, death and its related beliefs find no place in this book. And they shouldn't. They come along a little later–after roller skating and jump-rope and spin-the-bottle and love. Much later. However, the beliefs are universal, and even youngsters will have picked up some: When a dog looks at the moon and howls, it is a sign of death.—When a dog howls mournfully three times during one night, he is warning of death. —When a bird flies into a house or room where someone is sick and then flies out again (symbolic of the departure of the soul), that person will die.—When a pigeon pecks at the window-pane of a sick room, the person in that room will die.—If a dead tree falls in the forest and you hear the sound, it is a sign of death.—When a weeping willow tree that you have planted grows tall enough to cast a long shadow, it will shade your grave.

VIII   The Supernatural

Ghosts and witches! In the world of childhood, these are pleasantly concentrated in the goblins and pranks and doings of Halloween. Beyond that world, however, there is real fear of the supernatural, and of all its inexplicable terrors. (The great work here is Hyatt's *Hoodoo, Witchcraft*, cited in the bibliography.) For our purposes: You can see ghosts best on rainy nights.—If you wish to talk with a ghost, begin your conversation with, "What in the name of the Lord do you want?"—To kill a witch, draw a picture of it on the barn door, and shoot it with a silver bullet.—If your hair is tangled in the morning, it means that witches have been around during the night. To prevent their coming, throw salt over your left shoulder into the fire before going to bed.—Ghosts guard buried treasure.—Many ghosts are quite friendly.

IX Cosmic Phenomena, Time, and Numbers

In the text, this category is represented by the reasons for snow, the moon, stars, special days such as New Year's, Christmas, and St. Patrick's, and by the seasons and months of the year. Added items: The rainbow is God's promise that the world will never again be destroyed by a flood.— There is a pot of gold at the end of a rainbow.—It is bad luck to sit under a Christmas tree.—The number thirteen is unlucky.—Friday the thirteenth is very unlucky.—If there is a man in the moon, he was put there because he burned brush on Sunday.—Houses must be shingled in the dark of the moon or the shingles will turn up.—If you get up mad on your birthday, you will get up mad the rest of the year.

X Weather

This is universal as a subject, and there is no end to the sensible beliefs (based on local observations) and the wild superstitions relating to it: If it thunders in February, there will be a cool spell in April on the same day.—Wild geese going out to sea./Good weather there will be.—When terrapins and turtles go uphill, it won't rain.—When kittens play in the afternoon, it is a sign of rain before morning.—If a person falls down while walking, it means a storm: a large storm if the person is large; a small storm if the person is small.—As soon as you have finished washing and polishing your automobile, it will rain.—It is an indication of rain when a cow thumps her ribs with her tail.—A cat basking in a February sun will hug the stove in March.—Turkeys always hop up and down before a rain.—Rain on Monday,/Sunshine next Sunday.—As the weather is on November 21, so will it be all Winter.—An exceedingly loud quacking among ducks forecasts rain.—"My aunt always would put an egg, that was laid on Easter, in the top of the house on a rafter, little end pointing east, so the lightning would not strike the house."—And remember: If walnuts fall faster than squirrels can store them away, look for a big wheat crop next year.

XI Animals and Animal Husbandry

In this *Hodgepodge* text, animals, birds, and insects are fairly rampant: dogs, cats, birds, chickens, elephants, snakes, rats, mice, snails, guinea pigs, ladybugs, bees, ants, caterpillars, and such. This is, of course, as it should be. Children are wonderfully aware of animals and bugs. They are instinctively closer to nature and its ways than any of the rest of us. (After childhood, we become patronizing, and have the idiot notion that we control nature. Tsk, tsk! The little bugs go about their orderly business in a manner to shame us all.) Anyhow: When chickens drink, they lift their heads after each drink in gratitude to God.—If your dog barks at night, knock on the wall three times and he will stop.—When it thunders in January, goose eggs won't hatch.—If the first thing that you eat on Easter day is a green onion, you will not be harmed by snakes that year.— You will always be lucky if you know how to make friends with strange cats.—It is a sign of bad luck for a cow to enter the house.—If you do not see a white horse shortly after meeting a red-haired woman, you will have bad luck.—You will have bad luck on a trip if you meet a growling dog in your path.—Peppermint sprigs scattered about the house will keep mice away.—When a robin builds its nest near your house, you will have good luck.—To rid yourself of lice, take one of them into the graveyard and shoot it. The rest will leave at once.

XII Fishing and Hunting

This category belongs not alone to the so-called sportsman of today, but rather more to those who in earlier days depended for their livelihood on a catch of fish or the results of the hunt. The beliefs and superstitions carry over: If cats are jumping, it is a sure sign that fish will bite.—When dogwood trees are in bloom, the perch will bite.—Spit on the bait to make the fish bite. Tobacco juice is the best spit.—If you want to catch fish easily, fish on the even numbered days of the month.—A good time to fish is when the moon is a week old.—When the whippoorwill calls it is time to go fishing.—To teach a dog to bark let him run around with other dogs that bark.—If foxes bark in or near thick woods, there is no use going hunting, for the dogs will not trail them.—When the moon is bright, the dogs won't tree 'possums. The dogs can't see the 'possums, but the 'possums can see the dogs, and will go back into their holes.

XIII Plants and Plant Husbandry

Farmers, farm youngsters, and ladies with gardens have thousands of beliefs and superstitions here: If cutworms are in the garden, have your husband go out before sunrise and fire a gun across the garden.—Plant corn when the turtledove moans and the season is right and the ground is warm. (How can you lose?)—Eat the first daisy you see in Spring, make a wish, and it will come true.—Pick a four-leaf clover and say: One leaf for fame,/One leaf for wealth,/One leaf for honor,/One leaf for health.— It is bad luck to cut sweet pepper on Saturday.—It is bad luck to point your finger at a watermelon. It will fall off the vine.—When you plant corn, always drop four grains into a hole and say: One for the squirrel,/ One for the crow,/One for the earth,/And one for to grow.—Cucumbers should be planted while cherry trees are blooming.—Nine autumnal leaves kept under your bed make you lucky all Winter.

XIV   Miscellaneous

There must, of course, always be a final catch-all category: Miscellaneous. This is not the book or place to question that category in any detail, but folklorists seem to have given in to the enormity of the field of beliefs and superstitions and, with the completion of Category XIII, surrendered everything else to "miscellaneous." It does not make real sense. Here, for example, they have included baseball, dreams, good and bad luck, sneezing, wishes, and such. As a very first attack upon this "miscellaneous" category, I would create a strong category of "Sports, Games, and Entertainment," which would include all of the superstitions and beliefs relating to baseball, football, the theater, the opera, and all other aspects of the sports and entertainment world, as a starter. Other categories will suggest themselves as readily to you as they do to me. However, since "miscellaneous" does now exist: If a player breaks a bat, it means a batting slump.—If you rub a baseball bat with a bone, you will have power to hit the ball harder.—If you tell your dream before sunup, it will come true.—To step on an empty Lucky Strike pack brings good luck.—If you read a whole book on Christmas Eve, you'll have good luck.—It's bad luck to weep after dark.—If you dream the same dream for three nights straight without telling it, it will come true.—When you start to say something and forget what you were going to say, it was a lie.

PROVERBS AND PROVERBIAL SPEECH

Proverbs and proverbial speech are a second broad segment of folklore scattered throughout the book. The distinction between the two (proverbs and the proverbial phrase) is a relatively simple one: the proverb, with wide usage and acceptance, becomes fixed and unchanging (unlike most other items of folklore), while the proverbial phrase (or proverbial speech) is considerably more fluid. The proverb also, in sentence form, usually states a complete truth or truism in its few brief words, whereas the proverbial phrase is essentially descriptive and is not in itself a maxim, adage, saw, or complete saying.

The proverb: The early bird catches the worm; Great oaks from little acorns grow; Two heads are better than one. No single word here can be changed, without losing all. The proverbial phrase: Drunk as a skunk; drunk as a covey of boiled owls; so drunk he doesn't know George Washington is dead; so drunk he can't tell up from down; he looks like an accident going somewhere to happen; as red as a beet; as crazy as a loon; as crazy as a bedbug. Words in the proverbial phrase can be changed more readily (even though there must be some fixity to make them proverbial) than in the fixed proverb. Further, the proverbial phrases do not give advice, are not admonitory, do not pretend to full truth. They describe. ("I wouldn't be in his shoes for a hundred dollars.")

Proverbs and proverbial phrases are found in this *Hodgepodge* under proverbs, sayings, comparisons, rain, pennies, dumb as they come, health measures, weather, wishes, dreams, months, untidy, and varied other entries. They are so closely related to beliefs and superstitions (Rain before seven,/Stop before eleven) that they are in many instances inseparable. In consequence, I have not separated them in the bibliography: Every book and article dealing with beliefs–superstitions has in it proverbs and proverbial phrases; every book and article dealing with proverbs and proverbial phrases has in it beliefs–superstitions. For those who are hardily concerned with the proverb and proverbial phrase alone, the titles of the articles are fully adequate pointers and guideposts—but, the articles immediately beside them and dealing (by the titles) with beliefs and superstitions should not be overlooked, because they contain proverbs and proverbial speech, to boot. (Can you imagine an article on weather-lore without proverbs? Or on farming? Or on medicine? Or the upbringing of a child?) They touch each other. Placing them together in the bibliography is a reminder of their generally basic inseparability.

OTHER MATTER

The remaining matter in the book is either self-evident and needs no explanation; has already been described in the "Notes" to *The Nonsense Book* (riddles, puzzles, tongue-twisters, autograph album rhymes); is explained here in the *Hodgepodge* text itself (as, for example, Geography or Tattoos); or is otherwise noted and identified in the "Sources" and bibliography which follow.

SOURCES

The three main sources for the beliefs and superstitions included here are first, Harry Middleton Hyatt's *Folklore from Adams County, Illinois* (2nd revised edition, copyright 1965 by Harry Middleton Hyatt). Dr. Hyatt has generously permitted me to draw freely from that work, and

I am greatly in his debt. The second is the very extensive Works Progress Administration (WPA) manuscript collection of American folklore, housed now in the Library of Congress. It covers (in varying degrees of quality and quantity) every State in the Union, and is an invaluable record of many aspects of our country's folk traditions. The third is Ray B. Browne's *Popular Beliefs and Practices from Alabama* which I have used principally to illustrate the subdivisions of beliefs and superstitions given immediately above. A fourth source is my own pack-rat collection of odds and ends over the years.

The chief source for the proverbs and items of proverbial speech and phrase has been the WPA manuscript collection of folklore cited above. The great work on the proverb is Professor Archer Taylor's *The Proverb* (Harvard) Cambridge, 1931, reissued Hatboro, 1962. The best consideration of the difficult problem of definition is found in Professor Bartlett Jere Whiting's "Proverbs and Proverbial Sayings" in volume I of the *Frank C. Brown Collection of North Carolina Folklore*, Durham, 1952, which also includes his editing of the North Carolina proverbs and sayings. Another excellent State collection is Frances M. Barbour's, *Proverbs and Proverbial Phrases of Illinois* (Southern Illinois University Press) Carbondale, 1965. Additional works and articles will be found in the bibliography.

The jokes and riddle-conundrums (elephants, grapes, bananas, what is the difference between? and others) come from students in my folklore class at American University who work with children; from an excellent collection by Catherine Harris Ainsworth and a fine study by Meryl Wiener, both listed in the bibliography; and from a few long out-of-print conundrum-puzzle collections of the last century and the early part of this one.

I have not given sources (Maine-WPA; Hyatt-Illinois; Emrich-Nevada) for each and every one of the beliefs and proverbs since the great majority are found all over the lot and since this also is not that finely footnoted type of book. Such entries would be a little burdensome. On the other hand, the sources for some items do deserve special mention. *A Charm Against Evil Spirits:* This was given me by Maida Parker, (a student at American University, 1971), who learned it from her mother (and her mother before her) in Gloucester, Massachusetts. *Chickens and Hens and Roosters:* "My Grandfather Ben" from NYFQ, 1 (1945) 109, collected by Miss Lesley Brewer. *Clams:* Maine-WPA. *Counting-Out-Rhymes:* Whitney and Bullock, *Folklore from Maryland* (see bibl.). *Crows:* The "explanation" for Robin Hood's barn is my own and may or may not be the final answer. *Cumulative or Snowball Stories:* "The Old Hen" was sent to me at the Library of Congress by Joanna Colcord of Searsport, Maine, who had learned it from her grandmother, who was born in Vinalhaven, Maine, in 1834. Move the family back three generations into Massachusetts, and we are in the early 1700s. Think of the youngsters who must have enjoyed it along the way! Joanna Colcord is, of course, one of America's great authorities on the folklore of the sea, and her books on sea shanties and on sea language and speech are classics.—*"The Old Woman and Her Pig"* was sent me by Mrs. Hans Lemcke of Mahama Ranch, Durham, California, following one of my folklore broadcasts over the NBC radio network in 1954. It is, of course, like "The Old Hen," English in origin. It is pleasant to think of the "old woman's" travels—from what place in England and by what route to Mahama Ranch?—"The Little Old Lady Who Swallowed a Fly" was collected from Lee Martin (aged twelve at the time) in 1947 in Denver, Colorado, and published in HF, 6 (1947) 153–156. Variants of this are somewhat more extended, including a cat to eat up the bird, and the dog to eat up the cat. —*The Derby Ram:* "The Derby Ram" was collected by Vance Randolph at Walnut Shade, Missouri, in 1941, from the singing of Charles Ingenthron. It is available on long-playing record L12 from the Library of Congress. *Fleas:* This delightful tale comes from Evan Esar's *The Humor of Humor* (Horizon Press) New York, 1952. Copyright 1952, Evan Esar, used here by permission. Esar's work, an analysis (with examples) of folk and vaudeville humor belongs in every library of Americana and folklore. It is twice as good and instructive as anything in the field.— *I Saw A Ship A-Sailing:* A variant of this (from Maryland) is in the Opie's *Nursery Rhymes* (see bibl.).—*London Hill:* Maine-WPA.— —*Mrs. Vickers' Daughter:* Maine-WPA. Is it not a nice small poem?— *Replies to Taunts and Name Calling:* "You insignificant piece of humanity . . ." comes from the York State collection of Harold W. Thompson, reported in NYFQ, 1 (1945) 20–32 by Eugenia L. Millard.—*A Square Dance Call:* (WPA) Roswell, New Mexico, collected from Elza White. "Here's a little set I used to like to call to my crowd of girls and cowboys at Midland, Texas, in the 80's."—*Street Cries:* Rose Cohen's cry comes from the New York WPA collection. I hope that she sees this.—*Three Little Fish:* These were first drawn for me as a youngster and tattooed on my memory by an elderly passenger on shipboard out of the Mediterranean during World War I days. I have not seen them elsewhere.— *The Tree in the Wood:* This was recorded by Vance Randolph from the singing of Doney Hammontree at Farmington, Arkansas, in 1941. It is available on Library of Congress record L12.—*Upon a Christmas Morning:* Is this not completely and utterly delightful, and thoroughly American? It comes from W. W. Newell, "Old English Songs in American Versions," JAF, 5 (1892) 326.—*Washington's Birthday:* The song, "Washington the

Great," was recorded by John A. Lomax from the singing of Mrs. Minta Morgan at Bells, Texas, in 1937. It is available on Library of Congress long-playing record L29. Mrs. Morgan said, "Well, this song has been in our immediate family for a hundred years. My father was borned in 1824. He said he learned it when he was about thirteen years old at a country school that he went to, Cogshill school in East Tennessee, McMinn County."—*Wishes:* I have done a small book, *The Book of Wishes and Wishmaking* (American Heritage Press, 1970), which has many ways of wishmaking and wishes not given here. It is illustrated by Hilary Knight of Eloise fame. This mention of it here is simply an informative note. (Hah!) Read the last page of it, and do write.

In the bibliography which follows, I have listed books and articles by author and, in brackets, have given some suggestion of content in addition to that evident in most of the titles. No bibliography in the field of American beliefs and superstitions, proverbs and proverbial speech can be exhaustive. This one is not, but it is more complete than any that has appeared elsewhere to date: It contains all the major American books and folklore articles dealing with the subject matter, and a very goodly number of out-of-the-way and "minor" articles which—for their earthy and regional American color—deserve rescue here. I have attempted to make the bibliography not only informative, but pleasantly readable as well. I trust that I have in some measure succeeded and that the reader enjoys it.

Again, as with the "Notes and Bibliography" in *The Nonsense Book*, I must express my appreciation to the publishers for their willingness to permit the printing here of the bibliography. It increases the usefulness of the book to librarians, teachers, and students, and I hope as a reference tool that it will be as valuable to them as the main body of the book is entertaining to the youngsters to whom it is primarily directed.

As in *The Nonsense Book*, the journals chiefly cited in the bibliography, together with abbreviations for title are:

AS	*American Speech*
CFQ	*California Folklore Quarterly*
FF	*Folklore Forum*
HF	*Hoosier Folklore*
IF	*Indiana Folklore*
JAF	*Journal of American Folklore*
KFQ	*Keystone Folklore Quarterly*
KFR	*Kentucky Folklore Record*
MF	*Midwest Folklore*
MFR	*Mississippi Folklore Register*
N	*Names*
NCF	*North Carolina Folklore*
NEF	*Northeast Folklore*
NWF	*Northwest Folklore*
NMFR	*New Mexico Folklore Record*
NYFQ	*New York Folklore Quarterly*
PTFS	*Publications of the Texas Folklore Society*
SFQ	*Southern Folklore Quarterly*
TFSB	*Tennessee Folklore Society Bulletin*
WF	*Western Folklore*
WVF	*West Virginia Folklore*

BIBLIOGRAPHY

BELIEFS AND SUPERSTITIONS
PROVERBS AND PROVERBIAL PHRASES

A

Roger D. Abrahams, "Folk Beliefs in Southern Joke Books," WF, 23 (1964) 259–261. [Don't shake the tablecloth out of doors after sunset; you will never marry.]; **Roger D. Abrahams**, "Some Plantation Remedies and Recipes," TFSB, 29 (June 1963); **Charles C. Adams**, *Boontling: An American Lingo,* (Univ. of Texas Press) Austin, 1971. [A full and amazing book account of this incredible children's secret language which was adopted and taken over by an entire California community]; **Owen S. Adams**, "More California Proverbs," WF, 7 (1948) 136–144. [An empty wagon makes the most noise.— One is afraid, and the other dassn't.]; **Owen S. Adams**, "Proverbial Comparisons from California," CFQ, 5 (1946) 334–338. [142 generally well known: As quick as a flash.—To sell like hot cakes.—Like taking candy from babies.]; **Owen S. Adams**, "Proverbial Phrases from California," WF, 8 (1949) 95– 116. [Approximately 200 well known: To go like a house afire.—To go in one ear and out the other.—To fight like cats and dogs.]; **Owen S. Adams,** "Traditional Proverbs and Sayings from California," WF, 6 (1947) 59–64. [135 items—It's impossible to make a two-year-old calf in a minute.—He was biggest when he was hatched. (Hasn't measured up to his promise.)—A Southerner never sells what he can eat, and a Northerner never eats what he can sell.—Worry awhile and forget about it.—What one doesn't know doesn't give him a headache.—You can get a Southerner out of the South, but you can't get the South out of a Southerner.]; **Michael J. Ahearn**, "The Noell Madstone," PTFS, 29 (1950) 147–152. [Report of "more than a thousand cures" affected by madstone belonging to Dr. J. M. Noell of Alto, Texas, in the mid-1800's]; **Abbie L. Allen**, "Riddle Parallel to Children's Curse," JAF, 68 (1955) 282 ["Ca. 1900 in East Braintree, Mass., my father used to recite a riddle: 'Corn stalks twist your hair,/Mortar and pestle pound you,/ Fiery dragons carry you off,/Great cart wheels surround you.'—Ans. A train ride.—See also entry under H. H. Flanders]; **Hope Emily Allen,** "Connecticut Chat," JAF, 64 (1951) 223–224. [You're as thin as a June shad going down stream.]; **Hope Emily Allen**, "The Influence of Superstition on Vocabulary," *Publications of the Modern Language Association,* 51 (1936) 904–920; **Hope Emily Allen**, "Superstitions Attached to the Black-Beetle, the Lobster, Wood-Louse," *Notes and Queries,* 168 (1935) 460; **Prudence Allen**, "Love and Marriage in York State Lore," NYFQ, 5 (1949) 257–267. [If you should find an even ash/And put it in your glove,/The first young man you chance to meet/Will offer you his love.]; **Lelah Allison**, "Folk Beliefs Collected in Southeastern Illinois," JAF, 63 (1950) 309–324. [Good collection of 556 beliefs and superstitions: weather, folk cures, special days and numbers, weddings, birds, plants, birth and infancy, wishes, dreams, misc.—If you see a star fall with your mouth closed, you will get a new dress.—Thunder kills goslings in the shell.—A snake will swallow its young if danger approaches.—Smoke goes toward beauty.—Eat turnips to be pretty.]; **Lelah Allison,** "Folk Beliefs Regarding Weather in Southeastern Illinois," JAF, 61 (1948) 68–70. [Three accounts of true and unusual weather occurrences (cyclone carries girl over church steeple) and five methods of prognostication]; **Lelah Allison,** "Folk Speech from Southeastern Illinois," HF, 5 (1946) 93–102. [Hasn't the sense of a jackrabbit.—He knows as much about that as a hog does about Sunday afternoon.]; **Rudolph Altrocchi,** "Professor Source," CFQ, 2 (1943) 299–301. [Dialogue between student and "Professor Source," pointing up the antiquity of proverbs,]; **American Dialect Society** (Publication 4), *Proverbs and How to Collect Them,* 1945; [anon.], **"Ancient Eye Cures Are Preface to Modern Medicine,"** *Hygeia,* 14 (1936) 286; **John Q. Anderson,** "Carolina Courtship and Marriage in the 1840's," NCF, 10 no. 2 (1962) 1–10; **John Q. Anderson,** "Emerson and the Language of the Folk," PTFS, 25 (1953) 152–159. [The whole value of a dime is in knowing what to do with it.—There is always a best way of doing everything, if it be to boil an egg.—Old shoes are easy to the feet.—Each prophet comes presently to identify himself with his thought, and to esteem his hat and shoes sacred.]; **John Q. Anderson,** "Folk Remedies for the Cure of Warts," LFM, 2 (April 1965) 55–73. [120 "cures" grouped in eight useful categories.—Rub warts with a toad while sitting on a rotten stump in the moonlight.—Borrow a penny, rub it on the wart, and throw the penny away.]; **John Q. Anderson,** "Magical Transference of Disease in Texas Folk Medicine," WF, 27 (1968) 191–199. [The transfer of disease to animals, insects, trees. See also NCF, 13 (1965) 83–109, "The Magical Transference of Disease."]; **John Q. Anderson,** "Popular Beliefs in Texas, Louisiana, and Arkansas," SFQ, 32 (1968) 304–319. [174 entries.—When a horse or mule is punctured by a bull's horn, peel a green banana and stick it in the hole, then coat the hole with mud.]; **John Q. Anderson,** "Special Powers in Folk Cures and Remedies," PTFS, 34 (1968) 163–174. [45 Texas examples of power doctors and "powwowing."]; **Urban Anderson,** "A Comparative Study of Some of the Older Beliefs and Usages of East Tennessee," TFSB, 3 (Feb. 1937). ["A curious custom reported in Middle Tennessee attends the finding of water in digging a well. When the water is struck, the diggers shout, a whistle is blown, and a bell rung. Then one of the men jumps from the pit, seeks out a cow in a nearby field, and sends her sprawling by grasping her by the hind legs. I must confess that I am at a loss to account for this custom. . . . "]; [anon.], **"Anecdotes Illustrating the Folk Idiom in the American South,"** TFSB, 26 (March 1960). ["In this country, bullets have no eyes . . . "]; **G. L. Apperson,** *English Proverbs and Proverbial Phrases, An Historical Dictionary,* New York, 1929. [One of the basic reference works in the field]; **Shirley L. Arora,** "Spanish Proverbial Exaggerations from California," WF, 27 (1968) 229–254. [Fine collection with translations and annotated references.—He's so tall and she's so short it looks like a quarter past one.—He's so ugly you could use him to cure the hiccups.—He's so unlucky that if he fell over backwards he'd break his nose.];

Mary Jourdan Atkinson, "Familiar Sayings of Old Time Texas," PTFS, 5 (1926) 78–92. [A generous collection of proverbs, proverbial phrases, comparisons.—Just as well go out and bay at the moon as ask that old skinflint for money.—He hasn't got the sense God promised a louse.—She doesn't know A from izzard.—He's so ugly they have to put him down a well before the sun will rise.—I've seen wilder heifers than you milked in a gourd, ma'am.]; **Pearl Hamlin Augar**, "French Beliefs in Clinton County," NYFQ, 4 (1948) 161–171; **A. Monroe Aurand, Jr.**, *Popular Home Remedies and Superstitions of the Pennsylvania Germans*, Harrisburg, 1941; **Lucille Ayers** and others, "Expressions from Rural Florida," *Publications of the American Dialect Society*, 14 (Nov 1950) 74–80.

B

C. Merton Babcock, "Melville's Backwoods Seamen," WF, 10 (1951) 126–133. [Good introduction to Melville's use of folk materials, including the tall tale.—A storm for every calm.—If a man made up his mind to live, mere sickness could not kill him.]; **C. Merton Babcock**, "Melville's Proverbs of the Sea," WF, 11 (1952) 254–265. [There never was a very great man yet who spent all his life inland.—Anything that smacks of life is better than to feel Davy Jones's chest-lid on your nose.—Round the Cape of Good Hope is the shortest way to Nantucket.]; **C. Merton Babcock**, "Some Expressions from Herman Melville, *Publications of the American Dialect Society*, 31 (1959) 3–13. [28 sayings, chiefly proverbial phrases]; **Mrs. E. M. Backus**, "New England Folk Beliefs in the Last Century," JAF, 45 (1932) 501–502. [Approx. 25 items from a "rural hill town of Connecticut": When the first snow which falls remains on the ground until the next snow, there will be no more bare ground that winter.—A cold April and a wet May/Fills the barn with grain and hay.]; **Mrs. E. M. Backus**, "New England Folk Beliefs in the Last Century," JAF, 48 (1935) 196–197. [About 20 items of folk medicine: A chicken's gizzard dried, powdered and taken with molasses is a remedy for indigestion.]; **Emma M. Backus**, "Superstitions from Connecticut," JAF, 8 (1895) 192. [A pleasant pageful: If, while children are picking huckleberries, one picks from a bush already in possession of another, they say that the trespasser will spill his berries.]; **Emma Backus**, "Weather Signs from Connecticut," JAF, 8 (1895) 26. [Wild geese passing over is a sign of a storm.]; **E. R. Bain**, "Don't Cross the Bridge . . . ," *American Notes and Queries*, 2 (1942) 79. [Notes that Longfellow used the proverb "Don't cross the bridge before you come to it" in 1851.]; **Pearl Baker and Ruth Wilcox**, "Folk Remedies in Early Green River," *Utah Humanities Review*, 2 (1948) 191–192; **L. Karen Baldwin**, "A Sampling of Housewives' Proverbs and Proverbial Phrases from Levittown, Pennsylvania," KFQ, 10 (1965) 127–146. [249 items, all generally well known]; **Frances M. Barbour**, "Embellishment of the Proverb," SFQ, 28 (1964) 291–298. [Discusses changes rung on proverbs to modernize them or give them more vivid imagery. 89 examples—Hungry as a wolf. Hungry as a wolf after a week's snow.—Slow as the seven-year itch—and ten years behind in scratching.]; **Frances M. Barbour,** *Proverbs and Proverbial Phrases of Illinois,* (Southern Illinois University Press), Carbondale, 1965. [One of the basic American collections.—"To take off like a herd of turtles." To move slowly and with considerable disorganization.]; **Frances M. Barbour,** "Some Uncommon Sources of Proverbs," MF, 13 (1963) 97–100. [Parody-proverbs, proverbs from songs, and from advertising.—Easy as falling off a diet.—You can lead a fool to college, but you can't make him think.]; **Mary Barbour,** "Three Snake Stories," NCF, 15 no 2 (1967) 44–46. [Local experiences]; **Addison Barker,** "Anatomical Superstitions in *Blum's Almanac,*" NCF, 8 no 2 (Dec 1960) 47–48. [When your lips itch, someone is crying about you.—If your shins itch, you will travel to a strange place and have a painful illness.]; **Addison Barker,** "Weather Lore in *Blum's Almanac,* 1844–1950," NCF, 5 no 1 (July 1957) 11–19. [If the leaves of the paternoster pea plant droop vertically, expect a storm.—Thunder and lightning during Christmas week signify much snow for the remainder of the year.]; **Gertrude Barnes,** "Superstitions and Maxims from Dutchess County, New York," JAF, 36 (1923) 16–22. [92 items collected by students in a folklore class at Vassar College: Plant lima beans at the time when hickory leaves are the size of a squirrel's feet.—Beds should be placed north and south. "It's something about electric currents."]; **James H. Barnett,** *The American Christmas, A Study in National Culture,* New York, 1954. [History, customs, traditions, religious observation, commercialization]; **Viron L. Barnhill,** "Three Acadian Weather Practices," LFM, 2 (Aug 1968) 111–112. [Including the practice of storing charred pieces of the Christmas log in the attic as a protection against lightning]; **Mac E. Barrick,** "All Signs in Dry Spells Fails," KFQ, 9 (1964) 23–28 [57 South-Central Pennsylvania beliefs: Bullfrogs holler when it's going to rain.—If you can hear the South Mountain train whistling, it's a sign of rain. (Common saying along North Mountain, the train being then ten miles away.)]; **Mac E. Barrick,** "Early Proverbs from Carlisle, Pennsylvania (1778–1821)," KFQ, 13 (1968) 193–218. [Extensive collection from newspapers of the period]; **Mac E. Barrick,** "Folk Medicine in Cumberland County," KFQ, 9 (1964) 100–110. [If you chew your fingernails, they'll get in your appendix.—Feed a cold and starve a fever.—A long kiss is supposed to stop hiccups.—The best thing to do for a toothache is to take a mouthful of water and set on the stove till it boils.—Never rub your eye with anything but your elbow.]; **Mac E. Barrick,** "Popular Comparisons and Similes [from Cumberland County residents, Carlisle, Pennsylvania]," KFQ, 10 (1965) 3–34. [The quickest way to do many things is to do one thing at a time.—As sure as God made little apples.—As big as life and twice as natural.]; **Mac E. Barrick,** "Proverbs and Sayings from Cumberland County [Pa.]," KFQ, 8 (1963) 139–203. [Extensive collection.—Even a blind pig finds an acorn sometime.]; **Mac E. Barrick,** "Proverbs and Sayings from Gibbsville, Pa., John O'Hara's Use of Proverbial Materials," KFQ, 12 (1967) 55–80; **Julie Barrois,** "Herb Cures in an Isolated Black Community in the Florida Parishes," LFM, 3 (April 1970) 25–27. [Four "cures" checked for their efficacy with a professor of pharmacology at Loyola University]; **John Russell**

Bartlett, *Dictionary of Americanisms*, Boston 1877. [Major collection of colloquialisms, with some proverbial phrases]; **William W. Bass**, "Birthmarks Among the Folk," TFSB, 25 (March 1959). [Consideration of markings due to fright, craving for food]; **William W. Bass**, "Dog Days: Some Notes and a Few Superstitions," TFSB, 22 (Sept 1956). [Generally the period July 3–August 11, or the 40 days preceding the cosmical rising of the dog star Sirius.—Don't swim in small streams during dog days.—Sores won't heal during dog days.—Dish towels and other things mildew worse during dog days.]; **Fletcher S. Bassett**, *Legends and Superstitions of the Sea and of Sailors*, Chicago, 1885. [Good general collection]; **Wilbur W. Bassett**, "Illinois Folklore, Some Beliefs of Children and Youths," *The Folklorist*, London, 1 (1893) 157–158; **Ernest W. Baughman**, "Folk Sayings and Beliefs," NMFR, 9 (1954–1955) 23–27; **Ernest W. Baughman** and **Clayton A. Holaday**, "Tall Tales and 'Sells' from Indiana University Students," HF, 3 no 4 (1944) 59–70. [Good collection. "The Lion and the Mouse" in this book is drawn from it.]; **Richard Bauman**, "The Collecting of Proverbs," WF, 22 (1963) 271–272. [Synopsis of method by Jewish folklorist Yehude Loeb Cahan for collecting. Use key words: Do you know any proverbs about an *apple?*]; **John E. Baur**, *Christmas on the American Frontier, 1800–1900* (Caxton Printers) Caldwell, Idaho, 1961. [Christmas with the explorers, cowboys, miners, in the Rockies, Texas, the Yukon. With bibl.]; **Samuel P. Bayard**, "Witchcraft, Magic and Spirits on the Border of Pennsylvania and West Virginia," JAF, 51 (1938) 47–59. [Good first-hand accounts of witches, ghosts, ha'nts, as well as varied love charms, a few cures, and snake beliefs.— Telling the bees: "You must go to the hive immediately after there has been a death in the house, and say loudly and distinctly, 'Your master's dead!' Straightway all the bees will stop their humming for a moment, then recommence it loudly on a new note; and one bee will fly out of the hive and go directly to the death-chamber, where it will circle about the corpse, and after having assured itself of the truth of the report will return to the hive. The bees will then resume their normal activity, and will not leave the place." (In order to have this programme work out as it should, the window of the dead-room must be open.)]; **Richard K. Beardsley**, "A History of the Vanishing Hitchhiker," CFQ, 2 (1943) 13–25; **Richard K. Beardsley** and **Rosalie Hankey**, "The Vanishing Hitchhiker," CFQ, 1 (1942) 303–335. [Forty variants of this well-known ghost tale]; **Dorothy J. Baylor**, "Folklore from Socorro, New Mexico," HF, 6 (1947) 138–150. [History, customs, tales, beliefs, cures.—If you find a bobby pin, it means that you will have a date.— It will rain if you see bugs crawling out of a canyon.]; **H. P. Beck**, "Herpetological Lore from the Blue Ridge," MF, 2 (1952) 141–150; **Horace P. Beck**, *The Folklore of Maine*, Philadelphia and New York, 1957. [Fine state survey. Deserves reissue in paperback.]; **W. N. T. Beckett (R.N.)**, *A Few Naval Customs, Expressions, Traditions, and Superstitions*, The Hard, Portsmouth, 1931; **Martha Warren Beckwith**, "Signs and Superstitions Collected from American College Girls," JAF, 36 (1923) 1–15. [186 entries chiefly in the fun-belief category.—If you wish when you enter a covered bridge, and hold your breath all the way, you get your wish.—If you bury a dead bird, its song will make music in heaven.—It is good luck to say "rabbits" before you open your eyes on the first day of the month.—Roses are for luck: "I always took them to examinations."] **Helen Bellatty** (of Ellsworth, Maine, "Hallowe'en Superstitions of My Younger Days," NEF, 1 (Fall 1958). [Includes true-love divinations]; **Fanny D. Bergen,** *Animal and Plant Lore Collected from the Oral Tradition of English Speaking Folk,* (Memoirs of the American Folklore Society, 7) New York, 1899; **Fanny D. Bergen,** *Current Superstitions Collected from the Oral Tradition of English Speaking Folk,* (Memoirs of the American Folklore Society, 4) New York, 1896. [Both these volumes valuable for their basic collection and for dating beliefs, chiefly from New England]; **Fanny D. Bergen,** "Some Bits of Plant Lore," JAF, 5 (1892) 19–22. [Cites plants used for folk cures as well as for love "projects."—The familiar southernwood, *Artemisia abrotanum,* in England is known as lad's love, lad-love-lass, or lad's love-and-lasses' delight. In Maine and Woburn, Mass., this herb is called boy's love, and it is said that if a girl tucks a bit of it in her shoe she will marry the first boy whom she meets.]; **Fanny D. Bergen,** "Some Saliva Charms," JAF, 3 (1890) 51–59. [Spit, spat, spot,/Tell me where that bird's nest is.]; **Fanny D. Bergen, W. M. Beauchamp,** and **W. W. Newell,** "Current Superstitions," JAF, 2 (1889) 12–22, 105–112, 203–208. [Includes rhymes: Open your mouth and shut your eyes,/And I'll give you something to make you wise.—Shut your eyes and open your mouth,/And I'll give you something that comes from the south.]; **Rochele Berkovits,** "Secret Languages of School Children," NYFQ, 26 (1970) 127–152. [The best article to date. Some fifteen secret languages are fully reported through Q and A interviews with 6th and 7th graders.]; **Leonidas Betts,** "Folk Speech from Kipling [N.C.]," NCF, 14 no 2 (Nov 1966) 37–40. [. . . grinning like a mule eating briars.—To fling a Joe Blizzard fit. (Joe Blizzard lived in Kipling and had a violent temper, hence the local phrase.)]; **Pauline Monette Black,** *Nebraska Folk Cures* (University of Nebraska Studies in Language, Literature, and Criticism, 15) Lincoln, 1935; **William George Black,** *Folk Medicine: A Chapter in the History of Culture* (Publications of the Folk-Lore Society, 12), London, 1883. [Important early study]; **Marion E. Blair,** "The Prevalence of Older English Proverbs in Blount County, Tennessee," TFSB, 4 (March 1938). [Traces current proverbs to Layamon, Chaucer, *Piers Plowman,* Langland, Heywood, Hoccleve, Gower, and others. Fine study.]; **E. R. Bogusch,** "Superstitions of Bexar County [Tex.]," PTFS, 5 (1927) 112–125. [Approx. 300 items on varied subjects.—If a cat yells when it is held by the tail, her feet will point in the direction from which will come a letter telling of a death.—If you spit on more than three horseshoes in one day, you will have bad luck.]; **Henry George Bohn,** *A Handbook of Proverbs,* London, 1885. [Important collection and valuable reference source]; **Henry Carrington Bolton,** "Fortune-Telling in America Today: A Study of Advertisements," JAF, 8 (1895) 299–307. [Interesting review and useful for comparison with today's advertisements]; **Donald F. Bond,** "English Legal Proverbs," *Publications of the Modern Language Association,* 51 (1936) 921–935; **Donald F. Bond,** "The Law and Lawyers in English Proverbs," *Journal of the American Bar Association,* 21 (1935) 724–727; **Richmond P. Bond,**

"Animal Comparisons in Indiana, AS, 2 (1927) 42–58. [More than a thousand expressions.—High as a cat's back.—Awkward as a cow on skates.—Cross as a snapping turtle.—To scream like a panther.]; **Richmond P. Bond,** "More Animal Comparisons," AS, 4 (1929) 123–124. [150 more.—Saucy as a chipmunk.—Helpless as a turtle on its back.—Like a lost dog.]; **Robert W. Bond,** "Some Mysteries, Myths, and Methods of the Ancient Art of the Apothecary," TFSB, 15 (March 1949); **Wilfred Bonser, ed.,** *Proverb Literature: A Bibliography of Works Relating to Proverbs* (Publication of the Folk-Lore Society, 89), London, 1930; **Frances Boshears,** "Proverbial Comparisons from an East Tennessee County," TFSB, 20 (June 1954) 27–41. [1045 entries, all from personal memory.—I feel like something the cats drug in and couldn't eat.—As pert as a cricket.]; **George W. Boswell,** "Folk Wisdom in Northeastern Kentucky," TFSB, 33 (March 1967). [99 proverbial sayings, good collection.—Nothing but money is sweeter than honey.—Age steals upon us like a snowstorm in the night.—It's good for whatever ails you, and if nothing ails you, it's good for that.]; **George W. Boswell,** "Folkways in Faulkner," MFR, 1 (1967) 83–90; **Anna Mary Boudreaux,** "Proverbs, Metaphors, and Sayings of the Kaplan Area [Vermilion Parish, La.]," LFM, 3 (1970) 16–24. [Approx. 100 in French with English translation.—One is as good as the other, and both are good for nothing.—Everyone cracks pecans in his own way. (Each has his own way of doing things)]; **Audrey Boughton,** "Weather Lore: Winter Quarter," NYFQ, 1 (1945) 60–62; "Spring," 123–125; "Summer," 189–190; "Fall," 251–252. [Very pleasant selection of York State seasonal weather beliefs]; **John G. Bourke,** "Popular Medicine, Customs, and Superstitions of the Rio Grande," JAF, 7 (1894) 119–146. [Cures, charms, love philtres, chiefly Mexican.—A white comet means pestilence; a red comet, war.—To cure epilepsy in children take a newly born pig and rub the naked baby with this live pig from head to foot. The baby will break out into copious perspiration, and the pig will die.]; **Ruth A. Boyer,** "Farm Lore: Insects, Animals and the Weather," NYFQ, 2 (1946) 74–76. [When the peepers peep loudly at night, there will be rain the next day.—If a horse yawns, it will rain before sundown the next day.]; **Francis W. Bradley,** "South Carolina Proverbs," SFQ, 1 (1937) 57–101. [Excellent annotated collection of 612 proverbs and proverbial sayings.—Multiplication is vexation,/Division is as bad,/The rule of three perplexes me,/And practice drives me mad.]; **John Brand,** *Observations on Popular Antiquities Chiefly Illustrating the Origin of Our Vulgar Customs, Ceremonies and Superstitions* (ed. Sir Henry Ellis), 3 vols., London, 1901–1902. [Reissue. A fascinating work. Belongs on the shelf with Hone, Chambers, and other British antiquarians.]; **Elizabeth Brandon,** "Superstitions in Vermilion Parish [La.]," PTFS, 31 (1962) 108–118. [Fetishes, conjuring, ghosts]; **Thomas R. Brendle** and **William S. Troxell,** *Pennsylvania German Folk-Tales, Legends, Once-Upon-a-Time Stories, Maxims, and Sayings* (Pennsylvania German Society Proceedings, 50) Norristown, 1944; **Thomas R. Brendle** and **Claude W. Unger,** *Folk Medicine of the Pennsylvania Germans: The Non-Occult Cures* (Proceedings of the Pennsylvania German Society, 45) Norristown, 1935. [Important, since the Pennsylvania Germans as a group supplied the greatest quantity of folk medicine to the Midwest pioneers in the early 1800's.]; **Paul G. Brewster,** "Beliefs and Customs," in vol. I of *The Frank C. Brown Collection of North Carolina Folklore* (Duke University Press), Durham, 1952. [Extensive collection with comparative notes and bibliography.]; **Paul G. Brewster,** "Folk Beliefs and Practices from Southern Indiana," HF, 2 (1943) 23–38. [If a hen is set when the wind is from the north, the eggs will hatch but the chicks will stand around and "peep" until the wind changes.]; **Paul G. Brewster,** "Folk Cures and Preventives from Southern Indiana," SFQ, 3 (1939) 33–43. [Nosebleed can be stopped by wearing a necklace of flattened lead bullets.]; **Paul G. Brewster,** "Folk 'Sayings' from Indiana," AS, 14 (1939) 216–268. [His face is so long he could eat hay out of a churn.—Mistakes don't make haystacks or there'd be more fat cattle.]; **Paul G. Brewster,** "More Indiana Sayings," AS, 16 (1941) 21–25. [Meetin' ain't over till the benediction's said.—I wouldn't have it off a Christmas tree.—Not enough clothes on to pad a crutch.]; **Paul G. Brewster,** "Smart Sayings from Indiana," HF, 6 (1947) 50–54. [With addenda notes by Violet and William Hugh Jansen.—He's all right, but his feet ain't mates.—I'm gonna retire and build me a stump farm. Gonna build me a shack in the middle of a field of stumps and just listen to 'em rot.]; **Paul G. Brewster,** "Specimens of Folklore from Southern Indiana," *Folk-Lore,* 47, London, 1936, 362–368; **Paul G. Brewster,** "Still Another Batch of Indiana Sayings," AS, 19 (1944) 155–156. [80 sayings from immediately heard conversations]; **Harold E. Briggs,** "Folklore of Southern Illinois," SFQ, 16 (1952) 207–217; **D. G. Brinton,** "Reminiscences of Pennsylvania Folk-Lore," JAF, 5 (1892) 177–185. [Good review of charms, cures, planting, ghosts, etc., all from personal knowledge and dating from the 1850s]; **Hoyle S. Bruton,** "Miscellany," NCF, 1 (1948) 20–26. [Superstitions current as of 1915 in Montgomery County, N.C.]; **Lois Brock,** "Tarantula Lore," PTFS, 31 (1962) 41–52; **Henry M. Brooks,** "Weather Sayings of Salem, Mass.," JAF, 2 (1889) 309–310. [There's ne'er a Saturday of the year/In which the sun doth not appear.]; **Carleton F. Brown,** "The Long Hidden Friend," JAF, 17 (1904) 89–152. [The work of John George Hohman written in 1819: "Wonderful and Well-Tried Remedies and Magic Arts, As Well for Man as Beast." 2nd ed., Carlisle, Pa., 1863. Quite wonderful hex-doctor charms and cures.]; **Charles E. Brown,** *The Birds of the Campus,* Madison, Wisconsin, 1930; **Charles E. Brown,** *American Folklore—Insect Lore,* Madison, n.d.; **Roy M. Brown,** "The Treatment of Snakebite in Chapel Hill," NCF, 4 no 1 (1956) 1. [Report of a single cure]; **B. W. Browne,** "The Buzzard in the Folklore of Western Kentucky," KFR, 4 (1958) 11–12. [Brief, but interesting: "Buzzard Christians" are persons who attend church only for funerals.]; **Ray B. Browne,** *Popular Beliefs and Practices from Alabama* (Folklore Studies, 9), University of California Press, Berkeley, 1958. [Broad collection covering all fields; 4340 entries. Bibliography compiled by Wayland D. Hand.]; **Elizabeth Jones Browning,** "When They're Growed," TFSB, 25 (Sept 1959). [When they are little, they step on your toes;/When they're growed, they step on your heart.]; **Jan Harold Brunvand,** "Miscellany of Idaho Superstitions," WF, 22 (1963) 202–203. [15 from freshman students at University of Idaho.—Some people who are sick believe that if they bury a potato, they will get well faster. When my grandmother was sick, or thought she was, she felt better immediately after burying a potato.]; **Jan Harold Brunvand,** *Proverbs and Proverbial Phrases from Indiana Books Published before 1890* (Indiana University Folklore Series, 15) Bloomington, 1961. [Several hundred items in a basic collection.—A mule that whinnies and a woman that talks Latin never come to any good.—A handful of mother wit is worth a bushel of learning.]; **Jan Harold Brunvand,** *The Study of American Folklore: An Introduction,* New York, 1968. [With chapters and bibl. on proverbs and superstitions]; **Hoyle S. Bruton,** ed., "Miscellaneous Beliefs and Home Remedies" (pp. 20–26) and "Proverbs" (pp. 26–28) in NCF, 1 (1948). [Whatever you dream about cows is true about folks.—If you mock a screech owl, you'll get burnt.]; **Naomi Ruth Bryant,** "Children's Customs in San Mateo," WF, 8 (1949) 261. [Ten items.—Step on the discarded wrapper or package of Lucky Strike cigarettes and shout, "Lucky!" This brings good luck.]; **Margaret M. Bryant,** "Folklore from Edgefield County, South Carolina: Weather and Plant Lore," SFQ, 12 (1948) 279–291; **Margaret M. Bryant,** "Folklore from Edgefield County, South Carolina: Beliefs, Superstitions, Dreams," SFQ, 13 (1949) 136–148. [A woman who cuts thick slices of bread will make a good stepmother.—If you eat watermelon and drink whiskey at the same time, they will kill you. (A widely held belief, but I have proven it false in August. de.)]; **Margaret M. Bryant,** "The People's Sayings: How You Can Help Record Them," NYFQ, 1 (1945) 50–56; **Margaret M. Bryant,** "Proverbial Lore in American Life and Speech, WF, 10 (1951) 134–142. [Considers everyday use of proverbs in newspaper articles, advertising, radio]; **Mrs. Waller R. Bullock,** "The Collection of Maryland Folklore," JAF, 11 (1898) 7–16. [Reviews activity of Baltimore Folklore Society and suggests areas for collection, including superstitions]; **Roy E. Buren,** "A Butter Charm from the Ozark Mountains," JAF, 48 (1935) 196; **Charles Edward Burgin,** "The Extraction of Pain from Burns," NCF, 8 no 1 (1960) 17–18. [An account of "power-doctoring" or "powwowing"]; **Gaston Burridge,** "Does the Forked Stick Locate Anything? An Inquiry into the Art of Dowsing," WF, 14 (1955) 32–43; **E. E. Burris,** "The Place of the Dog in Superstition as Revealed in Latin Literature," *Classical Philology,* 30 (1935) 32–42; **Glynn Burton,** "Some Folkways of a Lincoln County Community," TFSB, 21 (March 1955). [Red bird, red bird,/Fly to my right,/And I'll see my sweetheart/Before Saturday night.—Do not raise an umbrella in the house or you will never marry.]; **John H. Bushnell,** "Medical Folklore from California," WF, 6 (1947) 273–275. [A piece of writing paper or newspaper placed against the skin in the pit of the stomach prevents train sickness as well as seasickness.]; **Norma Busse,** "Superstitions of the Theater," WF, 8 (1949) 66–67. [17 beliefs.—Never rehearse the last line of the play. To do so brings bad luck and the play will be a flop.—The leading man must kiss all the women in the cast. If he does not, he will never play a leading role again.]; **Ora S. Busse,** "Indiana Folk Beliefs, Omens, and Signs," HF, 6 (1947) 14–26. [Approx. 300 items: medicine, weather, planting, luck, love, marriage, body, misc.—To keep a hen from setting, put her head under her wing and dip her in a tub of water.—Eat chicken gizzards and you will be beautiful.]; **A. W. Butler,**

"Local Weather Lore," *American Meteorological Journal*, 1 (1884) 313–317; **Robert H. Byington**, "Popular Beliefs and Superstitions from Pennsylvania," KFQ, 9 (1964) 3–12. [Approx. 85 varied beliefs. (When the wind whistles around the corner, the devil is whipping his children.—Lots of rabbits out in the morning means it will storm shortly.—Squeezing a stone as hard as you can while holding your breath and counting backwards from eleven will cure a headache.]; **Robert H. Byington**, "Powwowing in Pennsylvania," KFQ, 9 (1964) 111–117. [Conjuring and "powwow cures" drawn chiefly from John G. Hoghman's *The Long Hidden Friend*, Berks County, 1819].

C

Ritchie Calder, *Medicine and Man, The Story of the Art and Science of Healing*, New York, 1958; [anon.], **"California Proverbs and Sententious Sayings,"** WF, 10 (1951) 248–249. [33 items.—Have you ever noticed that the knocker is always on the outside of the door?—Don't fret for what's not yet. You make trouble double when you borrow.—To get nowhere—follow the crowd.]; **Arthur L. Campa**, *Sayings and Riddles in New Mexico* (University of New Mexico Bulletin, 313) Albuquerque, 1937; **Arthur L. Campa**, "Some Herbs and Plants of Early California," WF, 9 (1950) 338–347. [Plants and remedies from the Spanish Mission of San Antonio in the early 19th century]; **Marie Campbell**, *Folks Do Get Born*, New York, 1946; **Marie Campbell**, "Folk Remedies from South Georgia," TFSB, 19 (March 1953); **Margaret Cannell**, "Signs, Omens, and Portents in Nebraska Folklore," (in University of Nebraska Studies in Language, Literature, and Criticism, 13) Lincoln, 1933, 7–50; **Loman D. Cansler**, "Madstones and Hydrophobia," WF, 23 (1964) 95–105. [Various accounts with good bibl notes]; **Terry M. Carbo**, "The Faith Healing Beliefs of a New Orleans Family," LFM, 2 (Aug 1968) 91–100. [Interesting personal reminiscences]; **George G. Carey**, *Maryland Folklore and Folklife*, Cambridge, Maryland, 1970. [Beliefs, superstitions, rhymes, riddles, tongue-twisters]; **Carl Carmer**, *Stars Fell on Alabama*, New York, 1934. [Classic volume on the beliefs, customs, traditions of the State]; **F. A. de Caro** and **W. K. McNeil**, *American Proverb Literature: A Bibliography* (mimeographed), *Folklore Forum* (Bibliographic and Special Series, No. 6), Bloomington, Ind., Dec 1970. [While dated 1970, the bibl. was not issued until Dec 1971. Its 374 annotated entries together with the items in this *Hodgepodge* bibl. constitute as definitive a coverage of the American proverb field as has appeared to date.]; **Emma Jean Caroland**, "Popular Beliefs and Superstitions Known to Students of Clarksville [Tenn.] High School," TFSB, 27 (June 1962). [If you break a churn, you will never marry.—For chills, take a bedbug, put it in a capsule and swallow it.—If the first caterpillar you see is a solid color, there will be a hard winter; if it is a mixed color, the winter will be half and half.]; **Lynwood Carranco**, "A Miscellany of Folk Beliefs from the Redwood Country," WF, 26 (1967) 169–176. [If you scratch your left ear twice every day, you will live to be 100 years old.—If you marry a plumber, you will have leaky faucets for life.—While driving in a car, if you don't lift your feet when you are going over a railroad track, you will lose your boyfriend.—Old pots make the best stew.]; **Lynwood Carranco,** "Northern California Superstitions, 1880's," WF, 25 (1966) 257. [Eight from a Mendocino County newspaper: He who proposes moving into a new house must first send in bread and a new broom.—The first tooth cast by a child should be swallowed by the mother to insure a new growth of teeth.]; **Jo Ann Carrigan,** "Early Nineteenth Century Folk Remedies," LFM, 1 (Jan 1960) 43–61. [From a North Carolina mss. of the 1830's. The full mss. is reproduced in the author's M. A. thesis, "Medicines and Miscellanies," Louisiana State University, 1956. Bibliographical notes.—For ear ache, put into the ear a clove of garlic, or a small baked fig, and bathe the face in warm water at bedtime.]; **Roland D. Carter,** "Mountain Superstitions," TFSB, 10 (March 1944). [Running account of varied beliefs.—When katydids begin to call, it is just six weeks until frost.—The mother of eight children (the last one two weeks old) in response to the suggestion of the Health Nurse who was visiting her that she should not plan to have another child, replied, "I reckon God wants me to have younguns. I didn't want all these, but for a long time there we didn't know what caused 'em."]; **Alexander F. Chamberlain,** *The Child and Childhood in Folk-Thought,* London, 1896. [Fine survey covering all aspects. Includes proverbs.—One good mother is worth a hundred schoolmasters.—Happy is he that is happy in his children.]; **Alexander F. Chamberlain,** "Proverbs in the Making: Some Scientific Commonplaces," JAF, 17 (1904) 161–170. [450 entries. Points out how readily "literary and scientific" commonplaces can pass into proverbial speech.— Laugh and grow fat.—Man is struggle; woman is love.]; **Mary E. Chamberlain,** "Certain Common Superstitions," JAF, 6 (1893) 145–146. [33 from Michigan, but generally diffused.—Remember the dream you have when sleeping for the first time in a strange room; it is sent for a warning.]; **Mary E. Chamberlain,** "Folklore from Northern New York," JAF, 5 (1892) 336–337. [Never eat the first strawberry you get; throw it where a bird will have it, and it brings you good luck.]; **Robert Chambers,** *Book of Days* (2 vols.), London, 1879. [Wonderfully readable collection of beliefs, customs, traditions, historical items, folklore relating to the days of the year]; **Selwyn Gurney Champion,** *The Eleven Religions and Their Proverbial Lore: A Comparative Study,* New York, 1945. [With bibl. Useful in tracing American proverbs with Biblical background]; **Selwyn Gurney Champion,** *Racial Proverbs,* London, 1938. [Proverbs arranged by nationality, with interesting American Negro material. Reissued New York, 1965]; **O. Chrisman,** "Secret Language of Children," *Science,* 22 (1893) 303–305; **Robert Christy,** *Proverbs, Maxims and Phrases of All Ages,* New York, 1904; **Mimi Clar,**" Negro Beliefs," WF, 18 (1959) 332–334. [From Virginia but collected from informant in Los Angeles. 33 entries, well known.]; **Mimi Clar,** "Weather Proverbs," WF, 16 (1957) 211–212; **Joseph D. Clark,** "North Carolina Superstitions," NCF, 14 no 1 (July 1966) 3–40. [1442 entries in all categories.—A snake can strike three times the distance of its own length.—Cows lie down on Sundays.—Always wear the sock that has the brand on the instep on the right foot.]; **Joseph**

D. Clark, "Proverbs and Sayings from North Carolina," SFQ, 26 (1962) 145–173. [Good definition of subject and fine collection of 712 items.—Sounds like a dying calf in a hailstorm.—I wouldn't know him from Adam's housecat.—He wouldn't give you air if you were in a jug.—More fun than pushing little biddies into the creek.]; **Joseph D. Clark,** "Similes from the Folk Speech of the South," SFQ, 4 (1940) 119–133 and 205–226. [More than two thousand items.—Happy as a barefoot boy in spring.—Sweet as apple cider.—Ugly as a homemade fence.—Aimless as a spent bullet.—Hot as a hen in a wool basket.]; **Joseph D. Clark,** "Superstitions from North Carolina," SFQ, 26 (1962) 198–224. [Don't allow women visitors on February 14. If you do, you will have bad luck with poultry.]; **Joseph D. Clark,** "Superstitions from North Carolina," NCF, 9 no 2 (Dec 1961) 4–22. [Don't have hair cut in March; it causes headaches all the year.—Rivers stop at midnight on Christmas.]; **T. D. Clark,** "The Snake in Mississippi Folklore,"in Arthur Palmer Hudson, *Specimens of Mississippi Folklore*, Ann Arbor, 1928; **Kenneth Clarke,** "The Folk Wisdom of Appalachia," TFSB, 34 (March 1968). [Review of the folklore of the region and its value]; **Kenneth W. Clarke,** "Popular Beliefs About the North Wind," WF, 19 (1960) 172. [Twenty beliefs from Chico, California.—The north wind imparts a bad taste to coffee and milk.—The north wind electrifies a person and makes him irritable.—Chickens will not lay when the north wind blows.]; **Mary Washington Clarke,** "As Jesse Stuart Heard It in Kentucky," KFR, 9 (1963) 75–86. [Folk speech in the writings of Stuart. Article adapted from Mary Clarke's Ph. D. dissertation, "Folklore of the Cumberlands as Reflected in the Writings of Jesse Stuart," U. of Pennsylvania, 1960]; **Mary Washington Clarke,** *Jesse Stuart's Kentucky,* New York, 1968. [Considers all aspects of folklore found in Stuart's writings, including proverbial matter throughout. The book is based on the author's doctoral dissertation.]; **Mary Washington Clarke,** "Jesse Stuart Reflects Kentucky Lore of Tokens and Ghosts," KFR, 9 (1963) 41–46; **Mary Washington Clarke,** "Proverbs, Proverbial Phrases, and Proverbial Comparisons in the Writings of Jesse Stuart," SFQ, 29 (1965) 142–163. [Daisies won't tell. (The dead do not tell tales.)—Make yourselves useful as well as good lookin'.]; **Mary** and **Kenneth Clarke,** *Introducing Folklore,* New York, 1963. [Handy paperback describing fields of folklore, with bibliographic notes. Chapters on proverbs and superstitions.]; **Robert** and **Martha Cochran,** "Some Menstrual Folklore of Mississippi," MFR, 4 (1970) 108–113. [Several superstitions and three recorded interviews]; **Tristram P. Coffin, ed.,** *Our Living Traditions,* New York, 1968. [Chapters by Ray B. Browne on proverbs and by Wayland D. Hand on superstitions]; **Joanna Carver Colcord,** *Sea Language Comes Ashore,* New York, 1945. [A remarkable study of the transfer of sea terms to everyday shore use, and a very great book for those who love the language. Copies of the first edition are still available from Tidewater Publishers, Cambridge, Maryland, at $3.00—while they last!]; **Yandell Collins, Jr.,** "Superstitions and Belief Tales from Louisville," KFR, 4 (1958) 71–78. [To cure yellow jaundice, place sheep lice in a capsule and swallow.—For good luck, place a clean silver dime in the pot of black-eyed peas.]; **Josiah Combs,** "The Language of the Southern Highlanders," *Publications of the*

Modern Language Association, 46 (1931) 1302–1322; **Josiah Combs** "Sympathetic Magic in the Kentucky Mountains: Some Curious Folk-Survivals," JAF, 27 (1914) 328–330; **Forest E. Conder**, *The Fisherman's Bible*, Marion, Ind., 1952; **Edward L. Conwell**, "Tennessee Remedies," JAF, 46 (1933) 89–90. [Four "cures" and a charm for stopping blood: God made the ocean,/God sent the flood,/God calms the ocean,/God stops the blood.]; **Gabriel Cordova**, "Black and White Magic on the Texas-Mexican Border," PTFS, 25 (1953) 195–199; **Elizabeth B. Cornett**, "Down Our Way: Belief Tales of Knott and Perry Counties," KFR, 2 no 3 (1956) 69–75. [Death omens, witchcraft]; **Ernest Cox**, "Rustic Imagery in Mississippi Proverbs (and Proverbial Speech)," SFQ, 11 (1947) 263–267. [A person feeling poorly: "I'm not fit to drive a hen from the door."]; **John Harrington Cox**, "The Witch Bridle," SFQ, 7 (1943) 203–209; **Betty Craft**, "Superstitions from Frenchburg, Kentucky," KFR, 10 (1964) 12–17. [97 varied items.—If it rains on Monday, it will rain three days that week.—Putting grape-vine juice on your hair will make it wavey.]; **Mrs. F. W. Crandall** and **Lois Gannett**, "Folk Cures of New York State," NYFQ, 1 (1945) 178–180; **Ed Cray**, "Cowboy and Rodeo Beliefs," WF, 22 (1963) 152; [anon.], **"Crickets and the Weather,"** WF, 23 (1964) 55. [Add 37 to the number of cricket chirps you hear in 15 seconds, and you'll be close to the actual temperature.] **Helen Creighton**, *Bluenose Magic*, Toronto, 1968. Nova Scotia beliefs and superstitions]; **John R. Crosby**, "Modern Witches of Pennsylvania," JAF, 40 (1927) 304–309. [Account of "witchcraft" and superstition among the immigrants of the Russian sect of Thoudrakians, near Pittsburgh]; **Tom Peete Cross**, "Folklore from the Southern States," JAF, 22 (1909) 251–255. [Slight collection made "in southeastern Virginia"]; **Stewart Culin**, "Concerning Negro Sorcery in the United States," JAF, 3 (1890) 281–287; **John McNab Currier**, (M. D.), "Contributions to the Folklore of New England," JAF, 2 (1889) 291–294. [Ghost and witch stories heard during a rural visit in New Hampshire]; **L. S. M. Curtin**, "Pioneer Medicine in New Mexico," in *Folk-Say*, Norman, Oklahoma, 1930; **Edith E. Cutting**, *Lore of an Adirondack County*, (Cornell University Press), New York, 1944; **Edith E. Cutting**, "York State Farm Lore," NYFQ, 7 (1951) 4–77. [With subdivisions on livestock, weatherlore, planting, harvesting, the year's special jobs, farmers' songs].

D

Gertrude C. Davenport, "Folk Cures from Kansas," JAF, 11 (1898) 129–132. [Approx. 50 medical superstitions obtained in 1890 from University of Kansas students who claimed they "knew no superstitions and believed none"]; **Henry Davidoff**, *A World Treasury of Proverbs*, New York, 1946; **Levette J. Davidson**, "Superstitions Collected in Denver, Colorado," WF, 13 (1954) 184–189. [75 items: dreams, wishes, weather, birth, seasons, death.—

Count the number of taxis going by, and the next boy you see after counting 100 will be your husband.—"It has become rather customary at a bridal shower to take down what the girl says as she opens the presents, and then read it back to her and tell her it will be part of her conversation on her wedding night."]; **Levette J. Davidson,** "Westernisms," AS, 17 (1942) 71–73. [Proverbs and "picturesque speech"]; **Kenneth W. Davis,** "Weather Signs in Central Texas," WF, 28 (1969) [Such as that of "a sow running about the pen with a stick in her mouth" before a severe storm]; **Gertrude Decrow,** "Folklore from Maine," JAF, 5 (1892) 318–320. [If a partridge is seen in the morning sitting on the doorstep, it is a sure sign of death.]; [anon.], **"Derogatory Comparisons—'So . . . That',"** WF, 18 (1959) 140. [18 from the UCLA archives.—So blind he couldn't hit a barrel if he was inside.]; **Jay K. Ditchy, ed.,** "Early Louisiana French Life and Folklore from the Anonymous Breaux Manuscript," LFM, 2 (May 1966). [Full issue of LFM devoted to this fascinating Acadian mss. Includes superstitions, farm life, marriage customs, death and funerals, schooling, clothing, food and drink, etc. The full mss. published: Jay K. Ditchy, *Les Acadiens Louisianais et Leur Parler*, Paris (E. Droz), 1932.—"The clocks stopped to indicate that they will no longer mark the hours for the dead man . . ."]; **Virginia Dober,** "We'll Tell 'Em," NCF, 4 no 1 (1956) 15–22. [In defense of the "folk." Varied beliefs and superstitions.]; **J. Frank Dobie,** "Do Rattlesnakes Swallow Their Young?", PTFS, 21 (1946) 43–64. [Numerous eyewitness accounts saying "Yes!"—Bibl. notes. —See also Jan 1936 issues of *Time* ("Letters") for contributions on "the snake-swallowing business"]; **J. Frank Dobie,** *Guide to Life and Literature of the Southwest,* (University of Texas Press), Austin, 1943. [A most important bibliographic guide to the region]; **J. Frank Dobie,** "Madstones and Hydrophobia Skunks," PTFS, 28 (1958) 8–17; **J. Frank Dobie,** *Rattlesnakes,* Boston, 1965. [A sympathetic and affectionate book-length study, with a chapter on snakes swallowing their young]; **J. Frank Dobie,** "Weather Wisdom of the Texas-Mexican Border," PTFS, 2 (1923) 87–99. [Personal collection gathered over "a goodly number of years"]; **J. Frederick Doering,** "Folk Remedies for Diverse Allergies," JAF, 57 (1944) 140–141. [Mistitled. Eight "cures" for hay fever.]; **J. Frederick Doering,** "Pennsylvania German Folk Medicine in Waterloo County, Ontario," JAF, 49 (1936) 194–198. [Powwowing, charms, folk remedies. For duodenal ulcers: Three tablespoons of castor oil, three tablespoons of whiskey, six tablespoons of boiling water, fifteen drops of Haarlem oil. Take every three days.]; **John Frederick Doering** and **Eileen Elita Doering,** "Some Western Ontario Folk Beliefs and Practices," JAF, 51 (1938) 60–68. [Weather and farm beliefs, medicine, omens, tokens, luck signs.—For each piece that one eats of Christmas cake baked by a different person, one will have a month of good luck.—Lucky, lucky white horse,/Lucky, lucky lee!/Lucky, lucky white horse,/Bring luck to me!— If a lady motorist drives by, pull your hair and you will have good luck.]; **Richard M. Dorson,** *American Folklore,* Chicago, 1959. [Basic overall survey of the field]; **Richard M. Dorson,** Blood Stoppers," SFQ, 11 (1947) 105–118. [Colorful and implicitly believed accounts]; **Richard M. Dorson,** *Blood-*

stoppers and Bearwalkers: Folk Traditions of the Upper Peninsula, Cambridge (Harvard), 1952; **Richard M. Dorson**, *Buying the Wind: Regional American Folklore*, Chicago, 1964; **Richard M. Dorson**, *Jonathan Draws the Long Bow*, Cambridge (Harvard), 1946. [Tales, speech]; **Fletcher Bascom Dresslar**, *Superstitions and Education*, (University of California Publications in Education, 5), Berkeley, 1907; **Harold E. Driver**, "A Method of Investigating Individual Differences in Folkloristic Beliefs and Practices," MF, 1 (1951) 99–105; **Hannibal Gerald Duncan** and **Winnie Leach Duncan**, "Superstitions and Sayings Among the Southern Highlanders," JAF, 42 (1929) 233–237. [Approx. 80 items, all well known]; **Alan Dundes**, "Brown County Superstitions," MF, 11 (1961) 25–57. [219 entries with references to other collections, good bibl., and suggested classification]; **Donald Dunn** and **Grant Thompson**, "Snakebite Cure," WF, 18 (1959) 112–113. [Mormon victim prayed to the Lord, and was told to eat hog grease. Did so, and was saved.]; **H. H. C. Dunwoody**, *Weather Proverbs*, War Department, Washington, D. C., 1883. [Excellent collection of United States weather lore gathered from all Army posts by order of Major General W. B. Hazen and edited by 1st Lieutenant H. H. C. Dunwoody, 4th Artillery. Some 2,000 entries. Unevenly annotated but basic to any study of American weatherlore.—Air bubbles over clam beds indicate rain.—In the Mississippi Valley, when fogs occur in August, expect fever and ague in the following fall.—When it rains in August, it rains honey and wine.]

E

Alice Morse Earle, *Customs and Fashions in Old New England*, New York, 1894; **Alice Morse Earle**, *Child Life in Colonial Days*, New York, 1899; **Alice Morse Earle**, *Home Life in Colonial Days*, New York, 1898. [All works by this prolific American "antiquarian" are valuable. She had an inbred taste for the curious, the out-of-the-way, and the fascinating items of the past, and a strong sense for rescuing the perishable. All her books are highly readable.]; **Glen Earthman**, "Superstitions from Denver," WF, 16 (1957) 132–133. [33, all well known]; **A. W. Eddins**, "Grandma's Sayings," PTFS, 26 (1954). [Talk is cheap, but it takes money to buy whiskey.—Short visits make long friends.—She'll soon wish she was back under her mammy's bed playing with the cats.—(All, of course, from Texas.)]; **A. W. Eddins** and **Mrs. Morgan Smith**, "Wise Saws from Texas," PTFS, 13 (1937) 244; **Lawrence Edwards**, "Warts and Witchery," TFSB, 17 (Dec 1951); **Frances Elliot**, "Stagestruck Luck: Beliefs from and about the Theatre," KFR, 10 (1964) 18–21. [Sarah Bernhardt liked to have someone kick her lightly on the rear just before she went on stage, and she always turned her head slightly and murmured "*merde*" . . .]; **Duncan Emrich**, *The Folklore of Love and Courtship*, New York, 1970. [Dear, dear doctor,/What will cure love?/Nothing but the clergy,/And white kid glove.—If you see a sparrow on a holiday, you will marry a man in love with a small house.]; **Duncan Emrich**, *The Folklore* *of Weddings and Marriage*, New York, 1970. [Feed a cat out of an old shoe, and your wedding day will be a happy one.—It is bad luck for a bride to drop her handkerchief either when stepping into or alighting from her carriage.]; **Duncan Emrich**, *Folklore on the American Land*, Boston, 1972. [With chapters on proverbs and proverbial speech, folk language, beliefs and superstitions]; **Duncan Emrich**, "Two Proverbial Phrases: 'Balled Up' and 'Neat as Apple Pie'," NYFQ, 25 (1969) 297–298. [Explains origins]; **Duncan Emrich**, *The Nonsense Book*, (Four Winds Press), New York, 1970. [Children's rhymes, riddles, tongue-twisters, autograph album rhymes, with full bibl. citing all folklore journal articles]; **George Allen England**, "Rural Locutions from Maine and Northern New Hampshire," *Dialect Notes*, 4, pt. 2 (1914) 67–83; **Eston Everett Ericson**, "Folklore and Folkway in the Tarboro [N.C.] *Free Press* (1824–1850)," SFQ, 5 (1941) 107–125; **Eston Everett Ericson**, "Nebraska Folklore and Popular Sayings," *Folk-Lore* (London), 49 (1938) 148–153; **Aurelio M. Espinosa**, "New Mexican Spanish Folk-Lore," JAF, 22 (1910) 395–418. [First extended article on subject. Describes richness of field and cites examples of legends, beliefs, superstitions, medicine, misc. Detailed articles on single subjects followed in subsequent issues of JAF.]; **Julia Estill**, "Customs Among the German Descendants of Gillespie County," PTFS, 2 (1923) 67–74. [Varied customs, including Christmas, New Year's, Easter]; **J. H. Evans**, "Weather-Lore," *Southern Workman*, 25 (1896) 16; **Alf Evers**, "Rattlesnake Lore of the Catskills," NYFQ, 7 (1951) 108–115; **James Ewell**, *The Medical Companion, or Family Physician*, (7th ed.), Washington, D. C., 1827; **James Ewell**, *The Planter's and Mariner's Medical Companion*, Philadelphia, 1807. [Medical "gospels" of the time, combining trial and error, folk medicine and the science of the day.]

F

T. J. Farr, "Middle Tennessee Folk Beliefs Concerning Love and Marriage," SFQ, 2 (1938) 165 ff; **T. J. Farr**, "Riddles and Superstitions of Middle Tennessee," JAF, 48 (1935) 318–336. [254: remedies, good and bad luck omens, beliefs relate to babies, death, love, marriage, the moon, plants, trees, weather, wishes, witchcraft, misc.—If you secretly bury a marble and go back in 3 days, all the marbles that you have lost will be there.—If you find a button and pick it up, the first person of the opposite sex with whom you cross running water is the person you will marry.]; **T. J. Farr**, "Tennessee Folk Beliefs Concerning Children," JAF, 52 (1939) 112–116. "I have made the collection over a period of several years, and have included only those beliefs which have been reported to me by at least five different informants." 105 entries.— To cure a baby of thrush, let a stallion snort in the baby's face.—A baby should be carried upstairs before downstairs so that it will rise in the world.— Let a chicken fly over a child's head to cure chickenpox.—If a baby is put in the first April shower, it will always be healthy.]; **T. J. Farr**, "Survivals of Superstition in Tennessee," TFSB, 21 (March 1955). [A good bibl. listing of all articles to date in TFSB on superstitions]; **T. J. Farr,** "Tennessee Superstitions and Beliefs," TFSB, 1 (April 1935); **Arthur Huff Fauset,** *Folklore from Nova Scotia,* (Memoirs of the American Folklore Society, 24) New York, 1931. [Includes weatherlore, dreams, omens, planting, divination, witchcraft, medicine, birth, death, customs relating to special days]; **Elza E. Fentress,** "Superstitions of Grayson County, Kentucky," (unpublished Master's thesis), Western Kentucky State College, 1934; **Austin E. Fife,** "More Similes from Moab, Utah," WF, 25 (1966) 195–196. [91, all well known: To yell like a hyena.]; **Austin and Alta Fife, eds.,** "Oregon Death and Funerary Beliefs," WF, 24 (1965) 6. [8 items: Cats go crazy when death occurs in their environment, and consequently are kept out of the house on such occasions.]; **Austin and Alta E. Fife, eds.,** "Oregon Folk Medical Beliefs," WF, 24 (1965) 6. [10 items]; **Austin and Alta S. Fife,** *Saints of Sage and Saddle: Folklore among the Mormons,* (reprint ed.), Gloucester, Mass., 1966. [The standard work in this regional and religious field]; **Austin E. Fife,** "Similes from Moab, Utah," WF, 25 (1966) 126–127. [53 folk comparisons from one informant]; **Margaret Gillis Figh,** "Folklore and Folk Speech in the Works of Marjorie Kinnan Rawlings," SFQ, 11 (1947) 201–210. [Poor as a lizard-eating cat.— She were settin' lookin' big-eyed and skeered like a little old scrooch owl on a limb in the daytime.]; **Margaret Gillis Figh,** "Folklore in Bill Arp's Works," SFQ, 12 (1948) 169–175; **Margaret Gillis Figh,** "Folklore in the 'Rufus Sanders' Sketches," SFQ, 19 (1955) 185–195; **Morris Fishbein,** *Shattering Health Superstitions,* New York, 1930. [Shame on him!]; **Barbara Fisher,** "Folksay in Johnstown, New York," NYFQ, 11 (1955) 210–211. [Fine idiocies:—Have you seen Mary? She just went around the corner with a rat in her mouth.—Head for the roundhouse, Nellie; they can't corner you there.]; **Helen Hartness Flanders,** "Children's Curse," JAF, 68 (1955) 210. [Remembered by her husband (Senator Flanders) as heard from children of Scottish descent near Pawtucket, Rhode Island: "Cartwheels surround you,/ Fiery dragons eat you up,/And mortar pestles pound you!"]; **Edwin M. Fogel,** *Beliefs and Superstitions of the Pennsylvania Germans,* Philadelphia, 1915. [Head, sleep on; buttocks stand guard!/Should anyone come, sound the alarm.]; **Edwin M. Fogel,** *Proverbs of the Pennsylvania Germans,* Lancaster, 1929; [anon.], **"Folklore Jottings in the District of Columbia,"** JAF, 1 (1888) 164. [When a dog moves his feet in his sleep, he is measuring the grave of a person who will soon die.—The whippoorwill is first heard every year on the 11th of April.]; **Ina B. Forbus,** "Orange County [N.C.] Home Cures," NCF, 8 no 1 (1960) 12–16. [Narrative account]; **Alcee Fortier,** "Customs and Superstitions in Louisiana," JAF, 1 (1888) 136–140. [When a woman whistles, it makes the Virgin Mary weep.—Put nails in the shape of a cross in the nest of a goose, that thunder shall not spoil the eggs and prevent them from hatching.]; **J. I. Fortune,** "Beautiful Legends of Texas Wild Flowers," *American Home,* 16 (1936) 24 ff.; **James R. Foster,** "Brooklyn Folklore," NYFQ, 13 (1957) 83–91; **Jerry Foster,** "Varieties of Sea Lore," WF, 28 (1969) 260–266. [Brief essay suggesting various areas for study]; **David C. and Mary Gene Fowler,** "More Kentucky Superstitions," SFQ, 14 (1950) 170–176. [Birds marry on St. Valentine's Day.—If you find a mare's nest and put a rock in it, a colt will hatch out.—To eat celery is good for the nerves.]; **Dr. Ben Fox,** "Folk Medicine in Southern Illinois," *Illinois Folklore,* 2 (1948) 3–7; **Benjamin Franklin,** *Poor Richard's Almanack,* (ed. B. E. Smith), New York, 1898; [Benjamin Franklin]: Thomas H. Russell, *The Sayings of Poor Richard: Wit, Wisdom and Humor of Benjamin Franklin in the Prefaces, Proverbs, and Maxims of Poor Richard's Almanacks for 1733 to 1758,* New York, 1926; **Neal Frazier,** "A Collection of Middle Tennessee Superstitions," TFSB, 2 (Oct 1936); **Florence Healy French,** "Cooper's Use of Proverbs in the Anti-Rent Novels," NYFQ, 25 (1970) 42–49. [As honest as noonday light.—All at once makes light work.—What is everybody's business is nobody's business.—Play and pay.]; **Hilderic Friend,** *Flowers and Flower Lore,* New York, 1889; **William D. Funk,** "Hiccup Cures," WF, 9 (1950) 66–67. [18 cures from Orland, Calif.—Drink warm milk through a straw.—Smell garlic.]

G

Stuart A. Gallacher, "Franklin's Way to Wealth: A Florilegium of Proverbs and Wise Sayings," *Journal of English and Germanic Philology,* 48 (1949) 229–251; **James W. Galley,** "Ancient and Modern Snakes," *The Argonaut,* March 20, 1880, included in Duncan Emrich, *Comstock Bonanza,* New York, 1950. [An amusing account of rattlesnakes in Nevada by one of the West's best and most overlooked writers]; **Emelyn E. Gardner,** "Folklore from Schoharie County, New York," JAF, 27 (1914) 304–325. [Chiefly tales and legends, but some beliefs: "If a farmer should keep a whiffet-dog, he would never be attacked by a lion."]; **Emelyn Elizabeth Gardner,** *Folklore from the Schoharie Hills, New York,* (U. of Michigan Press) Ann Arbor, 1937. [A broad collection including witchcraft, ghost tales, general superstitions: Cucumbers will grow when you can sleep on the outside of the quilts.—A cat with a red nose can be taught to do anything.—To like pepper is a sign that you are spunky.—To dream of a dog is a sign that you have a friend.—Fog at night,/Rain before light.—Carry hen's teeth in your pocket for toothache.]; **Edward B. Garriott,** *Weather Folk-Lore and Local Weather Signs,* (U. S. Department of Agriculture, Bulletin No. 33, Weather Bureau, No. 294) Washington, D. C., 1903. [Belongs with Dunwoody's work.—When Lookout Mountain (Tennessee) has its cap on, it will rain in six hours.—As the days lengthen,/So the cold strengthens.—Loud and long singing of robins denotes rain.]; **A. L. Gary,** "Proverbs from Rushville, Indiana," HF, 6 (1947) 72. [12 proverbs.—Short visits make long friends.—It is safest to cross in front of a mule and behind an automobile.]; **Wayne Geurin,** "Some Folkways of a Stewart County Community," TFSB, 19 (Sept 1953). [A good collection, edited by Herbert Halpert]; **Edward S. Gifford,** "The Evil Eye in Pennsylvania Medical History," KFQ, 3 (1960) 3–8; **Lanvil Gilbert,** "The Prairie Dog," PTFS, 28 (1958) 69–80. [Illuminating article, with bibl. notes. Example: In Texas alone he (the prairie dog) occupied 90,000 square miles, roughly one-third of the area of the state. In 1905 federal observers found that one continuous prairie dog town stretched from San Angelo on the south to Clarendon on the north, a distance of 250 miles. The width of the town varied from 100 to 150 miles. A conservative estimate set the population of this single colony at 400,000,000 prairie dogs.]; **Everett A. Gillis**, "Almanac Lore," PTFS, 28 (1958) 81–90. [Article suggesting almanacs as rich source for folklore materials]; **Everett A. Gillis**, "Weather Talk from Cap Rock," PTFS, 25 (1953) 200–204. [West Texas weather: "I'm over sixty years old, and I've noticed that this time of year we always have some kind of weather." —Whether it's cold, or whether it's hot,/There's gonna be weather, whether or not.—The fall of temperature in the Panhandle is as fast as a Texas ranger reaching for his gun.—A tarantula crossing a highway promises rain.]; **Everett A. Gillis**, "Zodiac Wisdom," WF, 16 (1957) 77–89; **Lew Girdler**, "Further Notes on 'A man must live'," WF, 22 (1963) 192. [Considers shades of meaning (apologetic, defensive, cynical) in use of the proverb, and need for noting context in which it is used.—This holds true of many, many proverbs and sayings, and the situation should perhaps always be noted.]; **Kenneth S. Goldstein** and **Robert H. Byington**, *Two Penny Ballads and Four Dollar Whiskey: A Pennsylvania Folklore Miscellany*, Hatboro, 1966; **George Laurence Gomme**, *Popular Superstitions*, Gentleman's Magazine Library, Boston, n.d.; **Luise Graalfs**, "Bad-Luck Superstitions on the Campus (University of California)," WF, 8 (1949) 264; **Dale Greer**, "Secret Speech," KFR, 10 (1964) 35. ["Double Dutch," an extremely complicated form of secret speech]; **Byrd Howell Granger**, "Of the Teeth," JAF, 74 (1961) 47–56. [Historical consideration of folklore of toothache, with solid bibl. notes]; **David B. Gracy III**, "Some Plantation Remedies and Recipes," TFSB, 29 (June 1963); **Marjory Titus Greene**, "Proverbs from Greene County, Indiana," HFB, 4 no 1 (March 1945) 1–9. [Approx. 200 generally well known]; **Felix Grendon**, "The Anglo-Saxon Charms," JAF, 22 (1909) 105–237. [Excellent article. Solid consideration of the Anglo-Saxon charms, with translation, commentary, analysis of type.]; **Mrs. Maude Grieve**, *A Modern Herbal, the Medicinal, Culinary, Cosmetic and Economic Properties, Cultivation and Folk-Lore of Herbs, Grasses, Fungi, Shrubs, and Trees With All Their Modern Scientific Uses* (ed. by Mrs. C. F. Leyel), 2 vols. London, 1931; **Hazel Griffin**, "Folk Remedies of the Roanoke-Chowan Section [N.C.]," NCF, 6 no 2 (1958) 30–31. ["Practically all homes were supplied with ingredients for home remedies. Many grew herbs or weeds by the yard fence as a measure against the day when illness would strike."]; **Hazel Griffin**, "Some Folk Expressions from Northeastern North Carolina," NCF, 15 no 2 (1967) 56–57; **Dan Gross**, "Folklore of the Theatre," WF, 20 (1961) 257–264. [61 taboos and superstitions]; **Dr. E. Grumbine**, *Folk-Lore and Superstitious Beliefs of Lebanon County* (Lebanon County Historical Society), Annville, Pennsylvania, 1905–1906; **Leon Guinn**, "Home Remedies from Scurry County," PTFS, 14 (1938) 268. [Some ranchers recommend for flu a quart of whiskey and a dozen lemons. Throw the lemons at a fence post and drink the whiskey.]; **Per E. Guldbeck**, "A Perspective on Folk Medicine,"

NYFQ, 18 (1962) 163–172. [Considers relation to academic medicine with mention of value of certain plants: quinine for malaria, ipecac for amoebic dysentery, foxglove for cardiac condition, etc.]

H

Howard W. Haggard, *The Lame, the Halt, and the Blind,* New York, 1932; **Howard W. Haggard,** *Mystery, Magic, and Medicine: The Rise of Medicine from Superstition to Science,* New York, 1933; **Joseph S. Hall,** "Witchlore and Ghostlore in the Great Smokies," (Pt. I), TFSB, 36 (March 1970). ["My uncle that lost his mind and died said: To witch you had to belong to the devil. You had to put one hand under your foot and another hand on top of your head, and you had to say that what was between 'em belonged to the devil. You put a handkerchief on the ground, and then said, 'There will be three drops of blood fall from the elements upon the handkerchief.' Then you could witch people."]; **Joseph S. Hall,** "Witchlore and Ghostlore in the Great Smokies," (Pt. II), TFSB, 36 (June 1970). [The use of salt, broom, and apple seeds as protection against witches. Witches in squirrel form.]; **Herbert Halpert,** "Cold Weather Comments," JAF, 61 (1948) 312. [Yukon Territory: Eleven months of winter and one month of damn poor sleighing.— Nome, Alaska: Eleven months of winter and one month damn late in the fall.]; **Herbert Halpert,** "Cold Weather Comments Again," JAF, 64 (1951) 222–223. [In Minneapolis you have two seasons of the year: eleven months winter—and August.—Considers possible age and spread of the phrase.]; **Herbert Halpert,** "Grapevine Warp an' Tobacco Stick Fillin'," SFQ, 9 (1945) 223–228. [His land's so poor a turkey can't gobble on it.]; **Herbert Halpert,** "More Proverbial Comparisons from West Tennessee," TFSB, 18 (March 1952). [291 items]; **Herbert Halpert,** "A Pattern of Proverbial Exaggeration from West Kentucky," MF, 1 (1951) 41–47. [162 items of the *so . . . that* type: She's so ugly she couldn't eat pumpkins through a rail fence.— She's so nosey she can hear the grass grow.—I'll slap you so hard your ears will ring like bells.—You're so green the cows will eat you if you don't watch out.]; **Herbert Halpert,** "Proverbial Comparisons from Idaho Territory," WF, 6 (1947) 379–380. [Well, there goes a ten-dollar Stetson on a five-cent head.]; **Herbert Halpert,** "Rhymed Proverbial Comparisons," WF 15 (1956) 196–197. [Rhymed similes from a Kentucky newspaper]; **Herbert Halpert,** "Proverbial Comparisons from West Tennessee," TFSB, 17 (Sept 1951). [So tight she screaks.—Looks like death eating crackers.]; **Herbert Halpert,** "Some Forms of a Proverbial Rhyme," JAF, 64 (1951) 317–318. [When you buy meat, you buy bones;/Buy land, you buy stones.]; **Herbert Halpert,** "Some Wellerisms from Kentucky and Tennessee," JAF, 69 (1956) 115–122. [62 Wellerisms with bibl. notes.—"I'm cutting quite a figure," said the chorus girl as she sat down on a piece of glass.]; **Herbert Halpert,** "A Tennessee Sheaf from the Folklore Archive at Murray State College," TFSB, 19 (Sept

1953); **Violetta Halpert,** "Folk Cures from Indiana," HF, 9 (1950) 1–12. [General survey]; **Violetta Halpert,** "Death Beliefs from Indiana," MF, 2 (1952) 205–219. [If you take flowers from a graveyard, you will take someone in your family back to the graveyard]; **Violetta Halpert,** "Indiana Wart Cures," HF, 8 (1949) 37–43. [Spunk water, spunk water,/Indian meal shorts,/ Spunk water, spunk water,/Remove my warts.]; **Wayland D. Hand,** "California Miners Folklore: Above Ground," CFQ, 1 (1942) 24–46, and same volume "Below Ground," 127–153. [Superstitions, beliefs, customs of hardrock-miners' daily work. Basic study.]; **Wayland D. Hand,** " 'The Devil Beating His Wife' and Other Folk Beliefs About the Sun's Shining While It Rains," KFR, 3 (1957) 139–143. [With bibl. notes]; **Wayland D. Hand, ed.,** "Folk Beliefs from Boise, Idaho," WF, 28 (1969) 41–42. [31 entries.—If you borrow salt, you must return sugar.—If you want to time something for one minute, recite the Lord's Prayer. It takes exactly one minute to recite.]; **Wayland D. Hand,** "The Folklore, Customs, and Traditions of the Butte Miner," CFQ, 5 (1946) 1–25 and 153–178. [Basic study of hardrock-mining folklore]; **Wayland D. Hand,** "Folklore from Utah's Silver Mining Camps," JAF, 54 (1941) 132–161. [Beliefs, customs, superstitions]; **Wayland D. Hand,** "Hat Burning at Childbirth," WF, 14 (1955) 52–54. [A curious custom, the husband required to burn all his hats]; **Wayland D. Hand,** "Hiccough Cures," WF, 27 (1968) 116. [13 well-known cures]; **Wayland D. Hand,** "The Magical Transference of Disease," NCF, 13 nos 1–2 (1965) 83–109. [Thorough essay with extensive source notes]; **Wayland D. Hand,** "A Miscellany of Nebraska Folk Beliefs," WF, 21 (1962) 257–276. [209 items with good bibliography.—If you leave the top off the sugar (bowl) at night, you might catch a leprechaun, because eating sugar makes them visible.— "In Allen, Nebraska, about 1920, I remember my aunt always placing us children on feather ticks to protect us when a tornado was coming."]; **Wayland D. Hand, ed.,** "Modern Taunts and Insults," WF, 25 (1962) 246. [Collected from students at UCLA.—Why don't you go out and play in the traffic?—Who put a nickel in your slot?—You're ugly and your mother dresses you funny.]; **Wayland D. Hand,** "Popular Beliefs and Superstitions from Oregon," CFQ, 4 (1945) 427–432. [From the Oregon WPA files. 103 entries.—Wishes made on new sidewalks will come true.—To see a mother cat carrying kittens in her mouth away from the nest is a sure sign that sneak thieves are about.]; **Wayland D. Hand,** "Popular Beliefs and Superstitions from Pennsylvania," KFQ, 4 (1959) 106–120. [Throwing rocks at swallows will cause cows to give bloody milk.]; **Wayland D. Hand,** *Popular Beliefs and Superstitions from North Carolina* in the multiple *Frank C. Brown Collection of North Carolina Folklore,* vols. VI and VII, 1961 and 1964 (Duke University Press), Durham, North Carolina. [Described in the preceding "Notes"]; **Wayland D. Hand,** "Popular Beliefs and Superstitions from Pennsylvania," in two parts, KFQ, 3 (1958) 61–72 and KFQ, 4 (1959) 106–120. [If you say "Rabbit, rabbit, rabbit" the first thing when you wake up in the morning on the first day of each month, you will have good luck all month.—At Bryn Mawr College: Do not walk under the viaduct at the station when the train is going over, because it means you will flunk.—Painting a four-inch square on alternate buttocks every three days will soon cause a goitre to disappear.]; **Wayland D. Hand and Marjorie Griffin**, "Inhalants in Respiratory Disorders," JAF, 77 (1964) 258–261. [To cure whooping cough, race a horse until it is hot and breathing hard; Then stop it suddenly and let it breathe into the mouth of the child affected.—Various cures and source notes.]; **G. L. Hanford**, "Metaphor and Simile in American Folk Speech," *Dialect Notes*, 5, pt. 5 (1922) 149–180. [Extensive list of similes and metaphors]; **Rosalie Hankey**, "Campus Folklore and California's 'Pedro!'," CFQ, 3 (1944) 29–35. [Origin of cry and references to 'Reinhardt' at Harvard and others]; **Rosalie Hankey**, "California Ghosts," CFQ, 1 (1942) 155–177. [40 different accounts]; **Ann Hansen**, "Folk Medicine from Clarkson, Utah," WF, 18 (1959) 107–112. [Early Mormon folk remedies]; **John Harden**, *Tar Heel Ghosts*, Chapel Hill, North Carolina, 1954; **Kelsie B. Harder**, "Beliefs and Customs in Perry County, Tennessee," TFSB, 21 (March 1955). [Approx. 30 items.—Don't point at the moon. Bad luck.—If a dog runs between your legs, you are going to get a whipping from your husband or wife.]; **Kelsie B. Harder**, "Home Remedies in Perry County, Tennessee," TFSB, 22 (Dec 1956). [For earache: Take a drop of blood out of a bessie bug and put it in ear.—For poison snake bite: Kill the snake and put the meat on the bite, or get drunk on tobacco and whiskey.]; **Kelsie B. Harder**, "Just an April Fool," TFSB, 27 (March 1961); **Kelsie B. Harder**, "Maybe Day Letter," TFSB, 21 (Dec 1955). [From Cedar Creek Community, Perry County, Tenn. " . . . the girls would all look to get a 'maybe' on the first of May . . . a great long letter, all lines except the first beginning with a 'maybe'. "—Grape vine warp,/Pine top fillin',/Me and you'll marry/If pap and mam's willin'./Maybe we will,/Maybe we won't;/Maybe we'll have a home,/Maybe we won't;/Maybe we'll have children . . . and so on]; **Kelsie B. Harder**, "Pert Nigh Almost: Folk Measurement," TFSB, 23 (March 1957). [Delightful country talk: pert nigh almost dry; ain't hardly none; jist enough to wetchy gizzard; them girl's is just fryin' size; I aim to raise a knot on ye head as big as a goose egg; John's wife's as big as a cow carryin' a calf; he's got more hair'n you could shake a stick at.]; **Kelsie B. Harder**, "Proverbial Snopeslore," TFSB, 24 (1958) 89–95. [I. O. Snopes' garbling of well-known sayings in Faulkner's *The Hamlet* and *The Town*]; **Kelsie B. Harder**, "Weather Expressions and Beliefs in Perry County, Tennessee," TFSB, 23 (Sept 1957). [It's a misty rain.—It's a gullywasher.—It's raining bullfrogs and pitchforks.]; **Margaret Hardie**, "Proverbs and Proverbial Expressions Current in the United States East of the Missouri and North of the Ohio Rivers," AS, 4 (1928–1929) 461–472. [524 items.—A task well begun is half done.—Beware of too great a bargain.—Don't whistle until you're out of the woods.—God gives us nuts to crack when we no longer have teeth.—Never cackle unless you lay.—He wants the whole world and a potato patch on the other side.—I wouldn't wear it to a dog fight.]; **Jesse W. Harris**, "Some Southern Illinois Witch Lore," SFQ, 10 (1946) 183–190; **Carl Hartman**, "Traditional Belief Concerning the Generation of the Oppossum," JAF, 34 (1921) 321–323. [Explodes the folk belief of copulation through the nostrils]; **Mildred Hatcher**, "The Influence of Geography on North American Folklore," TFSB, 19 (June 1953). [Self-evident, but needs stating and restating]; **Mildred Hatcher,** "Superstitions in Middle Tennessee," SFQ, 19 (1955) 150–155. [If a rabbit crosses the road in front of your car, tip your hat and say, "How do you do, Mrs. Rabbit?" If you do not, you will have car trouble.]; **Sadie Hatfield,** "Folklore of Texas Plants," PTFS, 18 (1943) 157–162. [A few folk cures, and reminiscenses in narrative form.—Mountain laurel beans, crushed, and put in liquor would make Indians wild as well as drunk. "The Texas law against marijuana includes the mountain laurel. So potent that one half bean will do the trick."]; **H. A. Hazen,** "The Origin and Value of Weatherlore," JAF, 13 (1900) 191–198. [Interesting explanations of certain origins, and debunks the obvious]; **William Carew Hazlitt,** *English Proverbs and Proverbial Phrases,* London, 1882. [Several thousand entries, major collection. Useful in tracing sources of "American" proverbs.]; **William Carew Hazlitt,** *Faiths and Folklore, A Dictionary of National Beliefs, Superstitions, and Popular Customs,* (2 vols.), London, 1905; **Atcheson L. Hench,** "To Come to Fetch Fire," JAF, 52 (1939) 123–124. [Chaucer's phrase still current]; **George D. Hendricks,** "More Texas Superstitions," WF, 24 (1965) 111–113. [From various informants.—"My grandmother firmly believed that Yankees had no souls. This troubled her until the day she died. Troubled her faith in the Good Book."—Washing the face in urine from a pregnant cow is good for the complexion. It must be the cow's first urination following the cow's first drink of the day.—If a boy wishes his date to be nice, he should climb a pecan tree and hammer a nail on the thirteenth branch from the top. With a three-foot string tied to the nail and a bottle of "My Sin" perfume tied to the other end of the string swinging, the girl will respond to his command. This will work only on Fridays before 8 p.m.]; **George D. Hendricks,** "Superstitions Collected in Denton, Texas," WF, 15 (1956) 1–18. [408 varied and interesting items.—When you start on a trip, you should never say out loud, "I have never been in a wreck."—It's bad luck for someone to kiss you on the right ear; he must then be kissed back on the right ear.—On Friday the 13th, stay in bed.—If you carry your books on your head, you'll forget your lesson.]; **George D. Hendricks,** "Texas Folk Proverbs," WF, 21 (1962) 92. [36 collected from students at North Texas State College, Denton, Texas. —The West is where a man can walk himself to death and get nowhere, like a mud turtle on a world cruise.—The world owes you a living, providing you earn it.—God made West Texas when he was a small boy wanting a sandbox.— The gestation period for the first child is often six months.—Stay away from the proud man who is ashamed to weep.—The noblest sight on earth is a man talking reason and his wife listening to him.]; **George D. Hendricks,** "Texas Folk Similes," WF, 19 (1960) 245–262. [639 sayings.—So tight he wouldn't give a dime to see an ant eat a bale of hay.—Crazy as a professor with nine degrees.—Walls so thin you can hear your neighbor's toenails growing.— Busy as a tumblebug in a cow track.—Pretty as bluebonnets on a hill.]; **Addie Suggs Hilliard,** "Applie Warme at Bedtyme," KFR, 12 (1966) 114–116. [Four chest "remedies" dating from 1562]; **Addie Suggs Hilliard,** "I Remember, I Remember," TFSB, 32 (Dec 1966). [Fine collection out of her own Scotch-Irish family tradition. Medicine, luck, wishes, death, domestic life, misc.]; **D. M. Hines,** "A Finder for Folk Cures," SFQ, 30 (1966) 301–304.

[Practical querying of the folk in this field]; **Donald M. Hines,** "Superstitions from Oregon," WF, 24 (1965) 7–20. [216 items in all categories.—A telephone call in the night means bad news.—Carry a coin of the year in which you were born for good luck.]; **Frank M. Hoadley,** "Folk Humor in the Novels of William Faulkner," TFSB, 23 (Sept 1957); **Dan G. Hoffman,** "Half a Dozen Repeating Games," NYFQ, 4 (1948) 207–212. [Circular or endless questions and tales]; **W. J. Hoffman,** "Folklore of the Pennsylvania Germans," JAF, 1 (1888) 125–135. [Saturday evening was considered to be the proper time for courting, though this delightful pastime often extended over the whole of Sunday.]; **W. J. Hoffman,** "Folklore of the Pennsylvania Germans," JAF, 2 (1889) 23–35. [Blisters on the tongue are caused by telling fibs.]; **W. J. Hoffman,** "Notes on Pennsylvania German Folk-Medicine," *Science,* (New York), 21 (1893) 355; **W. J. Hoffman,** "Folk-Medicine of the Pennsylvania Germans," *Proceedings of the American Philosophical Society,* (Phil.), 36 (1889) 329–353; **N. C. Hoke,** "Folk-Customs and Folk-Beliefs in North Carolina," JAF, 5 (1892) 113–120. [If two spoons are in the same cup of coffee or tea as it is handed, it is a sign of marriage.—Amber beads cure weak eyes.]; **N. C. Hoke,** "Folk-Customs and Folk-Beliefs in North Carolina," JAF, 20 (1907) 24; **Carl Holliday,** *Woman's Life in Colonial Days,* Boston, 1922; **William Hone,** *The Every-Day Book and Table Book,* (3 vols.), London, 1827, and *The Year Book,* London, 1832. [A great antiquarian whose works must be grouped with Brand, Chambers, and others. Most readable.]; **Quentin R. Howard,** "The Up-Side Down Stamp," KFR, 7 (1962) 125–126. [In this instance, the up-side down believed to be bad luck, rather than an invitation to a kiss]; **Arthur Palmer Hudson,** "Animal Lore in Lawson's and Brickell's Histories of North Carolina," NCF, 8 no 2 (1960) 1–15. [Excellent summary from two colonial works published in 1709 and 1737. Incredible accounts, but there they are.]; **Arthur Palmer Hudson,** " 'A Snake Can't Straddle a Log'," NCF, 9 no 1 (1961) 34–41. [Entertaining discussion of 18 localisms and proverbial sayings from Chapel Hill, N.C., including: "Good God in Goldsboro!"; "Let's go home and beat our wives"; "Thirty lashes with a wet noodle"; and others.—I like this for the situation and language and all: A country woman came to town to see the dentist. After drilling and blowing out the old lady's cavity with compressed air, the dentist asked: "Did that air hurt?"—The woman piped out: "That 'ere what?"]; **Arthur Palmer Hudson,** *Specimens of Mississippi Folklore,* Ann Arbor, 1928; **Charles H. Huguenin,** "A Prayer for Examinations," NYFQ, 18 (1962) 145–148. [Joseph of Cupertino, the "patron saint of the stupid is appealed to" with these letters on examination papers: JOC-PFM: Joseph of Cupertino, Pray for Me.]; **William Jackson Humphreys,** *Weather Proverbs and Paradoxes,* Baltimore, 1923. [Extensive treatment by a meteorologist of the scientific basis of weather proverbs]; **Frederick Edward Hulme,** *Proverb Lore,* London, 1902. [Problems of definition, structure, imagery. The use and "power" of proverbs.]; **Earl D. Hunter,** "Folk Remedies on Man and Beast," KFR, 8 (1962) 97–108. [Approx. 100 entries: For a crick in the neck, tie an old sock around the neck with the foot over the stiff area and go to bed.]; **Edwin R. Hunter,** "My Grandfather's Speech," TFSB, 8 (March 1942). [Good reminiscent and nostalgic study]; **Virginia Jo Hurdle,** "Folklore of a Negro Couple in Henry County [Tenn.]," TFSB, 19 (Sept 1955); **Elizabeth Hurley,** "Come Buy, Come Buy," PTFS, 25 (1953) 115–138. [Street cries]; **Zora Hurston,** "Hoodoo in America," JAF, 44 (1931) 317–417. [Charms, conjuring paraphernalia, witchcraft, cures. Fairly eerie, but see the more recent great collection by Hyatt.]; **Gerald T. Hurley,** "Proverbs Heard in California, 1948–1950," WF, 10 (1951) 323–324. [If you want something done, get a busy man.— Foresight's better than hindsight by a damn sight.] **Harry Middleton Hyatt,** *Folklore from Adams County, Illinois,* (Memoir of the Alma Egan Hyatt Foundation), New York, 1935, with second revised and enlarged edition, Hannibal, Missouri, privately printed, 1965. [16537 entries. The greatest collection of beliefs, superstitions, and related folklore from any one area in the United States. Basic to any American folklore library.]; **Harry Middleton Hyatt,** *Hoodoo—Conjuration—Witchcraft—Rootwork: Beliefs Accepted by Many Negroes and White Persons, These Being Orally Recorded Among Blacks and Whites,* (Memoir of the Alma Egan Hyatt Foundation), Hannibal, Missouri, privately printed, 1970. 2 vols., each of approx. 1000 pages. (Distributed solely by The American University Bookstore, Nebraska and Massachusetts Avenues, Washington, D. C., 20016. $31.50. Edition limited to 1000 sets.) [The greatest work in its field. Nothing will surpass it, and the material collected can never be recaptured. Covers the Southeast as well as Negro urban concentrations in Washington, New York, Baltimore, New Orleans.]

I J

[Anon.], **Idaho Lore,** (Caxton Press), Caldwell, Idaho, 1939. [WPA coverage]; **Richard Inwards,** *Weather Lore,* 3rd ed., London, 1898. [One of the half-dozen best collections on beliefs and superstitions on weather. See Dunwoody, Garriott, Sloane.]; **Moritz A. Jagendorf,** "Apples in Life and Lore," NYFQ, 18 (1962) 273–283. [Legends, rhymes, recipes]; **Thomas A. Janvier,** "Mexican Superstitions and Folk-Lore," *Scribner's Magazine,* 5 (March 1889) 349–359; **John Cordy Jeaffreson,** *Brides and Bridals,* (2 vols.), London, 1872. [Another British antiquarian producing a wonderful work]; **Lloyd N. Jeffrey,** "Snake Yarns of the West and Southwest," WF, 14 (1955) 246–258. [Considers folk "beliefs" and largely explains them away. Good article.]; **Richard Jente,** "The American Proverb," AS, 7 (1932) 342–348. [Examines proverbs in article by Margaret Hardie (previously cited) and concludes that 70 percent were in use in England 200 years ago]; **Richard Jente,** "Make Hay While the Sun Shines," SFQ, 1 (1937) 63–67. [Traces this widely known proverb back through Dekker and Shakespeare to John Heywood in 1546: "Whan the sunne shinth make hay."]; **Clifton Johnson,** "Some New England Superstitions," *New England Magazine,* 35 (1906) 161–168; **Clifton Johnson,** *What They Say in New England: A Book of Signs, Sayings, and Superstitions,* Boston, 1896; reissued (Columbia University Press) with added material (ed. Carl Withers), New York, 1963. [A delightful book]; **Helen Sewell**

Johnson, " 'To Give Someone a Yankee Dime': A Southern Proverbial Expression," JAF, 81 (1968) 71–72. [A Yankee Dime is offered by an adult to a child as an inducement to perform some small task. When the task is done, the child is disappointed by getting a kiss (the Yankee Dime) instead of the expected surprise.—The kiss is the Yankee Dime. Not unrelated to "he's not worth a Yankee damn."]; **Louis C. Jones,** "The Devil in York State," NYFQ, 8 (1952) 5–19; **Louis C. Jones,** "The Evil Eye Among European Americans," WF, 10 (1951) 11–25. [General survey covering possessors, effect, cures. See also Frederick Thomas Elsworthy, *The Evil Eye,* London, 1895 which LCJ says is "still the standard work."]; **Louis C. Jones,** "The Ghosts of New York State: An Analytical Study," JAF, 57 (1944) 237–254. [Basic survey useful to anyone engaged in study of ghostlore]; **Louis C. Jones,** "Hitchhiking Ghosts in New York," CFQ, 3 (1944) 284–292; **Louis Jones,** "Practitioners of Folk Medicine," *Bulletin of the History of Medicine,* 23 (1949) 480–493; **Louis C. Jones,** *Things That Go Bump in the Night,* New York, 1959. [An excellent collection of New York State ghostlore. Available now in paperback, Hill and Wang, New York]; **Michael Owen Jones,** "Toward an Understanding of Folk Medical Beliefs in North Carolina," NCF, 15 no 1 (May 1967). [A very good and useful general statement]; **William Jones,** *Credulities Past and Present,* (new ed.), London, 1898. [A British antiquarian on the loose. Fine items.]; **May Justus,** "Spring Calendar and Mountain Wife," TFSB, 8 (March 1947).

K

Ed Kahn, "Practical Poetry—Rhymed Proverbs," MFI, 10 (1958) 239. [Proverbial comparisons strung together into a rhyming 'poem']; **Harnett T. Kane,** *The Southern Christmas Book,* New York, 1958. [Customs, carols, cooking, beliefs, superstitions]; **Leo Kanner,** *Folklore of the Teeth,* New York, 1934; **Leo Kanner,** "Superstitions Connected with Sneezing," *Medical Life,* 38 (1931) 549–575; **Katherine T. Kell,** "The Folklore of the Daisy," JAF, 69 (1956) 13–21 and 369–376. [Solid study with bibl.: 1. The Daisy Family, 2. Daisy Stories, 3. Daisy Beliefs, 4. Folk Attitudes]; **Katherine T. Kell,** "Tobacco in Folk Cures in Western Society," JAF, 78 (1965) 99–114. [Good survey not only of "cures" but of other beliefs, with bibl. and notes, covering period from discovery of tobacco to the present]; **Walter R. Kelly,** *Curiosities of Indo-European Tradition and Folk-Lore,* London, 1863; **Blanche W. Keysner,** "Divining the Future," KFQ, 3 (1958) 5–9. [Love divinations]; **Marjorie M. Kimmerle,** "A Method of Collecting and Classifying Folk Sayings," WF, 6 (1942) 351–366. [A valuable essay]; **Marjorie M. Kimmerle,** "Thunder Stories," WF, 20 (1961) 264. [Collected by Dora R. Elan from third-grade class at Fairview School, Boulder, Colorado, 1959. Included in this present text.]; **Marjorie M. Kimmerle,** "A Weather Almanac for Colorado," *The Colorado Quarterly,* 7 (1958) 68–79; **Basil F. Kirtley, ed.,** "Folklore from Aroostook County, Maine, and Neighboring Canada," NEF,

1 (1958) 33–47 and 65–73; [anon.], **"Kissing Over a Candle,"** JAF, 1 (1888) 165. [In Southwest Missouri: "We-uns can marry ourselves by kissing over a candle."]; **George Lyman Kittredge,** *The Old Farmer and His Almanack,* Cambridge, Mass., 1924. [First study of this subject]; **G. L. Kittredge,** "Signs and Omens of the Eighteenth Century," JAF, 28 (1915) 191–194. [Undated broadside poem ca. 1790 citing numerous superstitions]; **George Lyman Kittredge,** *Witchcraft in Old and New England,* Cambridge, Mass., 1928. [Early and important study]; **Laurence M. Klauber,** *Rattlesnakes, Their Habits, Life Histories and Influence on Mankind,* 2 vols. Berkeley and Los Angeles, 1956; **William E. Koch,** "Hunting Beliefs and Customs from Kansas," WF, 24 (1965) 165–175. [200 items.—When the wind is in the west,/Hunting is the best.—Wear red laces in shoes for luck.]; **William E. Koch,** "More Wellerisms from Kansas," WF, 19 (1960) 196. [20 entries.— "Oh, I feel run down," said the man hit by a truck.]; **William E. Koch,** "Wellerisms from Kansas," WF, 18 (1959) 180. [17 items.—"I won't have guts enough to do that again," said the bug as he hit the windshield.—"I'll be a monkey's uncle," said the monkey as his sister had a baby.]; **Alexander H. Krappe,** "Proverbs" in *The Science of Folklore,* New York, 1964. [Good introduction to the proverb form.]

L

Mary Daggett Lake, "Superstitions about Cotton," PTFS, 9 (1931) 145–152. [Approx. 125 beliefs relating to marriage, weddings, good and bad luck, misc.—The first person that sleeps in the middle of a cotton field under a tree with a bird's nest in it will never hear wedding bells.—If one starts starts picking cotton in a row and leaves it uncompleted to pick another row, one is in danger of being bitten by a snake.]; **Thelma Lynn Lamkin,** "Telling the Time: Some Retorts from West Kentucky," MF, 2 (Summer 1952) 109–111. [What time is it?—Daytime, going on nightime.—Same time it was this time yesterday.]; **W. R. Lassiter,** "Why I'm an Old Bachelor," TFSB, 13 (1947) 27–35. [Calls on folk beliefs to "justify" bachelorhood. (There are, in this connection, folk beliefs and proverbs and one thing and another to "justify" anything.)]; **Amy Lathrop,** "Pioneer Remedies from Western Kansas," WF, 20 (1961) 1–22. [Excellent account of first-hand experience with ailments and cures at the turn of the century]; **Harry Law,** "Some Folklore of Macon County, Tennessee," TFSB, 18 (1952) 97–100. [Includes home remedies: Angry sores were treated by allowing a dog to lick them.—Burned whiskey was given children for colic.]; **Maria Leach,** *God Had a Dog,* (Rutgers University Press), New Brunswick, New Jersey, 1961. [The mythology and folklore of the dog from the earliest times to the present. Thorough bibl.—To stunt a puppy's growth feed him daisies in milk.—Kill cats, dogs, or frogs, and you'll die in rags.—Every dog thinks himself a lion in his master's house.—A man who kicks his hound will beat his wife.]; **Collins Lee,** "Some Negro Lore from Baltimore," JAF, 5 (1892) 110–112. [If you are robbed of anything, take a rooster, put him under a pot, and let everybody touch the pot: when the thief touches the pot, the rooster will crow.]; **Hector H. Lee** and **Donald Roberson**, *Lore of Our Land: A Book of American Folklore*, Evanston, 1963; **Charles Godfrey Leland**, *Gypsy Sorcery and Fortune-Telling*, London, 1891; **Gerald S. Lester**, "How Much Snow Next Winter?" KFQ (1961) 12–14. [An unusual way of using the first snow for forecast purposes involved bubble measurement. You took a pint of this snow, put it in a tin container, and put this on a hot stove. The number of bubbles that rose to the surface while the snow was melting gave the number of snows for the winter.]; **Anna Lett**, "Some West Tennessee Superstitions About Conjureres, Witches, Ghosts, and the Devil," TFSB, 36 (June 1970). [A circle of lime around a house will conjure an entire household.—The bone of a dead person is proof against conjure.]; **Beverly** and **Myron H. Levenson**, "Some Southern Folk Remedies and Related Beliefs," NCF, 8 no 2 (1960) 26–31. [For sunburn: Apply a one-half inch thickness of bread dough.—Dirt in the eyes: Swish tail of black cat across eye.—If you pull a tooth and a chicken eats it, none will grow in its place.]; **Gabe Lewis**, "Old-Time Remedies from Madison County (Tennessee)," PTFS, 14 (1938) 267–268; **Seraphia Leyda**, "Les Treateurs," LFM, 2 (Aug 1961) 18–25. [Good personal account of "power" doctoring in Louisiana]; **David E. Lick** and **Thomas R. Brendle**, *Plant Names and Plant Lore Among the Pennsylvania Germans*, (Proceedings of the Pennsylvania German Society, 33), Philadelphia, 1922; [anon.], **"A List of Similes,"** WF, 10 (1951) 174–175. [Poem from the *Golden Era*. Related to Halpert's contribution on "Rhymed Proverbial Comparisons."]; **Grady M. Long**, "Folk Customs in Southeast Tennessee," TFSB, 27 (Dec 1961). [Good collection.—"I don't hold with none of these strange and heathenish beliefs, but some things folks call superstitions is jest as true as God's Gospel."—"It took me a long time to ferret out the reason behind stopping the clock when a member of the family died. Actually it is to limit the power of death by breaking the cycle, and introducing a new period of time."]; **Grady M. Long**, "Folk Medicine in McMinn, Polk, Bradley, and Meigs Counties, Tennessee," TFSB, 27 (March 1962). [Practical herb remedies]; **C. Grant Loomis**, "Emerson's Proverbs, WF, 17 (1958) 257–262. [Cites 105.—"The seamen use another which has much true divinity: 'Every man for himself and God for us all.' "—He counts very unskillfully who leaves God out of his reckoning.]; **C. Grant Loomis**, "Folk Language in William MacLeod Raine's West," TFSB, 24 (Dec 1958). [An even break is good enough for any man.—Lots of good dogs bark.—They can't kill you twice.]; **C. Grant Loomis**, "Henry David Thoreau as Folklorist," WF, 16 (1957) 90–106. [Cites examples including proverbs in his writings]; **C. Grant Loomis**, "Indications of Miners' Medicine," WF, 8 (1949) 117–122. [Remedies for various ailments in the early mining camps, and a quoted hard comment on a physician: "He generally relieves you, if not of your disease, of your pocketbook. For three 'a-hems' and a 'ha' I paid in August last twenty-seven dollars."]; **C. Grant Loomis**, "Jonathanisms: American Epigrammatic Hyperbole," WF, 6 (1947) 211–227. [177 amusing entries.—There is a man so short in Quebec that he is obliged to stand on his own head to kiss his wife.—There is a man in Mississippi so lean that he makes all hungry who look at him, and when children meet him in the street they run home crying for bread.—A citizen of Wisconsin, while bathing in the river, discovered after an industrious scrub of five minutes a pair of drawers he had lost two years before.]; **C. Grant Loomis,** "Mary Had a Parody: A Rhyme of Childhood in Folk Tradition," WF, 17 (1958) 45–76. [Some 50 parodies.—Mary had a little lamb,/Likewise a lobster stew,/And ere the sunlit morning dawned,/She had a nightmare, too.]; **C. Grant Loomis,** "Proverbial Phrases in Journalistic Wordplay," WF, 23 (1964) 187–189; **C. Grant Loomis,** "Proverbs in Business," WF, 23 (1964) 91–94. [Selected from the *Cyclopaedia of Commercial and Business Anecdotes,* New York, 1868]; **C. Grant Loomis,** "Proverbs in the Farmer's Almanac(k)," WF, 15 (1956) 172–178. [Selected proverbs found in the *Almanac* from 1795 through 1834.—None is a fool always; everyone sometimes.—He that knows least commonly presumes most.—She that is born a beauty is half married.]; **C. Grant Loomis,** "Proverbs in the *Golden Era,*" WF, 14 (1955) 196–199. [Collection of 100.—Beauty will buy no beef.—Choose a wife rather by your ear than by your eye.—In a calm sea every man is a pilot.—Who has a bad wife, has purgatory for a neighbor.—She that hath a bad husband hath hell in her own house.—A good dog deserves a good bone.]; **C. Grant Loomis,** "Random Proverbs in Popular Literature," WF, 16 (1957) 133–135. [Plea for collection of proverbs from modern writers]; **C. Grant Loomis,** "Rhymed Proverbial Comparisons," WF, 14 (1955) 282–285. [See same title entry under Herbert Halpert]; **C. Grant Loomis,** "Some American Folklore of 1880," CFQ, 4 (1945) 417. [From *The Territorial Enterprise,* Virginia City, Nevada, Jan. 20, 1880.— Whoever reads epitaphs loses his memory.—To eat when a bell is tolling for a funeral causes a toothache.]; **C. Grant Loomis,** "Superstitions and Beliefs in Swift, being extracts from *A Complete Collection of Genteel and Ingenious Conversation,*" WF, 15 (1956) 126–128; **C. Grant Loomis,** "Superstitions, 1833–1851," WF, 24 (1965) 34–35. [*The Casket,* Philadelphia, 1833, pokes fun at the beliefs of a century before:—A ring made of the hinge of a coffin will prevent cramp.—A stone with a hole in it, hung at the bed's head, will prevent the nightmare.—Also cites *Harper's New Monthly Magazine* (1851) in the same vein:—A stick of brimstone worn in the pocket is good for them as has cramps.—The earache: Put an onion in your ear after it is well roasted.]; **C. Grant Loomis,** "Sylvester Judd's New England Lore," JAF, 60 (1947) 151–158. [Proverbs and beliefs in Judd's (1813–1853) writings:—I heard a dog howl in the streets the other night, and dreamed of seeing monkeys, and that is sartin death.—The dog that trots about will find a bone.]; **C. Grant Loomis,** "Traditional American Wordplay: The Epigram and Perverted Proverbs," WF, 8 (1949) 348–357. [Examples: A bird in the hand is worth two in the bush. Becomes: One girl in the kitchen is worth two at the front gate.—A bird in the hand is not good table manners.—A hair in the hand is worth two in the soup.—And also: You can lead a fraternity man to water, but why disappoint him.—Don't put off until tomorrow those you can do today.]; **C. Grant Loomis,** "Traditional American Wordplay: Definitions, Literal Cliches, Naming, and Occupational Punning," WF, 9 (1950) 147–

152. [Fine collection of rare idiocies: A Connecticut farmer has named his prize rooster *Robinson*, because Robinson Crusoe.—She was only a milkman's daughter, but she was cream of the crop.—The *lap* of *luxury:* A cat enjoying her milk.—*Horse Radish:* A radish that has a cold in the throat.]; **C. Grant Loomis,** "Traditional American Wordplay: Wellerisms or Yankeeisms," WF, 8 (1949) 1–21. [Major collection of 500 items.—"Ah-ha!" said the farmer to his corn. "Oh! hoe!" said the corn to the farmer.—"Don't touch me, or I'll scream!" as the engine-whistle said to the stoker.]; **C. Grant Loomis,** "Wellerisms in California Sources," WF, 14 (1955) 229–245. [326 Wellerisms.—"I may be down, but I'm not out," exclaimed the second baseman as he successfully slid into second.—"I guess I've lost another pupil," said the professor as his glass eye rolled down the kitchen sink.—"Eavesdropping again," said Adam as his wife fell out of a tree.]; **C. Grant Loomis,** "Wellerisms in the *Golden Era*," AS, 20 (1945) 303–305. [39 entries]; **Gabe Lewis,** "Old Time Remedies from Madison County [Texas]," PTFS, 14 (1938) 267–268. [15 cures remembered by Lewis's grandmother.—For crick in the neck: Rub your neck against a post that hogs have rubbed against.]; **Mary Lopez,** "Superstitions," WVF, 7 (1957) 38–44; **Burton Lowrimore,** "California Superstitions," CFQ, 4 (1945) 178. [12 relatively common beliefs.]

M

Flora MacDonald, "Home Remedies," NCF, 4 no 2 (1956) 17–18. [Cinders in whiskey for cough.—Pan of water under the bed at night for cramps.—Catnip tea for colic and soothing the nerves.]; **Kemp Malone,** "Negro Proverbs from Maryland," AS, 4 (1929) 285. [Three proverbs: Every like ain't the same.—Every shut eye ain't asleep.—Every good-bye ain't gone.—By way of comparison or relation, see *Julius Caesar*, II, 2, 128–129: That every like is not the same, O Caesar/The heart of Brutus yearns to think upon!]; **Roxie Martin,** "Old Remedies Collected in the Blue Ridge Mountains," JAF, 60 (1947) 184–185. [28 cures.—For slow childbirth a tea made of boiling water poured over browned egg shells.]; **Dwight Edwards Marvin,** *The Antiquity of Proverbs*, New York, 1922. [Good introduction to subject for general reader]; [anon.], **"Maryland Superstitions,"** JAF, 20 (1907) 159–160. [A dozen from Washington County.—A cure for fits: Take a live chicken and plunge it, feathers, protestations and all into a pot of boiling water; boil several hours and give a cup of the water thus obtained to the patient.]; **H. V. Massey,** "Birdlore," TFSB, 14 (Sept 1948); **James R. Masterson,** "Travelers' Tales of Colonial Natural History," JAF, 59 (1946) 51–67 and 174–188. [Wonderful accounts!]; **Helen M. McCadden,** "Folklore in the Schools," NYFQ, 3 (1947) 330–340; **W. L. McAtee,** "Home Medication in Grant County, Indiana, in the 'Nineties'," MF, 5 (1955) 213–216. [Chiefly herbal remedies, approx. 50 entries]; **W. L. McAtee,** "Medical Lore in Grant County, Indiana, in the 'Nineties'," MF, 8 (1958) 151–153. [Supplement to preceding, approx. 30 entries.—Fresh-churned, unsalted butter, and sour cream were used to cure sunburn.]; **W. L. McAtee,** "Odds and Ends of North American Folklore on Birds," MF, 5 (1955) 169–183. [With good bibl. Varied material on omens, medicinal uses, weather connected lore. Most useful.]; **W. L. McAtee** "Some Folklore of Grant County, Indiana, in the 'Nineties'," MF, 1 (1951) 243–267; **Eugene S. McCartney,** "Classical Weather Lore of Thunder and Lightning," *Classical Weekly,* 25 (1932) 183–192, 200–208, 212–216; **Eugene S. McCartney,** "Folklore Heirlooms," *Michigan Academy of Science, Arts and Letters,* 16 (1932) 105–210; **Cleo McGlasson,** "Superstitions and Folk Beliefs of Overton County, [Tenn.]," TFSB, 7 (Oct 1941). [Approx. 470 items.—Get up on the first day of May and count the live things you see, and it will be that many years till you marry.—For earache: Eat corn in February.]; **Dan McKenzie,** *The Infancy of Medicine, an Enquiry into the Influence of Folk-Lore Upon the Evolution of Scientific Medicine,* London, 1927; **Ida Mae McKinney,** "Superstitions of the Missouri Ozarks," TFSB, 18 (Dec 1952). [A reminiscent collection.—If you wish to keep a stray dog that comes to your house, trim one of your fingernails and put it in a biscuit. If the dog eats the biscuit, he will never leave.]; **Bruce McWhorter,** "Superstitions from Russell County, Kentucky," KFR, 12 (1966) 11. [Bad luck, cures, signs and weather]; **Jane Thompson Mead,** "Proverbs: Sayings from Westfield, Chautauqua County," NYFQ, 10 (1954) 226–227. [Expressions used within her family]; **Doret Meeker,** "Back to the Blanket: Lore of Steuben County," NYFQ, 8 (1952) 165–190; **Mamie Meredith,** "Prairie Schooner Slogans," AS, 7 (1932) 172–174. [Slogans painted on covered wagons from 1858 to the 1880's; **Eugenia L. Millard,** "Children's Charms and Oracles," Pt. I, NYFQ, 7 (1951) 253–268, and Pt. II, NYFQ, 8 (1952) 46–57; **Mary E. Miller,** "A Folklore Survey of Dickson County, Tennessee," TFSB, 24 (June 1958). [Bad and good luck, marriage, wishes, death, cures, weather, zodiac, proverbs, misc.]; **William Marion Miller,** "Smart Sayings from Southwestern Ohio," HF, 7 (1948) 20. [Make yourself useful as well as good looking.]; **Randall V. Mills,** "Superstitions," WF, 11 (1952) 43–45. (From the *Golden Era,* [S.F.], 12 [Feb 12, 1865] p. 2.) ["We have taken pains to collect a few of the popular superstitions with which some otherwise very sensible people are afflicted . . . "]; **Charles Frederick Millspaugh,** *Medicinal Plants, An Illustrated and Descriptive Guide to Plants Indigenous to and Naturalized in the United States Which Are Used in Medicine,* (2 vols.), Philadelphia, 1892; **W. E. Mockler,** "Moon Lore from West Virginia," *Folk-Lore* (London), 50 (1939) 310–314; **Adalene Moffat,** "The Mountaineers of Middle Tennessee," JAF, 4 (1891) 314–320. ["He's rotten enough to spile, but I reckon he'll keep."]; **George Monteiro,** "Hiccough Remedies on Television," WF, 23 (1964) 44–45. [Cures from the *Candid Camera* program (Nov. 19, 1961) and from Monteiro's family.—Put a penny between your toes.—Think of seven baldheaded men.—Pull a hair out of your ear.]; **George Monteiro,** "Parodies of Scripture, Prayer, and Hymn," JAF, 77 (1964) 45–52. [Good collection with bibl.—Blessed are they who run around in circles: for they shall be known as wheels.—Cast thy bread upon the waters and it will come back Lorna Doones.]; **George Monteiro,** "Proverbs and Proverbial Phrases of the Continental Portuguese," WF, 22 (1963) 19–76. [Portuguese with

English translation. 457 items collected in Massachusetts and Rhode Island.—
Any task is difficult for us when we have no taste for it.—Those who have
children have problems, and those who do not have them still have problems.—
I dislike my brother, but let no one lay a hand on him.]; **George Monteiro,**
"Proverbs in the Remaking," WF, 27 (1968) 128. [Quoted in Duncan Emrich,
Folklore on the American Land, Boston, 1972.—Very amusing account of
children being fed half of a true proverb and asked to complete it: A bird in
the hand is/warm—A rolling stone/plays a guitar.]; **Lynwood Montell,**
"Death Beliefs from the Kentucky Foothills, KFR, 12 (1966) 81–86. [Approx.
80 entries.—Domestic signs and portents; beliefs relating to infants and
adults; care of the dead.]; **Clare Moore Moody,** "Some Folk Beliefs and
Superstitions," MFR, 1 (1967) 25–33. [40 annotated entries.—If you put a
silver spoon in mushrooms when they're cooking, it will turn black if they're
poison.]; **James Mooney,** "Folklore of the North Carolina Mountains,"
JAF, 2 (1889) 95–104. [Sensitive account of the folk and their way of life.—
Folk speech, love charms, weather lore, witches, medicine, riddles.—A sun
shower is caused by the devil whipping his wife, the raindrops presumably
being her tears.]; **Merrill Moore,** "Hair into Snake," TFSB, 22 (Sept 1956);
Ruby Andrews Moore, "Superstitions from Georgia," JAF, 7 (1894) 305–
306. [To kill a ghost, it must be shot with a bullet made of a silver quarter-
dollar.]; [anon.] **"More Wellerisms from Kansas,"** WF, 19 (1960) 196.
[20 from Kansas State College Folklore Archives]; **B. Q. Morgan,** "Simile
and Metaphor in American Speech," AS, 1 (1926) 271–274; **Robert Morgan,**
"Witchcraft in Henderson County [N.C.]," NCF, 15 no 1 (1967) 4–6. [Local
accounts]; **Benjamin S. Moya,** "Superstitions and Beliefs Among the
Spanish-Speaking People of New Mexico," unpub. Masters dissertation,
Univ. of New Mexico, 1940; **Patrick M. Mullen,** "The Function of Magic
Folk Belief Among Texas Coastal Fishermen," JAF, 82 (1969) 214–225.
[Fine article placing beliefs in the context of the men's work]; **Charles H.
Murphy,** "A Collection of Birth Marking Beliefs from Eastern Kentucky,"
KFR, 10 (1964) 36–38; **Ruth Ann Musick,** "Folklore from West Virginia,
HF, 6 (June 1947) 41–49. [19 "superstitions": A beet may be used for rouge.—
It is bad luck to leave a house by a different door than the one you entered.];
Ruth Ann Musick, "Weather and Planting Signs," WVF, 3 (1953) 43–45;
Ruth Ann Musick, "West Virginia Folklore," HF, 7 (1948) 1–14. [Stories,
cures, children's rhymes.—For toothache: Hold a toasted persimmon between
the gum and the cheek.]

N

Keith A. Neighbors, "Mexican-American Folk Disease," WF, 28 (1969)
249–259. [Considers four afflictions: *empacho* (form of indigestion), *mal ojo*
(evil eye), *susto* (fright), *caida de la mollera* (fallen fontanel or upper palate);
Venetia Newall, "Easter Eggs," JAF, 80 (1967) 1–32. [European tradi-
tions]; **Venetia Newall,** *An Egg at Easter: A Folklore Study,* (Indiana Uni-

versity Press), Bloomington, 1971. [Definitive study with excellent bibl. Pastimes, games, the Egg Tree, decorated eggs, charms, magic]; **Jane H. Newell,** "Superstitions of Irish Origin in Boston, Mass.," JAF, 5 (1892) 242–243. [When a funeral goes by, you must say, "Lord have mercy on them."]; **W. W. Newell,** "Conjuring Rats," JAF, 5 (1892) 23–32. [On writing notes to rats and advising them to go down the street to a neighbor's house]; **W. W. Newell,** "Proverbs and Phrases," JAF, 2 (1889) 153–154. [From Massachusetts: Everything is all criss-cross.—He has no more blood than a turnip.—Pretty as a pink.]; **W. W. Newell,** "Topics for Collection of Folk-Lore," JAF, 4 (1891) 151–158. [A "reminder list" for the collector]; **Lucille F. Newman,** "Folklore of Pregnancy: Wives' Tales in Contra Costa County, California," WF, 28 (1969) 112–135. [Analytical study with 284 contemporary beliefs]; **Joseph Nicholas,** "How to Become a Witch," TFSB, 16 (March 1950); **George R. Nielson,** "Folklore of the German-Wends in Texas," PTFS, 30 (1961) 244–259. [Cures, wedding customs, death omens and beliefs, planting, the moon]; **Claire Noall,** "Superstitions, Customs, and Prescriptions of Mormon Midwives," CFQ, 3 (1944) 102–114; **G. K. Noble,** "Do Snakes Swallow Their Young for Protection?", *Copeia*, 98 (1921) 54–57. [With bibliography]; **Oran Warder Nolen,** "Some Odd Mexican Customs," PTFS, 19 (1944) 57–62. [Various cures, including one for snakebite]; **Ethel Todd Norlin,** "Present-Day Superstitions at La Harpe, Illinois: Survivals in a Community of English Origin," JAF, 31 (1918) 202–215. [Approx. 230 items on death, medicine, marriage, weather, and misc.—Make a rhyme, and you will see your beau before half-past nine.—A girl's freckles will disappear if she walks barefooted in the dew.]; **Ruby W. Norris,** "Folk Medicine of Cumberland County [Ky.]," KFR, 4 (1958) 101–110. [A good collection]; [anon.], **"A Note on an Early Superstition of the Champlain Valley: 'The Whip-Poor-Will', "** JAF, 4 (1891) 272–274. [Interesting statement by a 'non-believer' in superstition.]

O

Ruth Odell, "Mid-Western Saliva Lore," SFQ, 14 (1950) 220–223. [He knows enough not to spit to windward.]; **Ruth Odell,** "Nebraska Smart Sayings," SFQ, 12 (1948) 185–195. ["I knew him when he used to be able to get his hat on."—Shinny on your own side.]; **Ruth W. O'Dell,** "Before You Call Your Doctor," TFSB, 17 (June 1951). [47 home remedies]; **Ruth W. O'Dell,** "Signs and Superstitions," TFSB, 10 (Dec 1944). [When children misbehaved, they were often switched with a peach-tree switch, and it was termed administering peach-tree tea. Their mischief could generally be controlled completely by the mere suggestion from the parent.]; **Old Merry (Edwin Hodder),** *Queer Discourses on Queer Proverbs*, Philadelphia, 1869. [Witty, moralistic discourses which take as their starting point popular proverbs]; **Jack P. Olevitch,** "Proverbial Comparisons from Oklahoma and Missouri," HF, 3 (1944) 37. [You're slow as my grandmother, but she's a lot older.—I ain't had so much fun since the hogs ate my baby brother.]; **Katherine Oldmeadow**, *The Folklore of Herbs*, Birmingham [Eng.], n.d.; **Ellen Orr**, "The Black Coffee Fortune Cup," MFR, 3 (1969) 1–3. [How to tell fortune from black coffee]; **Ethel Owens**, "Witchcraft in the Cumberlands," KFR, 11 (1965) 76–77. [Precise instructions on how to become a witch, as well as protect oneself against them]; **J. G. Owens**, "Folk-Lore from Buffalo Valley, Central Pennsylvania," JAF, 4 (1891) 115–128. [If you pick your teeth with the nail of the middle toe of an owl, you will never have toothache.—To cure a boy of homesickness, put salt in the hems of his trousers and make him look up the chimney.]; **Welden Owens**, "Cross Country with Welden Owens," Dallas *Times Herald*, June 20, 1963. [Next time you're buying a watermelon, take along a broom straw, and do this: Place the straw crosswise on the melon. Then watch. By some strange chemical action, the straw will immediately begin turning itself parallel with the length of the melon—if it is ripe and ready to eat. But if it is still too green for slicing, the straw won't budge a bit. This performance of the straw requires less than ten seconds.].

P

Marion T. Page, "Superstitions at Home," TFSB, 20 (Sept 1954). [The first thunder in February, according to my mother, always waked up all snakes.—See a pin, pick it up,/All that day you'll have good luck./See a pin, let it lie,/You'll need a pin before you die.]; **Haywood Parker**, "Folk-Lore of the North Carolina Mountaineers," JAF, 20 (1907) 241–250. [Beliefs, superstitions, weather, medicine.—Circle around the sun,/Will rain none,/Circle around the moon,/Will rain soon.]; [anon.], **"Parodied Proverbs from Idaho,"** WF, 24 (1965) 289–290. [Give a woman an inch and she thinks she's a ruler.—If at first you don't succeed, don't be an idiot—quit!—A bird in the hand makes blowing your nose difficult.]; **Jerry S. Parr**, "Folk Cures of Middle Tennessee," TFSB, 28 (March 1962); **Albert Parry**, *Tattoo*, New York, 1933. [A solid survey of the art, practice, and superstitions of tattooing, with good bibliography]; **Mildred Parsons**, "Negro Folklore from Fayette County," TFSB, 19 (Sept 1953); **Coy Harlan Parsley**, "Ollie Oddities," KFR, 1 (1955) 61–79; **George E. Patten**, "Omens and Superstitions," *Appleton's Journal of Literature, Science, and Arts*, 2 (1869) 138–140; **Helen Pearce**, "Folk Sayings in a Pioneer Family of Western Oregon," CFQ, 5 (1946) 229–242. [That looks like last year's bird's nest.—He thinks he's some punkins.]; **T. M. Pearce**, "The English Proverb in New Mexico," CFQ, 5 (1946) 334–338. [Let's keep this a country where every man is entitled to scratch his own itch.—He weighed ten pounds less than a straw hat.]; **T. M. Pearce**, "Rhymes and Sayings," NMFR, 6 (1951–52) 23–25. [The room was as empty as a bride's nightgown.—She's as pretty as a red heifer in a flower bed.]; **Drew Pearson**, "Things I Didn't Know About Christmas," TFSB, 19 (Dec 1933); **Ted-Larry Petworth**, "Typical Protestant Modesty: Some Folk Cures of North-Central Louisiana," LFM, 2 (April 1965) 87–96. [The "modesty" being denial of power-doctoring capabilities by those possessing them]; **Sue Nell Pedigo,** "Chihuahua: Asthma Cure," KFR, 2 (1956) 135–136. [Cites case of the cure working and the transfer of disease]; **Louis Pendleton,** "Notes on Negro Folklore and Witchcraft in the South," JAF, 3 (1890) 201–207. [A few instances]; **James H. Penrod,** "Folk Beliefs about Work, Trades, and Professions from New Mexico," WF, 27 (1968) 180–190. [57 beliefs relating to sailors, actors, women, airplane pilots, rodeo performers, automobile racers.—There is something wrong with people who don't like watermelon, so don't do business with them.—It is bad luck to eat peanuts in the dressing rooms of theaters.—If a girl wears red on Friday, she is a whore.]; **Soledad Perez,** *"Dichos* from Austin," PTFS, 26 (1954) 223–229. [Approx. 75 proverbs and sayings in Spanish with translation.—Fifty years in the navy and he doesn't know a whale.—Flies do not enter a closed mouth.—He who takes no risks will never cross the sea.]; **Anne E. Perkins,** "More Notes on Maine Dialect," AS, 5 (1930) 118–131. [Greener than a gosling.—He's about as polite as a basket of chips.—So thin he looks like a knitting needle with a bean on it.]; **Anne E. Perkins,** "Vanishing Expressions of the Maine Coast," AS, 3 (1928) 134–141. [A wind that will blow all hell out by the roots.—The pullets are prating and will lay soon.]; **Henry A. Person,** "Proverbs and Proverbial Lore from the State of Washington," WF, 17 (1958) 176–185. [369 entries.—You don't have to buy a cow just because you want a glass of milk.—Apple pie without the cheese,/Is like a kiss without the squeeze.—Happy as a cat on Friday.]; [anon.] **"Perverted Proverbs,"** WF, 20 (1961) 200. [20 from UCLA Archives.—To err is human; to cover it up is, too. All work and no play makes Jack.]; **Gipsy Petulengro,** *Romany Remedies and Recipes,* New York, 1936; **Madge E. Pickard** and **R. Carlyle Buley,** *The Midwest Pioneer: His Ills, Cures, and Doctors,* New York, 1946. [Thoroughly readable with excellent bibl. and source notes. The tone of the work may be gathered from the dedication: To the Pioneer Doctor who boldly faced the wilderness; and to the Pioneer who bravely faced the Doctor.]; [anon.], **"Picturesque Speech,"** TFSB, 10 (March 1944). [A young girl from Knoxville, at the end of a long hard day, yawned, then settled down in a chair, remarking, "I could stretch from here to yonder if I didn't have to come back."]; **"Picturesque Speech,"** TFSB, 9 (May 1943). [I just backed my ears and did it.—I felt as though I'd turned a bird loose.]; **Gisela J. Plowman,** "Pedro-ing at California," CFQ, 3 (1944) 277–283. [22 variant explanations for origin of this campus cry]; **Genevieve Pope,** "Superstitions and Beliefs of Fleming County [Ky.]," KFR, 11 (1965) 41–51. [Approx. 300 items. General collection: birth, infancy, remedies, dreams, death, ghosts, animals, weather]; **Bernard H. Porter,** "Some Newfoundland Phrases, Sayings, and Figures of Speech," AS, 41 (1966) 294–297. [A fisherman is one rogue, a merchant is many.—Far as ever a puffin flew.—In a leaky punt with a broken oar,/'Tis always best to hug the shore.]; **J. Hampden Porter,** "Notes on the Folk-Lore of the Mountain Whites of the Alleghanies," JAF, 7 (1894) 105–117. [Witchcraft, ghosts, cures, charms, love divinations, and good note on the SATOR charm]; **Kenneth Porter,** "Humor, Blasphemey, and Criticism in the Grace Before Meat," NYFQ, 21 (1965) 3–18. [Bless these cakes and bless these pies,/And all the girls with pretty eyes.—Lord! have mercy upon us as we are about to partake of this food!—Good source notes and bibl.]; **Kenneth Porter,** "More Examples of Humor, Blasphemey, and Criticism in the Grace Before Meat," NYFQ, 24 (1968) 64–67; **Kenneth Porter,** "Some Central Kansas Wellerisms," MF, 8 (1958) 158–160. [With brief bibliographical suggestions]; **Kenneth Porter,** "The 'Possum in Midwestern Folklore," WF, 15 (1956) 23–25. [Considers the folk belief of birth through the nostrils.—See also Carl G. Hartman, *Possums*, Austin, Texas, 1952.]; **Louise Pound,** *Nebraska Folklore*, Lincoln, 1959. [Full volume on the folklore of the State]; **Louise Pound,** "Nebraska Snake Lore," SFQ, 10 (1946) 163–176. [Thorough collection of varied beliefs]; **Louise Pound,** "Old Nebraska Folk Customs," *Nebraska History*, 28 (1947). [31 pp., general survey]; **Sadie F. Price,** "Kentucky Folk-Lore," JAF, 14 (1901) 30–38. [Approx. 200 entries.—It never rains at night during July.—Place cornbread crumbs about your cucumber plants. It will attract the ants, and these will destroy the cucumber bugs.]; [anon.], **"Proverbial Material from the Western Kentucky Archive,"** KFR, 6 (1960) 47. [One today is worth two tomorrows. —So tall he could wade the Mississippi and never get his ankles wet.—One see is worth twenty hears.]; [anon.], **"Proverbs,"** NCF, 1 (June 1948) 26–27. [If you want a thing done, go; if not, send.—Bless the bridge that carries you over.]; [anon.], **"Proverbs and Phrases [from Massachusetts],"** JAF 5 (1892) 60. [God Almighty's overcoat wouldn't make him a vest.—There's no more peace here than for a cat in hell without claws.—Let them skin their own skunks.—As Irish as Biddy Murphy's pig.]; [anon.], **"Proverbs and Sayings,"** NYFQ, 2 (1946) 219–220. [He growls like a bear with a sore head.]; [anon.], **"Proverbs, Prophecies, Signs and Sayings,"** in *Nebraska Folklore*, pamphlets nos. 9 and 10 (Federal Writers' Project) Lincoln, 1937. [Broad collection of proverbs and superstitions]; **Virginia Pruitt,** "The Bold Hives in Tennessee," TFSB, 30 (June 1964). [The disease and some horrendous cures]; **Newbell Niles Puckett,** *Folk Beliefs of the Southern Negro*, Chapel Hill, N.C., 1926. [Thorough and basic study. Voodooism, cures, superstitions, beliefs.]

R

Samuel X. Radhill, "The Folklore of Teething," KFQ, 9 (1964) 123–143. [Traces beliefs to earliest times. Chiefly European sources.]; **Frank L. Rainey,** "Animal and Plant Lore," *The Kentucky Folk-Lore and Poetry Magazine*, 4 (April 1929) 8–15; **Vance Randolph,** "Folk Beliefs in the Ozark Mountain," JAF, 40 (1927) 78–93; **Vance Randolph,** *Ozark Superstitions*, (Columbia University Press), New York, 1947; reissued in paperback by Dover, 1964, with title *Ozark Magic and Folklore*. [A very great collection covering all beliefs and superstitions. Highly recommended: readable, entertaining, informative, based on skilled and affectionate field research.]; **Vance Randolph,** "Ozark Superstitions," JAF, 46 (1933) 1–21; **Vance Randolph** and **George**

P. **Wilson,** *Down in the Holler: A Gallery of Ozark Folk Speech,* (University of Oklahoma Press), Norman, 1953. [Belongs in every library of anyone who has any interest whatsoever in America. Most entertaining and readable. Treat yourself to a copy.]; **H. W. Ravenel,** "Recollections of Southern Plantation Life," (ed. Marjorie S. Mendenhall), *Yale Review,* 25 (1936) 748-777. [A document written in 1876 containing account of customs, superstitions, and vocabulary of South Carolina Negroes]; **Myrtle Read Rawles,** "'Boontling'—Esoteric Speech of Booneville, California," WF, 25 (1966) 93-103. [Secret language of children, adopted also by adults of the town. Quite incredible. With bibl.]; **Otto Ernst Rayburn,** "Blood Stoppers in the Ozarks," MF, 4 (1954) 213-215; **Joseph Raymond,** "Tensions in Proverbs: More Light on International Understanding," WF, 15 (1956) 153-158. [Important contribution to proverb study. Proverbs arise out of unity of thought: group, national, or otherwise.]; **J. Russell Reaver,** "Emerson's Use of Proverbs," SFQ, 27 (1963) 280-299; **W. Adelbert Redfield,** "Superstitions and Folk Beliefs," TFSB, 3 (April 1937). [470 beliefs in the major categories, from students at Pleasant Hill Adademy on the Cumberland Plateau, where students (from rural families) have to earn all of their way.—When a cow gets choked, get out in front of her and jump and holler, and she will get unchoked.—When a cow gets choked on shorts and dairy feed or cottonseed meal, pour water in her ear.—The nose will bleed every time it thunders.—The 27th of August is the "most poisonest" day of the year.—If you walk on your heels one-fourth of a mile, you will find some gold.]; **Kathleen Reecer,** "Folklore in Graves County [Ky.]," KFR, 5 (1959) 121-126. [Reminiscences of childhood and nice flavor of the country: food, toys, games, medical cures]; **Catherine M. Relihan,** "Farm Lore: Folk Remedies," NYFQ, 3 (1947) 81-84, 166-169. [For convulsions: Pour water from a baby's baptism over a peony bush, and catch as much as you can shake off. Bathe the eyes of the person having convulsions with it.—For boils: Soak lead BB shot in milk for eight days. Then pick the shot out of the rotten milk and take one daily. Use twelve BB shot to one pint of milk.—For colds: You crawl through a double-rooted briar toward the East.—For hiccoughs: Hold your breath, count to one hundred, repeat the first stanza of "The Star Spangled Banner."]; **Catherine M. Relihan,** "Farm Lore: Herb Remedies," NYFQ, 2 (1946) 156-158. [Bluebells for lung trouble.—Ragweed for summer complaint.—Balsam cone and gin for colds.]; **Catherine M. Relihan,** "Farm Lore: Wart Remedies," NYFQ, 3 (1947) 256-258. [Tortoise tail will cure warts. This is effective only in May.]; **Herbert Reynolds,** "Grandma's Handbook," TFSB, 16 (1950). [To cure the patient of tuberculosis a live skunk was placed in the room so the patient might inhale the fumes freely.—As a precaution against colds, keep a peeled onion lying on the end of the mantel. The onion absorbs germs from the surrounding air.]; **Ernest Rhys,** *The Dictionary of Best Known Quotations,* New York, 1939. [With proverbs]; **W. Edson Richmond,** "The Collection of Proverbs in Indiana," HF, 5 (1946) 150-156. [Urges preservation]; **W. Edson Richmond,** "Some Weather Lore from Indiana," MF, 8 (1958) 183-184; **Patricia K. Rickels,** "Some Accounts of Witch Riding," LFM, 2 (Aug 1961) 1-17. [Eerie accounts in Louisiana]; **A. H. Roberts,**

"We Aren't Magicians, But . . . . Verbal Charms Survive in the Machine Age," TFSB, 18 (1952); **Hilda Roberts**, "Louisiana Superstitions," JAF, 40 (1927) 144–208. [1585 entries in all fields. Fine collection.—If you wish to move a cat from one house to another, take it out through the window.—No man is ever exactly six feet high, for that was the height of Christ.]; **Leonard Roberts**, "Additional Exaggerations from Eastern Kentucky," MF, 2 (Fall 1952) 163–166. [Farm so steep he has to dig a hole behind the house for the dog to set in to bark.]; **Leonard W. Roberts**, "Floyd County Folklore," KFR, 2 (1956) 34–66. [Never sleep in a bed with your head downstream.— Cold weather when red buds are in bloom is called red bud winter; when blackberries, blackberry winter; when dogwoods, dogwood winter.]; **E. G. Rogers**, "Borrowing from the Moon," TFSB, 14 (1948). [Approx. 50 items of moon folklore]; **E. G. Rogers**, *Early Folk Medical Practices in Tennessee*, Murfreesboro, Tenn., 1941. [12 chapters, including Midwives and Childbirth Practices of Early Surgery, The Marking of Children, Paying the Doctor's Bill, The Undertaker]; **E. G. Rogers**, "Figurative Language the Folkway," TFSB, 16 (Dec 1950). [Good collection of similes and metaphors.—As sweet as julep.—Lipping full (as full as a pitcher filled to the lip).—Pumpkin head.— Beetle brain.]; **E. G. Rogers**, "Guideposts to Fortune," TFSB, 16 (June 1950). [Good and bad luck omens.—A squirrel following you will bring good luck.—It is good luck to cook turnips and pork together.—Do not fail to smile when passing the salt across the table.]; **E. G. Rogers**, "I Wish I May, I Wish I Might," TFSB, 13 (1947). [Approx. 60 ways of wishmaking]; **E. G. Rogers**, "Popular Sayings of Marshall County, [Tenn.]," TFSB, 15 (Dec 1949). [All water runs downhill.—Knee high to a duck.—A colt is good for nothing if it does not break its halter.]; **E. G. Rogers**, "Possible Origins of Some Common Idioms," TFSB, 14 (Sept 1948); **E. G. Rogers**, "Some Animal Superstitions from Marshall County, Tennessee," SFQ, 18 (1954) 233–238. [To stop an owl from hollowing, tie knots in the sheet.]; **E. G. Rogers**, "Some East Tennessee Figurative Exaggerations," TFSB, 19 (June 1953). [90 items. —A farm so poor that two red-headed women couldn't raise hell on it.— Eyes so red they looked like two cherries in a glass of buttermilk.]; **E. G. Rogers**, "Switching for Water," TFSB, 21 (Dec 1955); **Elzia G. Rogers**, *Early Folk Medical Practices in Tennessee*, Murfreesboro, 1941. [Pp. 68.— Basic.]; **W. Stuart Rogers**, "Irish Lore Collected in Schenectady," NYFQ, 8 (1952) 20–30. [Narrow title but broad matter]; **Thomas J. Rountree**, "More on the Southernism 'Yankee Dime'," JAF, 83 (1970), 461. [Personal recollection of use and meaning]; **Barbara C. Rumley**, "Superstitions in San Francisco," WF, 9 (1950) 159–160; **William J. Rupp**, *Bird Names and Bird Lore of the Pennsylvania Germans* (Proceedings of the Pennsylvania German Society, 52), Norristown, 1946.

S

S. J. Sackett, "Folk Medicine from Western Kansas," WF, 20 (1961) 256. [20 entries.—One remedy my mother used for colds and sore throats was skunk grease and a wool sock.]; **S. J. Sackett,** "German Proverbs from Around Hays, Kansas," WF, 18 (1959) 98. [He who trusts in God builds on a firm foundation.—Begin with God and end with Him, that is the best plan of life.]; **S. J. Sackett,** "Good Luck Charms from Western Kansas," WF, 21 (1962) 102; **S. J. Sackett** and **William E. Koch,** *Kansas Folklore,* Lincoln, Nebr., 1961. [Includes beliefs, proverbs; selected but generally well known]; **S. J. Sackett,** "Proverbial Comparisons from Western Kansas," WF, 19 (1960) 10. [29 entries, most well known]; **S. J. Sackett,** "More Folk Medicine from Western Kansas," WF, 23 (1964) 22 and 76. [Sneezing was good for dusting out the brain and making a person think more clearly.—If you eat too many wild onions, you will walk in your sleep.—Cat's hair will turn into worms in a child's stomach.—To cure rheumatism put a snake inside your shirt. After he crawls around for a while, take him out, and the rheumatism goes with him.]; **S. J. Sackett,** "More Folk Medicine from Western Kansas," WF, 24 (1965) 104. [4 common items]; **S. J. Sackett,** "More Signs of Bad Luck from Western Kansas," WF, 22 (1963) 112. [17 items.—Walking into a room which has an open closet door means bad luck.]; **S. J. Sackett,** "More Signs of Bad Luck from Western Kansas," WF, 24 (1965) 184. [Another thing that will cause you to lose your girl or boy friend is to walk across the steel elevator doors which are in the sidewalk. If I walked over a grate, I was sure to lose a date.—A lot of times when I take a girl to the movies, she makes me close my eyes when the newsreels start. They say that if you look at the front of the movie camera, which they show close up before the newsreels start, you will lose your girl or boy friend.]; **S. J. Sackett,** "Signs of Bad Luck from Western Kansas," WF, 23 (1964) 240. [It is bad luck to work the little horse on the right side of the team. Always work him on the left.]; **S. J. Sackett,** "Signs of Death from Western Kansas," WF, 20 (1961) 102. [If a cow moos after midnight, there will be a death in the family.]; **S. J. Sackett,** "Signs of Rain from Western Kansas," WF, 19 (1960) 190. [Comes a foggy morning or day, count ahead one hundred days, and that day will be rainy.]; **Martha Dell Sanders,** "Proverbial Exaggerations from Paducah, Kentucky," HF, 1 (1951) 191–192. [So weak that when he tried to raise the shade he got all wound up in it.—So gentle he'd go out of his way nine miles to keep from stepping on an ant hill.]; **Myra Sanders,** "Some Medical Lore," *Kentucky Folk-Lore and Poetry Magazine,* 5 no 2 (Oct 1930) 14–23; **Jean Sarrazin,** "Unwanted Company Lore," LFM, 3 (April 1970) 79. [To get rid of unwanted company, put a broom in a shoe behind a door.—The simplest way to get rid of guests who have stayed too long is to stand your broom upside down. It shouldn't stand straight up; it should lean against the wall.]; **Olan L. Sawey,** "Origins of Uvalde County Cattle Brands," PTFS, 25 (1953) 171–182; **Marilyn Schlesinger,** "Proverbs from High School," WF, 18 (1959) 322. [23 collected from students at Fremont High School, Los Angeles.—You can't drink water and whistle at the same time.—Two barrels of tears will not heal a bruise.]; **John Richie Schultz,** "Crawford County Folklore [Pa.]," KFQ, 4 (1959) 3–30. [Incl. superstitions, proverbs, proverbial comparisons.—Cure for a cow choked by an apple: put a board across her rump and hit it with a maul.—Little and often fills the purse.—If you kill a cat, you will have seven years bad luck.]; **Florence Johnson Scott,** "Customs and Superstitions Among Texas Mexicans on the Rio Grande Border," PTFS, 2 (1923) 75–84. [Wedding and funeral customs, omens and superstitions, the Evil Eye]; **Daniel Clayton Seely,** "New Orleans Survivals of Alsatian Superstitions," LFM, 2 (April 1965) 105–107. [From descendants of a family arriving in New Orleans in the 1860's.—When eggs are thrown against the side of a house, someone in it will get very sick.]; **Doris Seibold,** "Southern Arizona Weather Lore," WF, 26 (1967) 168. [If a coyote howls after daybreak, there will be a change in the weather.]; **Elizabeth Cloud Seip,** "Witch-Finding in Western Maryland," JAF, 14 (1901) 39–44. [19th century accounts of witches' activities]; **S. M. Sener,** "Local Superstitions," *Lancaster County Historical Society,* 9 (1904) 233–245; **Hubert Gibson Shearin,** "Some Superstitions in the Cumberland Mountains," JAF, 24 (1911) 319–322. [If one looks up at the sky and counts ninety-nine stars before lowering his gaze, he will fall dead.]; **Caroline Shelby,** "Folklore of Jordan Springs, Tennessee," TFSB, 25 (March 1959). [Keep babies in the dark until they are nine days old or they will go blind.—Take a large rose petal, gather the edges into a ball, and hit it on your head. If it pops, he loves you. If it doesn't pop, he doesn't love you.]; **Alfred L. Shoemaker,** *Christmas in Pennsylvania, A Folk-Cultural Study,* (intro. by Don Yoder), Pennsylvania Folklife Society, Kutztown, Penn., 1959. [Broad survey: Christmas trees, horns, cookies, mummers, fire crackers, Second Christmas. Illustrated. Bibl. notes.]; **Henry W. Shoemaker,** "Neighbors: The Werewolf in Pennsylvania," NYFQ, 7 (1951) 145–155; **Henry W. Shoemaker,** *Scotch-Irish and English Proverbs and Sayings of the West Branch Valley of Central Pennsylvania,* Reading, Penn., 1927; **Neva Shultis,** "Woodstock Lore," NYFQ, 13 (1957) 218–220; **Frank Simmons,** "The Wart Doctor," PTFS, 14 (1938) 192–194. [Account of meeting with Central Texas wart doctor]; **Mary H. Skeel,** "Superstitions of Childhood on the Hudson River," JAF, 2 (1889) 148. [Wear a piece of goldenrod and you will see your love before tomorrow.]; **Eric Sloane,** *Folklore of American Weather,* New York, 1963. [A very useful book for anyone teaching a class or two on weatherlore. Frontis listing of author's other books on subject.]; **Elmer L. Smith** and **John Stewart,** "The Mill as a Preventive and Cure of Whooping Cough," JAF, 77 (1964) 76–77. [Cites several instances in Virginia and West Virginia of parents curing child of whooping cough by placing it in the hopper of the mill and leaving it there until the grain is all ground out.]; **Grace Partridge Smith,** "Folklore from 'Egypt'," HF, 5 (1946) 45–70. [Weather, love, luck, dreams, death, cats, misc.—Under the window in stormy weather,/I marry this man and woman together./Let none but Him who rules the thunder/Put this man and woman asunder.]; **Grace Partridge Smith,** "Folklore from 'Egypt'," JAF, 54 (1941) 48–59. [Chiefly brief tales, with a few folk remedies: —For earache: a drop of buttermilk in the ear.—For toothache: pick the aching tooth with a hickory splinter, then stick the splinter in a newly made grave.]; **Grace Partridge Smith,** "Negro Lore in Southern Illinois," MF, 2 (1952) 159–162; **Grace Partridge Smith,** "A Yankee Proverb, Vermont Variety," JAF, 61 (1948) 392–393. [Your tongue is hung on a swivel and is loose at both ends.]; **Mrs. Lovisa V. Smith,** "Folk Remedies in Andes," NYFQ, 7 (1951) 229–298; **Mrs. Morgan Smith** and **A. W. Eddins,** "Wise Saws from Texas," PTFS, 13 (1937) 239–244. [Chiefly well known. However: Never speak of ropes in the house of a man whose father was hung.—Before my face, honey and sugar; behind my back, you old wooden-legged devil.]; **W. G. Smith** and **J. E. Heseltine,** *The Oxford Dictionary of English Proverbs,* 1935, and 2nd ed. rev. by Sir Paul Harvey, Oxford, 1948. [The most significant and useful collection of English language proverbs and proverbial phrases. Much orally collected material is, however, overlooked.]; **Walter R. Smith,** "Animals and Plants in Oklahoma Folk Cures," in *Folk-Say: A Regional Miscellany,* Norman, 1929, pp. 69–78. [" . . . to me there is something almost pathetic in the discrediting by a grown child of the home cures which brought it safely through the ills of childhood to maturity."]; **Walter R. Smith,** "Northwestern Oklahoma Folk Cures," PTFS, 8 (1930) 74–85. [Good account of pioneer ailments and cures.—"The settlers cared for their own sick before doctors came into the country; and when doctors did begin to locate in the few 'railroad towns' in the country, the people were slow to call for their assistance. In the first place, people who lived in dugouts or sod houses, ate beans and beef, drank black coffee and 'gyp' water, and worked outdoors rain or shine were hardy. In the second place, they had no money. Finally, the tendency to distrust doctors was not rare."]; **Walter R. Smith,** "You Can't Tell About the Weather," in *Folk-Say: A Regional Miscellany,* Norman, 1930, pp. 173–185; **Emma L. Snapp,** "Proverbial Lore in Nebraska," University of Nebraska Studies in Language, Literature, and Criticism, 13 (1933) 53–112; **Betty Snellenburg,** "An Introduction to Some Kalmyks' Ideas on Proverbs," KFQ, 13 (1969) 275–279. [Proverbs from Kalmyk Mongol informants living near Philadelphia:—It is better to throw seeds on top of the horns of a cow than to talk to someone who does not understand you.—He who is aware of his madness is healthy, and he who is aware of his foolishness is smart.]; [anon.] **"Some Wellerisms from Idaho,"** WF, 25 (1966) 34. [14, fairly common]; **James E. Spears,** "Some Negro Folk Pregnancy Euphemisms and Birth Superstitions," MFR, 4 (1970) 24–27. [In the family way; expecting; swallowed a watermelon seed; broke her leg; she is big, and "a man bigged his wife."]; **Frank G. Speck,** "Snake Folk-Lore: The Snake Who Swallows Her Young," JAF, 36 (1923) 298–300. [Good review of subject with reference to early accounts]; **F. Starr,** "A Page of Child-Lore," JAF, 4 (1891) 55–56. [Personal recollections, New York City (when it was more of a town).— "A common notion among us little lads was that lizards (newts) counted people's teeth. If they succeeded, the teeth fell out and the victim died. I *know* that our crowd of boys used carefully to keep our mouths shut when we passed a pond where these little amphibians abounded."]; **Frederick Starr,** "Some Pennsylvania German Lore," JAF, 4 (1891) 321–326. [To dream of falling means a disappointment in love.]; **Roland Steiner,** "Superstitions from Central Georgia," JAF, 12 (1899) 261–271. [139 items.—To strengthen your wind in running, eat half-done cornbread.—To make a girl love you, take a piece of candy or anything else she is likely to eat, and put it under either armpit, so that it will get your scent.]; **Claude E. Stephens,** "Witching for Water in Oregon," WF, 11 (1952) 204–207; **Burton E. Stevenson,** *The Home Book of Proverbs, Maxims, and Familiar Phrases,* New York, 1948. [2957 pages]; **Rosalyn M. Stewart,** "Forecasting the Weather," KFR, 3 (1957) 15–16. [Local forecasting by 'Granpa' Lee]; **Earl J. Stout,** *Folklore from Iowa,* (Memoir of the American Folklore Society, 29) New York, 1936. [1351 entries, including beliefs, customs, superstitions]; **John K. Strecker,** "Folk-Lore Relating to Texas Birds," PTFS, 7 (1928) 25–37. [Beliefs relating to weather, death, good and bad luck.—When crows form large flocks in Texas, a hard winter is sure to follow.—Never disturb a barn owl that sits between you and the moon: it will bring bad luck.]; **John K. Strecker,** "On the Origin of Reptile Myths," PTFS, 5 (1926) 70–77. ["Some superstitions have a practical basis. For example, in West Texas, it is said that if one kills a horned toad, his mother's cows will either go dry or give bloody milk. This is probably a 'scare' story to prevent children from killing the valuable horned toad which is a consumer of red ants and other injurious insects."]; **John K. Strecker,** "Reptile Myths in Northwestern Louisiana," PTFS, 4 (1925) 44–52. [The milk snake or cow-sucker, the joint snake, the hoop snake, the stinging snake, the thunder snake, snakes with legs, the coachwhip snake, mud-puppies (salamanders)]; **John K. Strecker,** "Reptiles of the South and Southwest in Folklore," PTFS, 5 (1926) 56–69. [Varied beliefs, and quotes from Spenser's *Faerie Queene* (1590) on belief that snakes swallow their young: "Soone as that uncouth light upon them shone,/Into her mouth they crept, and suddain all were gone.]; **Thomas B. Stroup,** "A Charm from North Carolina and *The Merchant of Venice,*" JAF, 49 (1936) 266. [The N. C. charm to cure a burn: There came two angels from the north;/One brought fire, and one brought frost./Go out fire and come in frost.]; **Thomas B. Stroup,** "A Charm from Pepys," JAF, 64 (1951) 319. [From Pepys' diary, Dec. 31, 1664: There came three Angells out of the East;/The one brought fire, the other brought frost./Out fire; in frost./In the name of the Father, and Son, and Holy Ghost./Amen.]; **Thomas B. Stroup,** "A Charm for Stopping Blood," SFQ, 1 (1937) 19–20; **Jesse Stuart,** "New Wine in Old Bottles," KFR, 12 (1966) 105–107. [Recalls early folk remedies]; **Jesse Stuart,** "The Yarb Doctor," *Kentucky Folk-Lore and Poetry Magazine,* 6 (March 1931) 4–10. [Poem]; **Betty Suffern,** " 'Pedro' at California," WF, 18 (1959) 326. [Seven added explanations for the origin of the campus cry]; [anon.], **"Superstitions of the 'Crackers' in Georgia,"** JAF, 5 (1892) 62. [If two persons going hand in hand meet an obstacle which divides them, the one on the left will go to hell and the one on the right to heaven.]; **Charles Swainson,** *The Folk-Lore and Provincial Names of British Birds* (Publications of the Folk-Lore Society, 17) London, 1886; **Charles Swainson,** *A Handbook of Weather Folk-Lore,* London, 1873.

T

Jeri Tanner, "The Teeth in Folklore," WF, 27 (1968) 97–105. [Wide variety of beliefs on toothache, dreams, growth of new teeth, pulling of old, etc.

Bibl. notes.]; **Archer Taylor**, "A Bibliographical Note on Wellerisms," JAF, 65 (1952) 420–421. [All entries relating to American material have been included.]; **Archer Taylor**, "A Few Additional Nineteenth-Century American Proverbs," NCF, 13 nos 1–2 (Special Number, 1965) 37–38. [Never dance with the mate if you can dance with the captain.]; **Archer Taylor**, "An Index to 'The Proverb'," (Folklore Fellows Communication, 113), Helsinki, 1934; **Archer Taylor**, "An Introductory Bibliography for the Study of Proverbs," *Modern Philology*, 30 (1932) 195–210; **Archer Taylor**, "Investigations of English Proverbs, Proverbial and Conventional Phrases, Oaths, and Cliches," JAF, 65 (1952) 255–265. [Fine bibl. references covering detailed studies of individual proverbs]; **Archer Taylor**, "More Proverbial Comparisons from California," WF, 17 (1958) 12–20. [200 from oral California tradition.—Poor as the day before payday.—Still as death.—Busy as a moth in a lighthouse.]; **Archer Taylor**, "Notes on North Carolina Proverbs in *North Carolina Folklore*," 1, 26–27, NCF, 12 no 1 (1964) 13–14; **Archer Taylor**, "Pedro, Pedro!" WF, 6 (1947) 228–231. [18 variants for this famous campus cry]; **Archer Taylor**, "Problems in the Study of Proverbs," JAF, 47 (1934) 1–21. [Historical account of studies in the field, sources and history of proverb collections, proverbial forms and types, proverbial comparisons, translated proverbs, the use of proverbs. One of the basic studies by the great authority in the field.]; **Archer Taylor**, "Proverb," in *Standard Dictionary of Folklore, Mythology, and Legend*, New York, 1950, pp. 902–905. [The best short introduction to proverbs]; **Archer Taylor**, *The Proverb* (and Index to "The Proverb,"), Cambridge, Mass., 1931, and 2nd ed. Hatboro, Pa., 1962. [The most valuable study of the proverb in English. Origins, content, style, proverbial phrases, comparisons, Wellerisms.]; **Archer Taylor**, *Proverbial Comparisons and Similes from California* (University of California Folklore Studies, 3) Berkeley, 1954. [Fine, and regrettably out of print]; **Archer Taylor**, "Proverbial Comparisons and Similes in *On Troublesome Creek*," KFR, 8 (1962) 87–95. [Novels of James Still: Not a speck o' nothing to eat the size of a chinebone of a gnat.—As quiet as the first day of the world.—The hours crawled turkle-slow.]; **Archer Taylor**, "Proverbial Materials in Two Novels by Harry Harrison Kroll," TFSB, 22 (June 1956). [They got as red as beets, like lovers caught kissing.—I are hongry as a wolf.—She's fixing to rain tadpoles and wild catfish.]; **Archer Taylor**, "Proverbial Material in Two More Novels by Harry Harrison Kroll," TFSB, 22 (Sept 1956). [He ain't got no more sense than a betsy-bug.—I may be crazy, but I ain't no fool.]; **Archer Taylor**, "Proverbial Phrases," in *Standard Dictionary of Folklore, Mythology, and Legend*, New York, 1950, p. 906. [Distinguishes between proverb and proverbial phrase: proverb form is fixed in a complete sentence, whereas proverbial phrase changes person and tense.]; **Archer Taylor**, "Proverbial Phrases in the Plays of Beaumont and Fletcher," TFSB, 23 (June 1957); **Archer Taylor**, "Proverbs and Proverbial Phrases in the Writings of Mary N. Murfree (Charles Egbert Craddock)," TFSB, 24 (1958); **Archer Taylor**, "The Study of Proverbs," in *Proverbium* 1 (1965) 1–10. [This is distributed free by the Society of Finnish Literature, Halituskatu 1, Helsinki, Finland]; **Archer Taylor**, "The Use of Proper Names in Wellerisms and Folk Tales," WF, 18 (1959) 287–293; **Archer Taylor,** "Wellerisms," in *Standard Dictionary of Folklore, Mythology, and Legend,* New York, 1950, pp. 1169–1170. [Definition with discussion of examples]; **Archer Taylor,** "Wellerisms and Riddles," WF, 19 (1960) 55–56; **Archer Taylor and B. J. Whiting,** *A Dictionary of American Proverbs and Proverbial Phrases, 1820– 1880,* (Harvard), Cambridge, 1958; **Walter Taylor,** "Home Remedies for Arthritis," PTFS, 27 (1957) 192–200. [Copper bracelets and rings, buckeye, horsechestnut, Irish potato, alfalfa seed tea]; **H. B. Teeter,** "Remedy: one Chihuahua," *Nashville Tennessean Magazine,* Jan. 18, 1953, pp. 6–7. ["In Mexico . . . the chihuahua is known as the 'asthma' dog . . .]; **Octave Thanet,** "Folk-Lore in Arkansas," JAF, 5 (1892) 121–125. [Unwillingness to kill cat because this would bring 'bad luck,' but no compunction or scruples about torturing it]; **T. F. Thiselton Dyer,** *British Popular Customs, Present and Past,* London, 1876; **T. F. Thiselton Dyer,** *The Folk-Lore of Plants,* New York, 1889; **Daniel Lindsey Thomas** and **Lucy Blayney Thomas,** *Kentucky Superstitions,* Princeton, 1920. [3954 items in all categories. One of the earliest extensive collections given over to a single State.—Music during a thunderstorm is very dangerous.—If your big toe itches, you will have a dear lover.—If you hold an apple in your armpit until it is warm and then eat it, your sweetheart will love you.]; **Harold W. Thompson,** *Body, Boots, and Britches,* Philadelphia, 1940, and reissued in paperback. [One of the best books dealing with regional folklore, York State in this instance. Fine chapter on proverbs.]; **Harold W. Thompson,** "Proverbs and Sayings," NYFQ, 5 (1949) 230–235. [Wouldn't know him if I met him in a cup of tea.]; **Harold W. Thompson,** "Proverbs and Sayings," NYFQ, 5 (1949) 296–298. [If it rained soup, he'd be there with a fork.]; **Lawrence S. Thompson,** "The Broom in the Ohio Valley," KFR, 9 (1963) 91–94. [Beliefs and superstitions: Parents should never strike children with brooms. Any child struck by a broom will become thin and gravely ill.]; **Lawrence S. Thompson,** "Hogs in Ohio Valley Superstition," KFR, 10 (1964) 59–61. [In the vicinity of Crab Orchard, Ky., pickled pigs' feet are eaten to insure fertility and good eyesight.]; **Lawrence S. Thompson,** "Marriage and Courtship Customs in the Ohio Valley," KFR, 9 (1963) 47–50. [If pigeons roost in any part of a bride's house in Clay County, she will lose her betrothed to another girl.]; **Lawrence S. Thompson,** "More Buzzard Lore," KFR, 4 (1958) 155–159. [If you talk to a buzzard flying overhead, it will vomit on you.—A sure way to learn the song of birds is to soak a buzzard's tongue in honey for three days and three nights, then lay it on your own tongue.]; **Lawrence S. Thompson,** "Rites of Sepulcher in the Bluegrass," KFR, 9 (1963) 25–28. [It is wise to pour a glass of corn whiskey into the open grave in Magoffin County.]; **Lawrence S. Thompson,** "Sparrows in Bluegrass Superstition," KFR, 9 (1963) 1–3. ["Sparrows are ornery, fussy cusses; they don't treat their womenfolk right . . . "]; **Lawrence S. Thompson,** "A Vanishing Science," KFR, 5 (1959) 95–105. [Folk medicine collected over a nine-year period.—A vermifuge: drink water in which a cat or dog has been dipped.]; **Helen M. Thurston,** "Sayings and Proverbs from Massachusetts," JAF, 19 (1906) 122. [Joy go with you and a good breeze after.—There's as much odds in folks as there is in anybody.—Don't know enough to be assistant manager to a corn crib.]; **James N. Tidwell,** "Adam's Off Ox: A Study in the Exactness of the Inexact," JAF, 66 (1953) 291–294. [Tongue-in-cheek article. Notes the ingenuity of the folk in making very exact, logical, almost scientific statements ("the exact") out of vague, virtually unknown elements ("the inexact").]; **Morris Palmer Tilley,** *A Dictionary of the Proverb in England in the 16th and 17th Centuries: A Collection of the Proverbs Found in English Literature and the Dictionaries of the Period,* (University of Michigan), Ann Arbor, 1950. [Most important collection. Magnificently produced.]; **Charles H. Titus,** "Political Maxims," CFQ, 4 (1945) 377–389. [A practical collection:—Do not drink your own soothing syrup.—If someone must get hurt, select an enemy.]; **Ruth B. Tolman,** "Proverbs and Sayings in Eighteenth Century Almanacs," WF, 21 (1962) 35–42. [Many literary, but others from tradition or have passed into tradition:—Poverty is no sin.— Death keeps no calendar.—Three removes is as bad as a fire. (Franklin: "remove," moving from one place of business or house to another).—With bibl. of 18th century almanacs]; [anon.], **"Traditional Barnyard Calls,"** NYFQ, 5 (1949) 170. [Pigs: poooie poooie pigpigpigpigpig]; **Phebe Allen Travis,** "Bird Lore of New York State," NYFQ, 1 (1945) 197–204. [I wasn't brought up in the woods to be frightened by owls.]; **Robert Chevenix Trench,** *On the Lessons in Proverbs,* New York, 1853. [A moralistic study of the meanings inherent in proverbs. Bishop Trench considers wit and beauty of proverbs, form, creation, morality, and national character.]; **Rodney H. True,** "Folk Materia Medica," JAF, 14 (1901) 105–114. [Considers the stock in trade and value of stock kept by drug dealers: folk "medicines" from mediaeval times to the present]; **C. O. Tullis,** "Folk Beliefs from Mt. Ayr High School," HF, 5 (1946) 35–36. [If you sweep dirt under a rug and the cat lies on it, the cat will have fits.]; **Tressa Turner,** "The Human Comedy in Folk Superstitions," PTFS, 13 (1937) 146–175. [Approx. 275 items: love and marriage, good and bad luck, death, news and company, wishes, money, cures, weather, misc.—All left-handed people owe the devil a day's work.—A fever blister means: "I've kissed someone that I had no business kissing."—To ride a horse with feathers in its mane is a sign of rain.]

V

L. J. Vance, "Weather Lore," JAF, 4 (1891) 166. [Pigs see the wind.—If the cat washes both ears many times, there will be a flood.—If the shells of mussels, clams, or crab-shells are thick, it is a sign of a cold winter.]; **Louis L. Vine,** "Dogs in Folklore and Fact," NCF, 7 no 2 (1959) 18–22. [A good collection]; **Evon Z. Vogt** and **Peggy Golde,** "Some Aspects of Water Witching in the United States," JAF, 71 (1958) 519–531; **Evon Vogt** and **Ray Hyman,** *Water Witching, U.S.A.,* (University of Chicago Press), Chicago, 1959.

W

Barbara K. Walker, "Folklore in the Schools: Collecting by Seventh Graders," NYFQ, 2 (1946) 228–236. [Brief tales, superstitions, rhymes]; John Walker, "A Sampling of Folklore from Rutherford County [N.C.]," NCF, 3 no 2 (1955) 6–16. [Omens, charms, medicine, weatherlore.—If mistletoe, untouched by human hands and not allowed to touch the ground, is made into a tea and given to a person with 'fits,' it will cure the patient. (The mistletoe must be shot from the tree and then caught in a sheet held at the corners by four persons.)]; Ralph S. Walker, "A Mountaineer Looks at His Own Speech," TFSB, 5 (Feb 1939). [Excellent first-hand study of grammar, speech, pronunciation]; Warren S. Walker, "Water-Witching in Central Illinois," MF, 6 (1956) 197–203; Warren S. Walker, "Proverbs in the Novels of James Fenimore Cooper," MF, 3 (1953) 99–107; Donald Wallace, "Beliefs and Belief Tales from McCreary County, [Ky.]," KFR, 3 (1957) 133–138. [Ghosts can't cross water.—The blood of a murdered person cannot be removed from anything.]; T/Sgt. Bill Wallrich, "Hyperbolic Similes of the U. S. Air Force," WF, 18 (1959) 253–254. [So good he can fly an unpainted barn door.—As useless as air-brakes on a turtle.—It (the plane) takes off like a wet brick.—Weather so bad that even the birds are walking.]; T/Sgt. Bill Wallrich, "Superstition and the Air Force," WF, 19 (1960) 11–16. [Good introduction to amulets, talismans, beliefs, superstitions]; Miranda Snow Walton, "Wyoming Pioneer Superstitions," WF, 9 (1950) 161–162. [As Monday goes, so goes the week.—Early thunder, early Spring.—A late Spring, a great blessing.]; Wheaton Phillips Webb, "The Wart," NYFQ, 2 (1946) 98–106; Wheaton Phillips Webb, "Witches in the Cooper Country," NYFQ, 1 (1945) 5–20; Joseph A. Weingarten, *Yiddish Proverbs and Proverbial Expressions, Compared with the Proverbs of Other Nations*, New York, 1944; Grace Pleasant Wellborn, "The Magic Art of Removing Warts," PTFS, 30 (1961) 205–217. [Account of "Uncle Dan" and his unusual ability to remove warts]; J. C. Wells, "Weather and Moon Superstitions in Tennessee," JAF, 6 (1893) 298–300. [Considers groundhog superstition (Feb 2) and includes other weather beliefs]; Roger L. Welsch, *A Treasury of Nebraska Pioneer Folklore*, Lincoln, Nebr., 1966; Howard D. Wesley, "Ranchero Sayings of the Border," PTFS, 12 (1935) 211–220. [Pleasant reminiscence. Spanish with translation.—He who attempts many things gets little done.— Swim, swim, and at the very bank drown.—The fish that sleeps is carried away by the current.]; Victor R. West, *Folklore in the Works of Mark Twain*, (University of Nebraska Studies in Language, Literature, and Criticism, 10) Lincoln, 1931. [Chapters on ghost-lore, demonology, witchcraft, luck and unluck, signs, omens, portents, proverbs, superstitions]; **"What's It a Sign of?"**, *Popular Mechanics*, 64 (1935) 888 ff. [Weatherlore]; Helen M. Wheeler, "Illinois Folk-Lore," *The Folk-Lorist*, 1 (1892–1893) 55–68; Edward Mitchell White, "The Vocabulary of Marbles in Eastern Kentucky," KFR, 9 (1963) 57–74. [Fine collection and study of terms]; Gertrude White, "Folk-Medicine Among Pennsylvania Germans," JAF, 10 (1897) 78–80. [Powwowing]; Newman Ivey White, ed., *The Frank C. Brown Collection of North Carolina*

Folklore, (7 vols.), (Duke University Press), Durham, 1952–1964. [A very great collection with volumes on beliefs, superstitions, proverbs]; **William Tinsley White**, "Proverbs and Picturesque Speech from Claiborne Parish, Louisiana," LFM, 2 (Aug 1961) 85–86. [The kiss sounded like a mule pulling his foot out of a mudhole.—Busy as a cat trying to scratch a hole in a tin roof.—Beauty is skin deep,/Ugly's to the bone;/ Beauty fades away,/Ugly holds its own.]; **Vallie Tinsley White**, "Superstitions from Claiborne Parish, Louisiana," LFM, 2 (Aug 1961) 88–90. [The first dove you hear in the Spring will tell you where your troubles are. If the dove is behind you, so are your troubles; if in front of you, your troubles are still to come.—If you can step on the heel of a person walking in front of you, you can get that person's sweetheart.—Go out and count nine stars for five successive nights and you may have a wish.]; **B. J. Whiting**, "American Wellerisms of the Golden Age," AS, 20 (1945) 3–11. [Fine selection from *Spirit of the Times, Wit and Wisdom, Yankee Notions*. ("I see through it now," as the maid servant said when she knocked the bottom out of the pail.—"I'm down on you," as the feather said to the goose.); **B. J. Whiting**, "The Earliest Recorded English Wellerisms," *Philological Quarterly*, 15 (1936) 310–311. [Whiting notes an example of the form in the writings of Bede]; **B. J. Whiting**, "A Handful of Recent Wellerisms, *Archiv*, 169 (1936) 71–75; **B. J. Whiting**, "The Nature of the Proverb," in *Harvard Studies and Notes in Philology and Literature*, 14 (1932) 273–307. [Considers the "troublesome matter of a definition for the proverb," and treats history of attempts at definition]; **B. J. Whiting**, "The Origin of the Proverb," *Harvard Studies and Notes in Philology and Literature*, 13 (1931) 47–80. ["Proverbs are the creations of individuals, but their nature is such that they capsulize the experience of those many persons who hear and repeat them."]; **B. J. Whiting**, "Proverbial Material in the Popular Ballad," JAF, 47 (1934) 22–44; **B. J. Whiting, ed.,** "Proverbs and Proverbial Sayings," in vol. I of *The Frank C. Brown Collection of North Carolina Folklore*, (Duke University Press), Durham, 1952. [With solid introduction defining the proverb and the special North Carolina field; selected bibliography]; **B. J. Whiting**, "Proverbs in North Carolina," SFQ, 11 (1947) 173 ff.; **B. J. Whiting**, *Proverbs, Sentences, and Proverbial Phrases from English Writings Mainly before 1500*, (Harvard University Press), Cambridge, 1968; **B. J. Whiting**, "Proverbial Sayings from *Fisher's River*, North Carolina," SFQ, 11 (1947) 173–185. [The world wasn't made in a day—took six, I think.]; **B. J. Whiting**, "Some Current Meaning of Proverbial," *Harvard Studies and Notes in Philology and Literature*, 16 (1934) 229–252; **Annie Weston Whitney** and **Caroline Canfield Bullock**, *Folklore of Maryland*, (Memoir of the American Folklore Society, 18) New York, 1925. [2837 entries. General coverage, including beliefs, customs, superstitions, rhymes, riddles]; **Milton Whitney**, "Weather Sayings from Maryland," JAF, 48 (1935) 195–196. [Cold will the winter be, for thick is the fur of the foxes.—Winter never rots in the sky.—When a fire fizzes, it is blowing for snow.]; **H. M. Wiltse**, "Some Mountain Superstitions of the South," JAF, 12 (1899) 131–135. [When you get up in the morning, be sure that you put both feet out of bed exactly at the same instant. Otherwise you will have trouble all day.—If the crickets do not chirp in your hearth, go to a neighbor's house and borrow some. If these do not remain and chirp for you, wisdom dictates that you move out of the house at once, as you will never know happiness there.— You should never take a broom with you when you move, unless you throw it clear through the house you are about to occupy before taking in any other article whatever.]; **Paul R. Wieand,** *Folk Medicine Plants Used in the Pennsylvania Dutch Country,* Allentown, 1963; **D. K. Wilgus** and **Archer Taylor,** "Proverbial Material from the Western Kentucky Folklore Archive," KFR, 6 (1960) 47–49. [Approx. 50 items: You wouldn't know beans if you had your head in the pot.—Nervous as a long-tailed cat in a room full of rocking chairs.]; **Cratis D. Williams,** "Metaphor in Mountain Speech," *Mountain Life and Work,* (Winter) 1962, 9–12. [Relate to fighting and drinking, with comparisons for degrees of drunkenness]; **Cratis D. Williams,** "Metaphor in Mountain Speech," *Mountain Life and Work,* (Spring) 1963, 50–53. [Hypothetical monologues. Rich and comic similes.]; **Cratis D. Williams,** "Lawrence County [Ky.] Superstitions: Pregnancy, Childbirth, and Infancy," KFR, 2 (1956) 137–140. [A snake will not bite a baby if its mother is not around.]; **Jacqueline Williams,** "Mottoes and Slogans of the Curio Shop and Business Establishment," NCF, 3 no 1 (1955) 25–32. [A good collection of proverbial and smart-aleck advice found on back-bar cards]; **Mrs. Robert Williams,** "Connecticut Chat," JAF, 62 (1949) 63–64. [Reports phrases used by her "Connecticut Yankee Grandmother": "She steps around all day in a peck measure," (Anyone who worked in a haphazard, inefficient manner.)—A dingy washing hung to dry: "Those clothes look as though they had been washed in a mud puddle and dried on a gridiron.]; **George Williamson,** "Superstitions from Louisiana," JAF, 18 (1905) 229–230. [If one plants a cedar tree, he will die when the tree is large enough to shade a grave.]; **George Bundy Wilson,** "Notes on Folk Medicine," JAF, 21 (1908) 68–73. [German-American remedies from Eastern Iowa. For good health: Eat slowly. Always have on your table salt, pepper, parsley, sage, garlic, and a raw onion.—For nosebleed: Pull out hairs from under the arms of the one whose nose bleeds. Take an uneven number (three, five, seven, or nine) and hold them in the nose of the patient. The bleeding will stop at once.]; **Charles Morrow Wilson,** *Backwoods America,* (University of North Carolina Press), Chapel Hill, 1935; **Charles Morrow Wilson,** "Elizabethan America," *Atlantic Monthly,* 144 (1929) 238–244. [Discussion of the speech of the Southern mountaineers]; **Charles Morrow Wilson,** "Folk Beliefs in the Ozark Hills," in *Folk-Say: A Regional Miscellany,* Norman, Okla., 1930, pp. 157–172; **Eddie W. Wilson,** "The Onion in Folk Belief," WF, 12 (1953) 94–104. [General survey, including use of onion in magic, dreams, weatherlore, riddles, folk remedies, beauty aids]; **Eddie W. Wilson,** "Some American Fishing Superstitions," MF, 5 (1955) 217–220. [Introductory essay, with source notes]; **George P. Wilson,** "Josiah H. Combs and Folk Speech," KFR, 6 (1960) 104–107. [An appreciation of Combs and his work]; **George P. Wilson,** "Some Folk Sayings from North Carolina," NCF, 6 no 2 (Dec 1958) 7–17. [He's going to hell as straight as a blue-wing hawk.—"How are you?" "I'm just sort o' sticking together."]; **Gordon Wilson,** (ed. Lawrence S. Thompson), *Folklore of the Mammoth Cave Region,*

(Kentucky Folklore Series, 4), Bowling Green, Kentucky, 1968. [A collection of writings previously published, chiefly in KFR, SFQ, and TFSB. Available from the Kentucky Folklore Society.]; **Gordon Wilson**, "Local Plants in Folk Remedies in the Mammoth Cave Region," SFQ, 32 (1968) 320–327. [Good survey.—Wild Grape: Both fox grapes and possum grapes appear in many folk remedies; the sap will help you grow a fine head of hair and will also remove freckles and warts.]; **Gordon Wilson**, "Some Galloway County [Ky.] Animal Lore," KFR, 3 (1957) 9–13. [Cabbage snakes, hoop snakes, hair snakes, joint snakes, as well as cats, dogs, and cows]; **Gordon Wilson**, "Similes from the Mammoth Cave Region with a Farm Flavor," KFR, 14 (1968) 44–50, 69–75, and 94–99. [Smells like an acre of garlic.—Nosey as a pet coon.—Crumbly as cornbread.—Needs that no more than a hog needs a spelling book.—Busy as an ant at a picnic.]; **Gordon Wilson**, "Sayings with a Farm Flavor," KFR, 15 (1969) 12–21. [He doesn't know beans from bird eggs.—You were raised in a barn with the north door open.—The more you see some people, the better you like dogs.—I'll put a spider in his biscuit!]; **Gordon Wilson**, "Accepting the Universe or 'Grin and Bear It'," KFR, 15 (1969) 69–74. [Better be alone than in bad company.—Age makes a man older, not wiser.—Well begun is half done.—You'll die when your time comes and not before.]; **Gordon Wilson**, "Folk Beliefs about People," TFSB, 32 (June 1966). [Name a fire for a lover; if it burns well, his love will be warm.—No baby should be bathed all over until it is a month old: just grease its body with unsalted lard or with mutton tallow, and wipe it off with a soft cloth.]; **Gordon Wilson**, "Folk Beliefs about Times, Seasons, and Weather," TFSB, 33 (March 1967). [Approx. 120 items.—When hogs carry leaves, look for cold weather.—If you run around the house barefooted in the first snow of winter, you will be free of colds all that season.]; **Gordon Wilson**, "Folk Remedies," TFSB, 31 (June 1965). [For toothache, carry a hog's tooth in your pocket.—To have beautiful, glossy hair, wash it in snow water or May dew.]; **Gordon Wilson**, "Luck," TFSB, 32 (Sept 1966). [114 items of good and bad luck.—It is good luck to wear borrowed clothes.—Bad luck to break a tooth.]; **Gordon Wilson**, "Plants and Animals in Folk Beliefs," TFSB, 31 (Dec 1). [Approx. 22 entries, all from Mammoth Cave Region.—It is bad luck to kill a bat.—Plant watermelons on May 1, before sunup, in your shirttail (i.e., without wearing trousers).]; **Gordon Wilson**, "Proverbial Lore," TFSB, 31 (Dec 1965). [If you had another brain, they would rattle.—You don't have the sense of a night-old baby.]; **Gordon Wilson**, "Swallow It or Rub It On: More Mammoth Cave Remedies," SFQ, 31 (1967) 296–303; **Gordon Wilson**, "Talisman and Magic in Folk Remedies in the Mammoth Cave Region," SFQ, 31 (1967) 192–201. [153 items.—To prevent heart trouble, wear a gold watch nearest your heart.]; **Gordon Wilson** and **W. Willard Cockrill**, "The Weatherman and Folklore," TFSB, 34 (June 1968). [Traditional weather beliefs]; **Gordon Wilson** and **Jesse Funk**, "The Physician and Folklore," TFSB, 35 (March 1969). [Various folk remedies, concluding with fear of hospitals: "To the hospital in a buggy, home in a coffin."]; **Gordon Wilson** and **Mr.** and **Mrs. Raymond Hazelip**, "The Pharmacist and Folklore," TFSB, 35 (Dec 1969). [" . . . some people seem to take medicine as a sort of effort to overcome loneliness or the creeping ailments of age; taking something gives an oldster something to do to relieve the tedium of thumb-twiddling."]; **Frank J. Wilstach**, *A Dictionary of Similes*, Boston (new ed.), 1930. [A basic work]; **Henry M. Wiltse**, "In the Field of Southern Folklore," JAF, 14 (1901) 205–208. [Beliefs about dog bites, snakes, planting, measuring cures, marriage signs.—"Hon. C. C. Coltus of Elizabethton, Tennessee, informs me of a quite common belief that, in order to raise gourds, it is necessary for the planter of the seeds to throw them over his left shoulder, one at a time, and utter an oath as each seed is thrown, before planting them."]; **Martin L. Wine**, "Superstitions Collected in Chicago," MF, 7 (1957) 149–159. [175 entries, varied subjects.—Laugh today,/Cry tomorrow.—Any money found is lucky, so keep it.—Before you throw out bread, kiss it.]; [anon.], **"Witchcraft in New Mexico,"** JAF, 1 (1898) 167–168; **N. F. Woodall**, "Old Signs in Alabama," JAF, 43 (1930) 325–326. [20 items from the files of the Folklore Society of Hampton Institute.—If you are going up hill when you hear the first dove mourn in the New Year, you will have good luck all year; if you are going down the hill, you will have bad luck all year.]; **Hensley C. Woodbridge**, "Asthma and the Chihuahua," KFR, 2 (1956) 133–135. ["It is believed in Kentucky and Tennessee that the chihuahua is a cure for the asthma." Sleep with it, and the asthma passes to the dog.—*Business Week*, Sept. 19, 1953, notes increased demand for the chihuahua: registered pups which sold for $35 and $50 each now fetch $125.]; **Frost Woodhull**, "Ranch Remedios," PTFS, 8 (1930) 9–73. [Excellent firsthand, extensive collection of folk cures for man and beast, with running comment.—"It is perfectly obvious that a chicken will thrive although its gizzard be filled with a collection of rocks and other indigestible matter; the lining of the gizzard must logically possess some remarkable power. The president of a San Antonio land bank told me that his father was never without some dried chicken gizzard lining in his pocket. Whenever the old gentleman felt an attack of indigestion coming on, he pulled out a piece of dried chicken gizzard lining and chewed on it. Relief was immediate."]; **F. G. Woodward**, "An Early Tennessee Almanac and Its Maker: Hill's Almanac, 1825–1862," TFSB, 18 (March 1952); **Carey Woofter**, "Dialect Words and Phrases from West-Central West Virginia," AS, 2 (1927) 347–367. [Fine collection of several hundred words with phrases illustrating their use.—She just suffered from all kind of ailments.—You talk like your mouth was full of mush.—He started for home quicker'n hell beating tanbark.]; **Letitia Humphreys Wrenshall**, "Incantations and Popular Healing in Maryland and Pennsylvania," JAF, 15 (1902) 268–274. [Powwowing and witchcraft, with reports on fraudulent use of mails]; **Lillian Mayfield Wright**, "Mountain Medicine," NCF, 12 no 1 (1964) 7–12. [Personal recollections, colorful, valuable]; **John Wyllie**, "Short Dictionary of Slang, Jargon, Cant, and Popular Customs Now or Formerly Current at the University of Virginia," University of Virginia Alumni News, 24 (1936) 80–81. [18 entries].

Y

Irene Yates, "A Collection of Proverbs and Proverbial Sayings from South Carolina Literature," SFQ, 11 (1947) 187–200; **Irene Yates**, "Conjures and

Cures in the Novels of Julia Peterkin," SFQ, 10 (1946) 137–149; **Leah Rachel Yoffie,** "Popular Beliefs and Customs Among the Yiddish-Speaking Jews of St. Louis, Missouri," JAF, 38 (1925) 375–399. [The Evil Eye, amulets, exorcism, magic numbers, days, women, children, the human body, clothing, food, eggs, lights, signs of death.—Step over and never on the threshold.—Tuesday is a very lucky day.—A man must not pass between two women.—Never curse your children.—Do not curse an orphan; its mother protects it in heaven.]; **Leah Rachel Yoffie,** "Yiddish Proverbs, Sayings, Etc. in St. Louis, Missouri," JAF, 33 (1920) 134–165. [Excellent collection with translations covering all subjects. 420 entries.]; **Kimball Young** and **T. D. Cutsforth,** "Hunting Superstitions in the Cow Creek Country Region of Southern Oregon," JAF, (1928) 283–285.

MISCELLANEOUS (Riddles, Tongue Twisters, Jingles, Rhymes, and such)

Carleton Britton Case, *Case's New Book of Conundrums and Riddles with Their Answers,* Chicago, 1916. [Subtitled "2000 of the World's Wisest and Wittiest Catches." Uneven in quality, with only a few true riddles.]; **Josiah H. Combs,** "Spellin' 'Em Down in the Highlands," KFR, 3 (1957) 69–73. [Nonsense spelling at its best]; **Maurice Crane,** "Bop Jokes," JAF, 73 (1960) 249–250. [Describes type and illustrates.—Stranger: "Pardon me, sir. How do I get to Carnegie Hall?" Bopper: "Practice, man!"—New York cabbie drives precariously through city traffic. Bopper: "Just drive the melody, man."—Bopper: "Let me have some apple pie." Waitress: "I'm sorry, sir. It's gone." Bopper: "Crazy, chick! I'll have two pieces."]; **Ed Cray,** "Wellerisms in Riddle Form," WF, 23 (1964) 114–116. [22 items.—What did one light say to the other light? Bet I'm brighter than you are.]; **Mary A. A. Dawson,** *Puzzles and Oddities: Found Floating on the Surface of Our Current Literature, or Tossed to Dry Land by the Waves of Memory,* New York, 1876. [Conundrums, riddles, puzzles, transpositions. Nice title?]; **Martha Dirks,** "Teen Age Folklore from Kansas, WF, 22 (1963) 89–102. [Cruel jokes, knock-knocks, elephant jokes, nonsense. 210 items.—The last words of Eli Whitney were, "Keep your cotton-pickin' hand off my gin!'"]; [anon.], **"Down Your Way,"** KFR, 2 (1956) 76 ff. [Poking and tickling rhymes for babies]; **Charles B. Eaton,** *Riddles and Their Answers, Amusing and Entertaining Riddles, Enigmas, Charades and Puzzles,* New York, 1890; **Duncan Emrich,** *The Book of Wishes and Wishmaking,* New York, 1971. [Illustrated by Hilary Knight. A hundred and more traditional ways of making wishes.]; **Duncan Emrich,** *The Nonsense Book,* New York, 1970. [Rhymes, riddles, tongue-twisters, puzzles, jokes from American folklore. Illustrated by Ib Ohlsson. Extensive bibliography.]; **Evan Esar,** *The Humor of Humor,* New York, 1952, and reissued without date by Bramhall House. [A valuable book for student, teacher, and folklorist. Jokes, jokes, jokes, with perceptive and knowledgeable breakdown into categories.]; **Paul Flowers,** "Rhymes, Songs, and Ditties," TFSB, 10 (Sept 1944); **Martha Freedle,** "Children's Games and Amusements in Sumner County in the 'The Good Ol' Days'," TFSB, 27 (1961) 23–31. [Homemade toys, games, counting-out rhymes]; **C. Grant Loomis**, "American Limerick Traditions," WF, 22 (1963) 153–157. [Statement of the field with examples from print]; **C. Grant Loomis**, "American Pre-Weller Wellerisms," WF, 16 (1957) 51–52. [Notes several appearing in the United States prior to the use of the form by Sam Weller in Dickens' work]; **C. Grant Loomis**, "Traditional American Wordplay: The Conundrum," WF, 8 (1949) 235–247. [Approx. 300 from 19th century source, chiefly the *Golden Era*]; **Clayton Man**, "Pity the Pupil," NYFQ, 15 (1959) 93–98. [Rhymes, school lore]; **Lee Martin, Eva McIntosh, Mildred Newcomb, contribs.**, "The Little Old Lady Who Swallowed a Fly," HF, 6, (1947) 153–156. [Three variants from Colorado, Georgia, Ohio]; **Irene A. McLean**, "Rhyme," HF, 2 no 2 (Dec 1943) 46. [I am a little curly head,/My father is a preacher;/I like to go to Sunday School/Because I love my teacher!]; **Alice Crissman O'Brien**, "Tongue-Twisters from California," WF, 22 (1963) 164. [20 entries, most widely known, but spotted here in California]; **T. M. Pearce**, "Some Spanish Riddles from New Mexico," WF, 6 (1947) 237–239. [10 riddles.—It lives on high,/On high is its place;/It is believed in/But not worshipped. A clock.]; **Frederick d'Arros Planche**, *Guess Me, A Curious Collection of Enigmas, Charades, Acting Charades, Double Acrostics, Conundrums, Verbal Puzzles, Hieroglyphics, Anagrams, Etc.*, New York, 1879. [Add also "Transpositions", some of which are included in this book]; **John A. Reinecke**, "The Language of Marbles Games in New Orleans," LFM, 2 (April 1965) 107–109; **J. A. Rickard**, "Riddles of Texas-Mexican Children," PTFS, 18 (1943) 181–187. [33 riddles from Laredo. Spanish with translation. —A live man scratches a dead man,/And the dead man falls over with laughter. A guitar.]; **E. G. Rogers**, "Family Folk Fronts in Rime and Rhythm," TFSB, 11 (1945). [Good collection of love rhymes]; **Marilyn Ruth Schlesinger**, "Riddling Questions from Los Angeles High School Students," WF, 19 (1960) 191–195. [Approx. 100 from sophomores at Fremont High School.— What's the difference between a Texas flea and other fleas? Texas fleas have their own dogs.]; **Gwladys H. Simon**, "Riddles from Hawaii," WF, 18 (1959) 254–255. [19 from 8th grade students.—What was the color of George Washington's white horse? White.]; **Brian Sutton–Smith**, "The Kissing Games of Adolescents in Ohio," MF, 9 (1959) 189–217. [Description and study of 22 games, with reference bibliography]; **Archer Taylor**, "A Riddle for the Sun, Sky, and Stars," CFQ, 3 (1944) 222–231. [Thorough study with bibl. notes for this well-known riddle]; [anon.], **"Tongue Twisters,"** WF, 19 (1960) 64. [18 items from UCLA Folklore Archives); Meryl Weiner, "The Riddle Repertoire of a Massachusetts Elementary School," *Folklore Forum* (Indiana University), 3 (Jan 1970) 7–38. [300 riddles in current, oral circulation collected from 1st through 5th grade students, aged $6\frac{1}{2}$ to $10\frac{1}{2}$, Auburn, Mass.—Fine collection with most informative analysis.]; The **WHIM WHAM: or, Evening Amusement for All Ages and Sizes. Being an Entire New Set of Riddles, Charades, Questions, and Transpositions. By a Friend to Innocent Mirth.** Philadelphia, 1811. [With that happy bibliographical note, this *Hodge-Podge* comes to an end.]